Vintage Science Fiction Films, 1896–1949

Vintage
Science Fiction
Films, 1896–1949

MICHAEL BENSON

McFarland & Company, Inc., Publishers
Jefferson, N.C., & London

Frontispiece
John Barrymore plays a man with tooth personalities
in *Dr. Jekyll and Mr. Hyde* (Paramount, 1920).

Library of Congress Cataloging in Publication Data

Benson, Michael.
Vintage science fiction films, 1896–1949.

Filmography: p.
Bibliography: p.
Includes index.
1. Science fiction films — Plots, themes, etc.
2. Science fiction films — Catalogs. I. Title.
PN1995.9.S26B4 1985   791.43′09′0915   83-42889

ISBN 0-89950-085-4

Printed in the United States of America

McFarland & Company, Inc., Publishers
Box 611, Jefferson, North Carolina 28640

for lisa

Table of Contents

Acknowledgments

The author's sincere thanks go to the following for helping with materials and ideas during the preparation of this book: L.M. Grasso, Rick Erickson, Steve Rossi, David Jacobs, Seth Lapidou and his mom, Ronn Mullen, Diane Konowitz, Mark Ricci at *The Memory Shop* for his cooperation in supplying the stills, and the Library and Museum of the Performing Arts at Lincoln Center.

"The scientific dreams of today may very well become the scientific fact of tomorrow." — John Colton, in his script to *The Invisible Ray* (1936, Universal)

Silents

All that's conjurable can be reproduced on film. Cinema is as flexible as the imagination. Almost as soon as moving pictures were invented they were used to transport viewers into virgin worlds where known limits of time and physics were shattered.

Like an unwanted child of destiny, cinematic science fiction was born by mistake in 1896. French filmmaker Georges Méliès (1861–1938) was shooting the Place de l'Opéra in Paris when his camera jammed. Though it didn't take him long to fix the problem, he was annoyed, thinking the interruption would cause an awkward jump in image. Only after the film was processed did Méliès realize that the result was far more impressive than his intention. Legend has it he saw an omnibus eerily transform into a hearse. This is the first known example of stop-motion photography.

Filmdom's first special effect.

Being a magician by trade, Méliès recognized the illusionary potential of film and quickly expanded on his accidental discovery, inventing many of the trick photography techniques still used by moviemakers today: fast- and slow-motion, the dissolve, the fade, multiple exposures and underwater photography.

As a young man, Méliès wanted to be a painter—an occupation scorned by his parents. When he expressed an interest in magic, his father gave him the money to buy the *Théâtre Robert-Houdin* for his act. The older Méliès would have done anything to keep his son from being an artist. The young man's skills as an illusionist soon made him the most famous magician in France. When he learned of the moving pictures developed by Louis Lumiére in France and Thomas Edison in America, he was immediately interested. Since the flickers were a novelty, what was filmed was unimportant, and Méliès first efforts were mundane—usually street scenes of famous Paris sites. It wasn't until he had his pre-ordained mechanical difficulties that he recognized film as a suitable forum for an extension of his act, and fantastic cinema was the result.

In 1896 Méliès made *The Devil's Castle*, including the first screen appearance of a vampire. The fiend was forced to disappear by an uplifted

1

crucifix, obviously without much impact, as it was 26 years before another vampire picture was made.

Meanwhile, in England, pioneers G.A. Smith (1864–1959) and James Williamson were experimenting with the interpolation of close-ups in their narrative films. Smith made a comical 54-foot film called *X-Rays* (1897). A professor points the rays at lovers, revealing a pair of embracing skeletons. Other than this, Méliès' work stands alone among known 19th century science fiction films.

The Frenchman's first full-fledged science fiction effort was *The Astronomer's Dream* (1898). To make it, Méliès constructed the world's first film studio in the Parisian suburb of Montreuil. The walls and ceilings were made of glass for illumination, and translucent curtains produced ghost-like effects. The stage was equipped with trap-doors, secret panels, gigantic moving cut-outs, and the ability to combine painted backdrops with live sets.

Also known as *La Lune a un Mètre*, it shows a scientist falling asleep and dreaming of a visit from the man in the moon who sneaks into his home through an open window. The short-subject was hand painted frame-by-frame to simulate color photography, which was unknown at the time.

Four years later, Méliès filmed his undisputed masterpiece, *A Trip to the Moon* (*Le Voyage dans la Lune*) (1902). He wrote, directed, photographed, and starred in this fantasy about a rocketship propelled into outer space by cannon. The missile imbeds itself in the right eye of the Man in the Moon, whose pasty face contorts in agony. All is surreal on the moon's surface. Plant-life abounds. Even an umbrella, when planted in the soil, takes root and begins to grow. Pretty ballerinas from the *Théâtre du Châtelet* in Grecian costumes and acrobats from the *Folies-Bergère* fly through the air. The astronauts, wearing no spacesuits, tumble into a crater where they encounter insect-people called Selenites.

The film was not intended to be taken seriously and did not attempt to depict an actual trip to the moon, as might be indicated by the credits claiming that it was based on both H.G. Wells' *The First Men in the Moon* and Jules Verne's *From Earth to the Moon*. It is a crazy pantomime designed to be wholly comedic. Modern audiences often mistake Méliès' whimsy for naivetè, producing unwarranted condescension.

A Trip to the Moon was often imitated and outright pirated by opportunistic filmmakers taking advantage of tardy copyright legislation. In 1903 a very hastily pirated version of the same vehicle was released in the U.S. by Lubin Film, with the name changed to *A Trip to Mars*. Thomas Edison, always willing to steal what he could, released a version of *A Trip to Mars* in 1910. Méliès himself made a derivative picture called *The Impossible Voyage* (1904), which starred himself and merely changed his space journey's target to the sun.

The French innovator, to be discussed later, showed surprising lack of growth after *A Trip to the Moon*. He insisted on keeping his stories frivolous rather than realistic, frustrating his increasingly sophisticated

Méliès' lunacy: *A Trip to the Moon* **(Star, 1902).**

audience, and was eventually abandoned by theater-goers for meatier stuff. Being a lousy businessman, he was forced to sell his theater, went broke, and spent the last twenty years of his life as a newsboy on Parisian streets. Méliès' unwillingness to be adventurous was reflective of the young industry as a whole for the first two decades of its existence. Considering its potential as a burgeoning new art-form, its creative sparks were few. Most productions were only marginally adequate, and few bothered to tell narrative stories at all. Filmmaking was considered by all to be a shoddy occupation, and filmmakers considered themselves grinders of cheap entertainment. Though Méliès never moved his camera during his cinematic career, his influence came in discovering the narrative potential of film — as opposed to the early documentary ideals of Edison or Lumière.

A 1905 film produced by American Robert William Paul called *The ? Motorist*, rivaled — and in some opinions surpassed — the best of Méliès' work. A motoring couple exceed the speed limit and hurtle off the Earth into space where they encounter heavenly bodies before returning safely to the ground. One impressive scene shows them cruising the rings of Saturn.

Also in 1905, French filmmakers Gaston Velle and Gabriel Moreau first used invisibility as an excuse for trick photography with *The Invisible Thief* for Pathé. The same company produced *An Adventure at the Bottom of the Sea* (1906), where sea fairies were prevalent.

An automated man went berserk, smashed furniture, and exploded in British Alpha's *The Motor Valet* (1906) directed by Arthur Cooper.

Méliès returned on his last cinematic legs in 1907, making *Tunneling the English Channel.* The film was about efforts to unite France and England, and it borrowed from *20,000 Leagues Under the Sea*, the first film adaptation of Jules Verne's classic. The latter is notable today for its primitive yet ingenious special effects. Stop-motion photography, split-screen multiple exposures, giant moving cut-outs, and live action combined with full-scale mechanical backgrounds to relate the adventures of a subaquatic explorer who discovers, among other things, half-naked sea nymphs. It was remade twice, first in 1916 by Universal.

The year 1907 produced two other science fiction films. Accelerated motion was the effect of a fluid called *Liquid Electricity*, also known as *The Inventor's Galvanic Fluid*, produced and directed by J. Stuart Blackton. In *A Trip to Jupiter*, a jovial French short originally hand-colored, an adventurous monarch ascends an endless ladder, receiving a salute from each solar system satellite. Segundo de Chomon directed.

Robert Louis Stevenson (1850–1894) was the offspring of a comfortable Scottish family of engineers best known for their work with lighthouses. He attended Edinburgh University and considered both engineering and law before becoming a writer at 23. Although he achieved his popularity as a fiction writer, he began his literary career as an essayist, his early works expressing a blasé fatalism.

When Stevenson was 36, he published his most popular work, *The Strange Case of Dr. Jekyll and Mr. Hyde*, which during the following century was adapted to film more times than any other science fiction vehicle. With cinematic adaptation so plentiful, it should be no surprise that his work suffered greatly in translation. The book is a colloquial metaphor for the personality antithesis living within all humans, representing a touchstone of Victorian sensibilities.

Because of Hollywood's insistence on simplification, those who have not read the book tend to think of Dr. Jekyll and Mr. Hyde as separate beings — a white soul and a black soul — rather than the intricately meshed polar facets of a single 19th century psyche. The point was not that one man could become two, but that two men could become one. Hyde didn't prove man can escape his conscience — he proved he cannot.

Dr. Jekyll and Mr. Hyde was first filmed in 1908 in Chicago by the Selig Polyscope Company and was a primitive one-reeler of a touring stage troupe performing Luella Forepaugh and George Fish's 1897 play. Sometimes known as *The Modern Dr. Jekyll*, it was shot from a stationary camera, each scene beginning with a curtain rising. The unknown actor playing the title characters is courting the vicar's daughter in the church garden when the initial transformation changes the "admirable scholar" into a "furious brute of a maniac." The only cinematic touch is the replacement of Jekyll's climactic monologue with visions of creepy gallows. After attacking Jekyll's girlfriend, Alice, and killing her father, the fifteen-minute picture ends with Hyde's suicide to "rid himself of Jekyll forever."

In 1910, two versions were made: *The Duality of Man*, a British

Production, and *Den Skaebnesvangre Opfindelse*, a Danish film known in the U.S. as *Dr. Jekyll and Mr. Hyde* (and listed thus in the filmography). The British version expanded on the story; at one point Hyde, while gambling in a garden, steals the winnings and is chased by police, evading them by transforming back into the kindly doctor. When his fiancée (here known as Hilda) arrives with her father, Jekyll again becomes Hyde, kills the old man, and swallows poison before police arrive.

The Danish version stuck more closely to Stevenson's original plot. Shot in Copenhagen and produced by Ole Olsen, the movie was written and directed by August Blom. Starring Alwin Neuss, it was the first to take advantage of the transformation's illusionist potential. The disappointing ending revealed the entire episode to be a bad dream, a delusion of Jekyll's feverish mind.

In 1912 Thanhauser's American one-reeler was unique, featuring two actors as the polar nature of a single psyche. James Cruze and Harry Benham performed in the leads. Director Lucius Henderson shot from a single camera position with no changes in lighting, achieving his transformation through careful cuts and quick dissolves in camera.

Three more *Hydes* were made in 1913: A British edition was filmed in a primitive color process (Kinemacolor) by the Kineto Company, while the same year's Universal release starred and was directed by King Baggot, whose sparse acting ability was given a full workout. In Germany, *Der Anderer* (*The Other*) was an altered version based on Paul Lindau's derivative play. The Vitaskop production was directed by Max Mack and starred Albert Basserman in the leads.

After an unnotable American effort in 1914, the subject vacationed six years before returning full force when four films popped up in quick succession in 1920. First and foremost of these starred the great stage and screen actor John Barrymore (1882–1942) and was directed by the merely competent John S. Robertson. Though some scenes no doubt made Stevenson flop in his grave, this film stands up well against the more sophisticated sound films with Fredric March and Spencer Tracy. For the first time Hyde's sexuality was clear cut: Barrymore plays a sadistic sex killer rather than the book's child-beating murderer.

The film also added a second female lead, a working-class girl to serve as Hyde's victim, to the usual aristocratic and virginal fiancée. Nita Naldi portrayed the sexy Soho dancer, displaying incredible cleavage in the invented role.

Writer Clara S. Berenger went so far as to change Jekyll's motivation by borrowing the Lord Henry character from Oscar Wilde's *The Picture of Dorian Gray* (played by Brandon Hurst and referred to as Sir George Carewe). She posed him as Jekyll's mentor while directly lifting Wilde's epigrams.

Produced by Paramount and filmed on Long Island, this was Barrymore's thirteenth film, and his first wearing make-up to enhance his evil gestures. It's frequently been said that Barrymore made his transformation from good to evil without make-up, but a screening proves this untrue. Still, the acting skill that Barrymore demonstrates far surpasses that of his predecessors. The possible exception is Richard Mansfield, who made a critically acclaimed career of playing the roles in T.R. Sullivan's play. Unfortunately, there is no filmed record of his performance. Barrymore is self-indulgent but effective as he dislocates his regular features into the grotesque countenance of Hyde even before he stiffens, twitches, and falls out of camera range so the illusion can be completed. It was no doubt that Barrymore's screen dynamism made viewers believe the effect was accomplished without make-up.

Until usurped by Lon Chaney several years later, the role established Barrymore as the king of the macabre. He enjoyed wearing the Hyde make-up so much that he later donned a facsimile as Captain Ahab in a silent version of Melville's *Moby Dick* called *The Sea Beast*.

As Jekyll, Barrymore is a distinguished Victorian, yet ominous foreshadowing comes early when his libido is aroused at his own stag party. As Hyde, he is an old degenerate with a horrible leer, rotten teeth, deeply shadowed eyes, and a pointy skull. His corrupt caricature was more insect than animal, symbolized by a tight shot of an arachnid ascending his bedpost during a later offscreen transformation. Martha Mansfield played Jekyll's harassed fiancée, Millicent.

The film was very popular and heralded by critics. Because of its success, there were three attempts to cash in. Along with an obscure Arrow Film Corporation release starring Hank Mann, there was producer Louis B. Meyer's opportunistic vehicle starring Sheldon Lewis (1869–1958), switching the time to the present and the setting to New York City. It showed the card-title "An Apostle of Hell!" as Lewis took his satanic quaff. The German version of 1920, *Der Januskopf* (*The Head of Janus*), was adapted freely from Stevenson by Hans Janowitz in an attempt to avoid paying rights to the author's estate and derived its title from the two-faced Roman deity. It was helmed by F.W. Murnau (1889–1931), later to be one of the German silent cinema's greatest directors. Known in America as *Janus-Faced*, the film featured the cinematography of Karl Freund (1890–1969), who was the cameraman for *Metropolis* in 1926. Unfortunately, only the script and a few stills remain. Conrad Veidt (1893–1943), in his follow-up role to Césare in *The Cabinet of Dr. Caligari* (the two films were released four months apart), played both Dr. Warren, a scientist obsessed with his Janus bust, and Mr. O'Connor, a lustful, murdering fiend. As O'Connor (presumably a hideous satyr of Irish extraction) Veidt drags his pretty fiancée (Margarete Schlegel) into a brothel and murders a little girl in the street. Warren manages to consume lethal poison before O'Connor can consume his personality.

The Stevenson story was laid to rest for 12 years after the 1920 eruption. It reappeared with sound by Robert Mamoulian—a classic featuring Fredric March's Oscar-winning performance.

In the film *She* (the first one, in 1908), based on H. Rider Haggard's novel, a beautiful but savage queen possesses the secret of eternal youth. A 1911 version, starring James Cruze and Marguerite Snow, a 1916 version produced in Great Britain, a 1917 Fox production, and a 1926 British film with Betty Blythe in the title role all followed during the silent era.

The year 1908 began a slew of short subjects featuring scientifically impossible acts, most frequently used for cheap laughs, yet still taking advantage of the illusionary powers discovered by Méliès twelve years before. Here is a quick rundown of the year's known science fiction entries:

After a mad scientist changes several men into apes with injected serum, he can't reverse the simian symptoms. Instead, he puts his creations on display in British-Gaumont's *The Doctor's Experiment; or, Reversing Darwin's Theory*. In France's *A Wonderful Fluid*, a growth elixir turns plants into trees and causes women to grow facial hair. The opposite follicle effect was the focus of England's *The Wonderful Hair Remover* (1910). The French also produced *Latest Style Airship*, directed by Ferdinand Zecca for Pathé, about a flying bicycle. The same gimmick had been used by Zecca in *Conquest of the Air* (1901) and in a French film of the same title by Gaston Velle. Turning men into monkeys was *The Professor's Secret* in France, while in the U.S. the title character was a human wearing a vanilla-colored suit visiting Earth with his glass bubble in *The Man in the Moon Seeks a Wife*. Flight 100 years in the future was envisioned in *The Airship*, produced and directed by J. Stuart Blackton. A knockout talc was *The Debilatory Powder*, while a liquid rendered both people and objects transparent in *The Invisible Fluid*.

The volume of sf short subjects was even greater in 1909 as Gaumont and Pathé competed to catch the attention of a newly discriminating audience. Most either predicted technological advances or depicted fantastic dreams. Here are the ones history has chosen to remember:

Fast-motion photography dominates Gaumont's *The Times Are Out of Joint*, which is about a speeding clock that accelerates the world. Gaumont's *The Electric Policeman* and *Police of the Future* forecast crime prevention. In the former, a French flatfoot runs at superhuman speed after donning a pair of electric shoes. The same company made *Man in the Moon* (not to be confused with the Méliès film occasionally listed under the title) about outer space travel by hot air balloon. Heavenly bodies come alive—the moon and stars wink and smile at the hero balloonist. Pathé made *Moonstruck* about a sleeping drunk who dreams of his frightening visit with evil lunar inhabitants. Chemical technology's accompanying fears were examined in Pathé's *A Wonderful Remedy* about a newly discovered lotion that turns ugliness into beauty and vice versa. *Professor Puddenhead's Patents*, directed by Walter Booth, featured an antigravitational auto able to fuel from the ground while aloft. In England's *A Professor's Twirly-Whirly Cigarettes*, directed by H.O. Martinek, future campus life is seemingly predicted when a liver-based powder mixed with tobacco produces spinning smokers. Defect-correcting surgery was forecast in Lux' *Professor Zanikoff's Experience of Grafting*. Long before amphetamines became socially accept-able under the euphemistic guise of diet pills, Italian filmmakers invented *Wonderful Pills*, which "cured laziness." More elaborate was *The Airship Destroyer*, directed by Walter Booth, about a dogfight over London. In England, all are joyous about the effects of *The Professor's Strength Tablets*, directed by Percy Stow, until the pills are revealed to have explosive after-effects. Great intelligence was possible with *Professor Weise's Brain Serum Injector*, a Lubin release.

Rounding up the long list of 1909 pictures are two vehicles strong enough to warrant remakes. The first of three versions of Richard Gan-thony's successful London play, *A Message from Mars*, was made in New Zealand, a Franklyn Barrett production about a Martian's earthly visit to help pitiful humanity with its problems. It was remade in Ganthony's native England in 1914, written and directed by J. Wellett Waller, and again in 1921 America by director/producer Maxwell Karger with Aphonz Ethier as the Martian.

An inventor learns to create artificial diamonds through condensation in *The Diamond Maker*, directed and produced by J. Stuart Blackton. The picture was remade in 1913 as a two-reeler by Rex Films and in 1914 in Italy by Cines. The same subject appeared in *The Diamond Maker* (1929), a silent Universal serial directed by Jack Nelson.

Before the motion picture copyright law was passed in 1912, it was legal to duplicate films by another and take credit for them. As happened to Méliès, stolen films had their credits stripped and replaced. Most notorious of the film pirates were the studios of New York-based Thomas Edison (1847–1931). It is therefore ironic that one of Edison's most original and discussed films was a miserable failure when released. This was the first adaptation of Mary Shelley's classic, *Frankenstein*, directed in 1910 by J. Searle Dawley. All prints of the movie are now gone forever; sole surviors of the effort are a scenario of 25 scenes and some stills. According to the film's press release, the monster is created in "a cauldron of blazing chemical." Unlike more popular versions to follow, the monster here is defeated by the power of love, leaving Dr. Frankenstein and his pretty wife to live happily ever after.

The monster was portrayed by a member of the Edison acting team, Charles Ogle (1865–1940), whose self-designed make-up consisted of a pasty face, hunchback, no neck, and wild silver hair. Ogle later played the first serial villian in Edison's *What Ever Happened to Mary?* (1913).

Frankenstein, considered too weird in its day, was a disaster for Edison. The only other attributed silent version of Shelley's novel was Italy's obscure *The Monster of Frankenstein* (*Il Mostro di Frankenstein*) (1920). Giovanni Diovetti wrote the scenario for the Albertini Film release at the directorial helm of Eugenio Testa. Unattributed, but clearly derivative, was the Ocean Film Corporation's *Life Without Soul* (1915), filmed in New York

Charles Ogle as the Monster in *Frankenstein* (Edison, 1910).

and directed by Joseph W. Smiley. It starred Percy Darrell Standing as the monster and ended with a typical "all a dream" copout.

The same year Shelley's creation made his movie debut, the other sf entries were predominantly trick films — inventors displaying their latest impossible and usually silly fare.

Films of 1910: *The Inventor*, about the discovery of an impenetrable material; Germany's *Motor Car of the Future*, similar to *The ? Motorist*, about a car that flies to avoid an oncoming train and heads for the rings of Saturn; England's *Professor Piecan's Discovery*, about a strength elixir; *The Wonderful Chair*, about a criminal intruder trapped by a mechanical seat; *Algy Tries Physical Culture*, about a super-strength formula; and the self-explanatory *The Aerial Submarine* directed by Walter Booth.

There was more of the same in 1911: Another diamond-creating method is discovered in England's *The Inventor's Son*, directed by David Miles. A super-explosive was *The Inventor's Secret*, made in Italy. In *The Aerial Anarchists*, a British forecast directed by Walter Booth, frightening futuristic planes bomb large cities. *The Effects of a Rocket* was more a prediction of the jet plane than space travel. *From Death to Life* featured an animating solution, while the Italians produced *The Motor Chair* and the French envisioned *One Hundred Years After*.

Méliès' final contribution to the genre he invented was *The Conquest of the Pole*, casting himself as Mabouloff, inventor of a flying bus on its way to the North Pole. But the hero of the picture is the "Abominable Giant of the Snows," who insists on eating expedition members. The fearsome tundra beast is the sole exception to Méliès gentle yet fantastic universe.

Foreign films were the rule in 1912's science fiction roster. *Fire of Life*, a Danish dream film directed by Schedler Sorenson, features invented immortality. England's *Lieutenant Rose, R.N., and His Patent Aeroplane*, predicts remote control. The Italians made *The New Microbe*, about a newly discovered weakness-causing germ. In Britain's *Overcharged*, directed by Frank Wilson, Caspar Milquetoast is almost electrocuted, but emerges from the experience a magnetic superman.

Domestically, in 1912 Edison made *Dr. Brompton-Watt's Adjustor*. It concerns a scientist's youth-serum transformation into a chimp.

Influencing science fiction to come, French director Victorin Jasset adapted a novel by Gaston Leroux (who later wrote *The Phantom of the Opera*) to make *Balaoo the Demon Baboon* (1913). In it, Darwinist Dr. Coriolis (Henri Gouget) half-humanizes the title creature (actor Bataille). When a poacher gets Balaoo to kidnap the doctor's daughter (Camille Bardon), the ape rebels, traps his tormentor, and ends up getting shot for his trouble. The novel was filmed in Hollywood as *The Wizard* (1927) and *Dr. Renault's Secret* (1942).

Also trying to transform animals into human beings was the tropical scientist in France's *The Island of Terror* (1913), a thinly disguised version of H.G. Wells' *The Island of Dr. Moreau*, later horrifically filmed as *Island of Lost Souls* (1933).

The other science fiction films of 1913 were: Italy's *After Death* about a life-preserving suspended animation serum; Germany's *The Air Torpedo* about the invention of an automated prolonged-flight bomb, not unlike those that ravaged London 30 years later; and England's *Professor Hoskin's Patent Hustler*, directed by Dave Aylott. Here, the title invention accelerates everything via fast-motion photography.

The form of special effects demanding the most skill and patience is model-animation through stop-motion photography. A model is placed in a desired position, a single frame is exposed, the model is moved slightly, another frame is exposed, and so on. When the film is projected, the figure appears to be moving by itself. As early as 1897 filmmakers were using the painstaking technique to make kiddiefare, a category where such work remained until turned into an art form by Willis H. O'Brien (1882–1962), the man who later made *King Kong* real.

Born in Oakland, O'Brien began his professional life as a marble cutter but always had interest in serious sculpture and cartooning. He began to experiment privately with stop-motion photography, first animating two small clay boxers. Encouraged by the results, he switched the subject matter to prehistoric monsters, a career motif which became his key to success. His ambitious 60-second interaction between a dinosaur and a caveman impressed one producer enough to front O'Brien $5,000 for expansion on the film. After two months of work, Edison bought *The Dinosaur and the*

Missing Link (1914) and released it under the name of Manikin Films. The figures—clay molded to wooden frames—were crude but impressed Edison enough to contract O'Brien for nine more similar films. All were five-minute whimsical Stone Age subjects costing $500 apiece. Only one title is known: *Rural Delivery, Million B.C.* (1918).

His Edison contract fulfilled and his reputation boosted by his product's quality, O'Brien supplied the effects for World Films' *The Ghost of Slumber Mountain* (1919) directed, produced, and written by Herbert M. Dawley. Returning $100,000 on a $3000 investment, it was the first film ever to combine animated models with live actors. O'Brien appears as Mad Dick, an old hermit's ghost who sees into prehistoric times through his magic telescope. With his career in full swing, O'Brien immediately began pre-production planning for the silent era's greatest model-animation achievement. [See: *The Lost World* (1925)]

The other 1914 science fiction films were *The Master of the World*, a Karl Warner production about a newly invented gold-making process; *The House That Went Crazy*, where an intruder disrupts the smooth operation of an automated home; *By Radium Rays*, about an insanity cure; England's *Perpetual Motion Solved*, starring a flying automobile; *Professor Oldboy's Rejuvenator*, about a scientist and his dog transformed by youth serum into a baby and his pup; *A Trip to the Moon* (unassociated with Méliès), which combined crude animation with live action to show an airplane that visits the rings of Saturn and races a comet; and *The Fifth Man*, directed by F.J. Grandon, about a future time when people are kept in zoos.

The golem, a clay statue animated according to Jewish/German legend to protect a ghetto, is not technically a creature of science fiction, but golem movies will be discussed because of their spiritual parallel to Shelley and influence on Karloff's *Frankenstein*.

The golem is the original man-made monster. According to legend, the creature was molded by a magician of ancient Thessaly and animated in Prague during Emperor Rudolph II's reign by Rabbi Ben Yehuda Low to protect Jews from terrorism.

The Golem (1914), a German-Bioscop production, was directed by Paul Wegener (1874–1948) and Henrik Galeen, written by Galeen and starring Wegener as the monster. Known in America as *The Monster of Fate*, the picture was released the week diplomatic relations with Germany were broken off prior to World War I, so reaction here was never favorable.

Discovered in a vault beneath a worksite, the golem is sold to a merchant and brought to life by the *Shem*, a magic word written in the Star of David on his chest. Ordered to protect the merchant's daughter (Lyda Salmonova), the golem grows increasingly human and falls in love—going berserk when the girl sneaks off to her nobleman lover's ball. After destroying much of the city, the golem chases the girl and her beau to a tower top and threatens to toss his competitor to a plunging death. But he is stiffened when the girl utters a magic word, and it is the statue that topples.

After a 1916 Danish version, Wegener made a whimsical sequel *Der Golem und die Tänzerin* (*The Golem and the Dancing Girl*) (1917), with the director playing himself, clay-costumed for seduction purposes. The original "two monsters are better than one" film was *Alraune and the Golem* (1919).

More worthy of note was Wegener's 1920 sequel (or perhaps prequel), *The Golem* (*How He Came into the World*), recounting the original Jewish legend. The film had an easier time making it stateside with world frictions eased. With Wegener repeating as the monster and Salmonova as the girl of his dreams, it is remembered for the unreal studio settings of Hans Polzig. Again the golem is felled from a tower while trying to kill his competition. James Whale, director of Universal's *Frankenstein*, was obviously influenced by the mob scenes, final fire, and the creature's pained movements. It was 16 years before the clay man made another film appearance in Julien Duvivier's 1936 sound version.

The other science fiction films of 1915: A remote-control ray detonates bombs from afar in *Pawns on Mars*; illumination by electric ray is provided in *Let There Be Light*, directed by William Bertram; a "negative electricity machine" causing levitation is the star of *The Mysterious Contragrav*, written and produced by Henry McRae; a statue is animated electrically in *Niobe*, a Daniel Frohman/Paramount production; and E.A. Martin directed *War of Dreams* about a scientist's losing battle with his conscience after inventing an explosive detonated by "dream waves."

Other gimmick films from the early silent era, all with self-explanatory titles, were:

The Automatic House (1915), *The Automatic Laundry* (1908), *The Automatic Monkey* (1909, French), *The Automatic Motorist* (1911, British), *The Automatic Servant* (1908), *The Electric Policeman* (1909, French), *The Electric Villa* (1911, French), and *The Electric Girl* (1914).

The potentially comic shtick of super-magnetism was examined in *The Magnetic Fluid* (1912, French); *The Magnetic Kitchen* (1908, French); *Magnetic Removal* (1908, French), about a man cleaning his house with a magnet; *The Magnetic Squirt* (1909, French), about an elixir enabling the lame to walk; *The Magnetic Vapor* (1908), about a henpecked husband who uses magnetism to become a forceful ruler; and *The Wonderful Electro-Magnet* (1909). There was also *The Mechanical Legs* (1908, French), *The Mechanical Husband* (1910), *the Mechanical Man* (1915), *Mechanical Mary Anne* (1910, British), and *The Mechanical Statue* (1907).

Borrowing from the golem and Prometheus legends, Otto Rippert made *Homunculus* in 1916, a sprawling marathon about the extraordinary life of a laboratory-created man. The German film was shown in six weekly hour-long parts, with Danish matinee idol Olaf Fønss as the soulless creature. Wearing no dreadful make-up, though somberly dressed, Fønss' portrayal was restrained and heroic enough to make *Homunculus* a popular German cult film.

The monster falls in love with a pretty girl (Maria Carmi), gets rejected, and attempts world destruction in his wrath. At first a superman in moral integrity and intellect, he becomes evil upon learning of his unnatural origin. Gaining great political power, he becomes dictator of a large, unnamed country until nature re-establishes normality with a well-placed lightning bolt.

Stuart Paton directed the second version of Jules Verne's *Twenty Thousand Leagues Under the Sea* (1916). The Carl Laemmle/Universal production was the first to make use of J. Ernest Williamson's efficient underwater photography technique. The "photosphere," a thick steel, spherical chamber with one large porthole, when attached to a floating barge overhead, could be submerged 80 feet. In the sea the hero once again encountered scantily-clad sea-nymphs.

Model work was considered cheating by contemporary filmmakers; so Williamson built his own 100-foot "Nautilus" which could be operated by one man. A giant octopus, the film's most memorable menace, was rubber and had a man inside operating the arms.

The release date assured the film's success. It was distributed the same week a German U-boat slipped blockades to sink a dozen ships outside New York.

With the world racked by war, the volume of sf cinema dwindled. Sadly, many fearful visions of science fiction were becoming scientific fact.

In an adaptation of Owen Davis' play *Lola*, produced and written by James Young and called *Without a Soul* (1916), a scientist returns his daughter (Clara Kimball Young) from the dead by electric ray, only to find her in the title condition and unmanageably evil. When she expires a second time, he lets her stay that way.

One of the first disaster pictures was Denmark's *The End of the World* (1916), directed by August Blom. Tidal waves, flooding, and unnatural lightning storms destroy Earth when a comet passes too close. Another passing comet doses Earth with laziness gas in Mutual's *The Comet's Comeback* (also 1916). These pictures were probably delayed reactions to Halley's Comet's last passing in 1910.

Other science fiction films of 1916: A super-explosive and an oversized spider are featured in Selig's *The Germ of Mystery*, directed by William Robert Daly, while Arthur Tavares starred in Vogue's *Germanic Love*, a one-reel comedy, as a professor trying a love potion on college tramps. An X-ray device causes invisibility in both *The Hand of Peril*, directed, written and produced by Maurice Tournier, and *Rays That Erase*, directed by E.J. Collins. A crazed warmonger tries to annihilate London with huge guns and futuristic airships in London Films' *If*, a bullseye forecast by Stuart Kinder, while in Pathé's *The Iron Claw*, directed by Edward José, a ray-gun arsonist succumbs in the finale to a strange virus.

In 1917, Mutual produced a frightening prophecy with *Zeppelin Attack on New York*. Unfortunately, the short subject about a German fleet invading the Big Apple is long lost and little is known about it.

In *The Greatest Power* (1917), directed by Edwin Carewe, a scientist (William B. Davidson) accidentally invents an "exonite" super-bomb while searching for a cancer cure. After some soul searching, he decides to limit his invention's accessibility to the U.S. Government.

Alfred Désy directed Hungary's *The Prehistoric Man* (1917) about a ray that temporarily increases the rate of evolution, turning a monkey into a politically powerful womanizer before regressing it to normality.

Denmark's *Sky Ship* (1917), directed by Holger-Madsen, better resembled the science fiction of the Fifties than the Teens. Astronauts, after discovering an all-woman society on Mars, return to Earth with natives. There a human menace mauls an innocent Martian girl before being zapped by a divinely intervening lightning bolt. In General's *The Violet Ray* (1917), a typical potboiler in the "Grant, Police Reporter" series directed by Robert Ellis, the villian possesses the title weapon.

The first adaptation of Hans Heinz Ewer's controversial German novel *Alraune* was Hungarian and made in 1918. The book stirred a fuss in the early 20th century for its construction around scientifically impossible and blasphemous artificial insemination. A scientist impregnates a prostitute with a convicted murderer's seed, producing a baby girl whom the doctor raises to test the association of character with environment. Genetics prevail when she matures hopelessly affected by her true parents' natures and her unholy conception. She delights in driving men to suicide with her seductive charms.

The film was directed by Michael Curtiz (who directed *Dr. X* in 1932) and Odor Fritz from a screenplay by Richard Falk. The first German version made later the same year by Luna-Film is obscure. The soulless girl met the clay monster in *Alraune and the Golem* (1919), while German remakes of the original followed in 1928, 1930, and 1952.

There were two other science fiction efforts in 1918: Hungary's *The Mind-Detecting Ray*, a short directed by Alfred Désy, is about the betrayal of a villain's underworld activities by his stolen mind-reading machine. *The Kaiser's Shadow*, directed by R. William Neill, tells of a German spy's attempts to steal ray rifles.

Germany's *The Cabinet of Dr. Caligari* (1919) is not science fiction, unless controlled somnambulism is based on unknown science, but its influence on genre films to follow make its discussion here essential. Direction (Robert Wiene, 1881–1938), cinematography (Willy Hameister), and set designs (Hermann Warm, Walter Reimann and Walter Röhrig) were a major advance from their fantastic predecessors. As it occurs inside a madman's mind, all is surreal. The Cubist-style sets have no right angles.

Because of lingering anti-German feelings, *Caligari* did not surface in the U.S. until several years after its release. It was ridiculed by German and American establishment filmmakers whose tunnel vision focused on captured reality. *Caligari* offered subjective, prestyled reality, and despite stodgy criticism its fans were many. By transporting viewers into an impossible existence where physical laws oscillated, dreams became possible — and so did nightmares. *Caligari* taught filmmakers to successfully suspend disbelief, propelling sf cinema into worlds both brilliant and ludicrous.

It is no coincidence that this same production crew later combined to make silent science fiction's greatest achievement, Fritz Lang's *Metropolis* (1926).

The scenario, written by Hans Janowitz and Austrian poet Carl Meyer (with doctoring by Lang), told of Dr. Sonnow (Werner Krauss, 1884-1959), operating under the name Caligari, and his somnabulist carnival attraction Cesare (Conrad Veidt, 1893-1943). At night, the sleepwalker is sent out to murder. Bespectacled Caligari is a squat man with a Hitler mustache, black top hat, cloak, and walking stick, while his sleeping henchman, also in black, is tall, thin, walks stiffly, and has darkly underscored eyes. Cesare's mannerisms were a major influence on Boris Karloff's *Frankenstein* performance.

Young Czech writer Hans Janowitz based *Caligari* on personal trauma. He once saw a strange man prowling the bushes at a German fair and later learned that a woman in the vicinity had been murdered that night. Attending the girl's funeral, Janowitz was haunted by the presence of the same man. The script may have been heavily influenced by or stolen from an 11th-century German folk tale. Janowitz and Meyer were paid $200 apiece for their work by producer Erich Pommer.

The other science films of 1919 were headed by a British adaptation of H. G. Wells' *First Men in the Moon*, directed by J.V. Leigh. It starred Bruce Gordon as lunar expedition leader Professor Cavor.

In France's *The Wonderful Rays*, an electronic device recreates crimes, while Germany's *The Arc*, a forecast of civilization's destruction directed by Richard Oswald, was notable for the photography of Karl Freund. In Britain's *The Green Terror*, directed by Will Kellino, the title menace is an evil chemist's wheat-destroying substance.

Most noted for the expressionistic set designs of poet/architect Paul Scheerbart was Germany's *Algol* (1920), directed by Hans Werkmeister, about Mephisto (Emil Jennings), an alien from the distant planet Algol bent on conquering Earth with his eradicating death machine. He fails when his machine goes berserk, wipes out his family, and destroys him. There are no extant prints of the film and reports on its contents vary greatly.

Marshall Neilan produced and directed *Go and Get It* (1920), a picture similar to the creaky Forties potboilers. A man and woman reporting team race a rival newspaper to solve a series of mysterious murders, in the end learning that a famous scientist has transplanted the brain of a condemned criminal into the body of a gorilla (Bull Montana, 1887-1950). Montana also played an ape in *The Lost World* in 1925. The ape, having killed the scientist, stalks the streets in search of those responsible for his conviction.

The first version of Pierre Benoit's 1919 novel *L'Atlantide* was made in

France in 1921. Written and directed by Jacques Feyder, it told of undersea Queen Antinea, whose insatiable man-lust includes mounting her decapitated conquests in a bizarre trophy room. A better adaptation of the novel was made in Germany in 1932 with Brigitte Helm.

Lon Chaney (1883–1930) was born of deaf and dumb parents and maintained a life-long sympathy for human abnormalities. Inflicting incredible self-pain, Chaney bent himself into some of the movie's greatest monsters. Chaney's pantomimic skills, enhanced by the observation of his parent's handicaps, always added a touch of pathos to the grotesque beings he portrayed, most notably in *The Hunchback of Notre Dame* (1923) and *The Phantom of the Opera* (1925).

In 1922, the press in the United States and Great Britain was giving a lot of coverage to the Voronoff theories that transplanting monkey glands into human beings could promote and prolong life. The controversy birthed Barry Pain's novel, *The Octave of Claudius*, and the book became one of Chaney's most underrated films, *A Blind Bargain* (1922). Chaney is given a meaty double role, playing both Dr. Lamb, a crazed surgeon performing hideous experiments, and the pathetic results of a botched operation.

The J.G. Hawks scenario told of young down-and-out Robert (Raymond McKee) who submits to be Lamb's guinea pig in return for free treatment for his sick mother. Robert's nerves are rattled when he learns the doctor's hunchbacked assistant (Chaney) is actually part ape. The quasi-simian shows Robert the doctor's grotesque creations in various stages of human completion, kept in the operating room. When Lamb straps Robert to his table and prepares animalization, the hunchback releases a huge gorilla monster from its cage and the antagonist is hairily crushed. Also in 1922, Hal Roach produced the Pathé one-reeler, *Years to Come*, about when women rule the world.

The manipulation of time provided the basis for France's *The Crazy Ray* (1923) by whimsical director René Clair. Known in France as *Paris Qui Dort* or *Paris Asleep*, a scientist actually freezes Paris into a split second of time with his experimental ray. Only a few Parisians are unaffected, and most take the opportunity to frolic in the streets. Only the young hero, an Eiffel Tower watchman, takes the phenomenon seriously and seeks out its source. Paris is normalized and the hero is rewarded for his efforts by winning the heart of the scientist's pretty daughter. The comedy retains much of its innocent charm when viewed today.

The other science fiction films of 1923: Universal's *Legally Dead*, directed by William Parke, is about a kindly scientist's unwitting rejuvenation with adrenaline of a hanged murderer; *Radio Mania*, a Herman Holland production filmed in a primitive 3-D process about a young man's dream of friendly Martian visitation and the secrets of producing gold and diamonds; *The Sky Splitter*, directed by Ashely Miller and J. Norling, about a scientist's winged rocket that, being faster than the speed of light, allows him to view his own childhood; and *The Unknown Purple*, routinely produced and directed by Roland West, about a wrongly imprisoned scientist (Henry B. Walthall) who, after parole, becomes invisible with purple light and avenges his corrupt partner and cuckolding wife.

In a thinly veiled piece of Marxist propaganda came Russia's 45-minute *Aelita: The Revolt of the Robots* (1924). The lavishly accoutered movie, written by Fyodor Otzep and Alexei Faiko from a play by Alexei Tolstoy, tells of Muscovite engineer Los (Nikolai Tseretelli) who, after murdering his cheating wife, takes his space travel machine to Mars. Accompanying him is Red soldier Gusev (Igor Ilinski), seeking to spread Marx's cause throughout the cosmos. Oddly enough, a detective pursues him for his crime. On Mars, Los falls for Martian Queen Aelita (Yulia Solntseva), but romance is interrupted when the Prime Minister has the Earthlings imprisoned with Martian slaves wearing metallic garments and spiked helmets. Aelita's servant girl helps them escape. When betrayed by his blueblooded paramour, Los organizes a revolt before waking to find it all a nightmare. The moral is, never trust an aristocrat.

The mature sets and costumes, in the Constructivist style of Naum Gabo, were the work of an art direction team headed by Isaac Rabinowitch from the Kamerny Theater in Moscow. Not released in the United States until 1929 (and then with severe editing), it is intentionally comedic—though laughs are hindered by domestic cropping and bruised by partial extant prints. One memorably funny scene has the hero teaching Aelita how to kiss.

Other science fiction films of 1924: A searchlight-like aircraft-destroying device is the genius villain's weapon in Pathé's *The Death Ray*, while a similar ray forces criminals to kidnap a scientist's daughter in *The Perils of Paris*. Fox's *The Last Man on Earth*, produced and directed by Jack G. Blystone, takes place in 1954 when plague decimates the male population to one (Earle Foxe). Based on a story by John D. Swain, the lightweight action centers around the catty competition for his affections between two powerful senators. Though similar, this is a different story than *The Last Man on Earth* (1963), starring Vincent Price, and *The Omega Man* (1971), starring Charlton Heston, both based on Richard Matheson's novel, *I Am Legend*.

Willis H. O'Brien [See: *The Dinosaur and the Missing Link* (1914)] brought stop-motion photography into its own with his effects for *The Lost World* (1925), a tale of prehistoric monsters based on Sir Arthur Conan Doyle's novel. This was by far his most ambitious project before *King Kong* (1933) and marked a jump in the art of film illusion.

For the first time O'Brien used rubber rather than clay models for *The Lost World*. This not only made the monsters more realistic but enabled them to be lit adequately while filming without melting. The models were constructed with complicated wooden frames and wire veins for increased mobility and were equipped with internal air bladders so they appeared to breathe. Varnish was used to make the monsters salivate while chocolate syrup simulated blood. An aerial brace with thin wires attached enabled pterodactyls to fly and land-bound dinosaurs to leap.

Over forty models were used, constructed by Marcel Delgado, the same sculptor responsible for giving King Kong his lifelike appearance eight years later. O'Brien had to ask Delgado to work on the film several times. Only after O'Brien built and fully equipped Delgado's studio did Delgado agree to sculpt the beasts.

The Lost World was a predecessor to *King Kong* in terms of plot line as well as special effects. The story involves a group of British explorers, led by Professor Challenger (Wallace Beery, 1885–1949), who discover an isolated South American valley and plateau where a dateless habitat has survived intact. Challenger and crew escape the world just before volcanic destruction and return with a fertile brontosaurus egg. Predictably, the embryonic monster hatches, grows to full-size, and escapes into the streets. "My brontosaurus is loose," Challenger exclaims. The city is ravaged and London Bridge is destroyed before the reign of terror is thwarted.

A contemporary review of the picture in the British magazine *Kine Weekly* applauded the realism of the models but faulted their movements as mechanical. "There is hardly enough scope allowed for size comparisons except in the London scenes. London Bridge seems very unfamiliar," the review added.

The movie was produced by Earl Hudson and Watterson R. Rothacker, and directed by Harry O. Hoyt from a script by Marion Fairfax. The cameraman was Arthur Edeson, who later created the stark cinematography in Universal's *Frankenstein*.

The Lost World was remade by spendthrift producer-director Irwin Allen for 20th Century–Fox in 1960. Though veteran actors Claude Rains and Michael Rennie struggled to give the modern version integrity, the script by Allen and Charles Bennett was prohibitively inane. Cheap rear-projection of live lizards rather than models were used for the effects while shapely but talentless Jill St. John portrayed the spoiled-brat heroine.

Lon Chaney returned in *The Monster* (1925), produced and directed by Roland West. Chaney plays mad Dr. Ziska, who kidnaps passing motorists into his secret lab, murders them, and attempts to enliven their cadavers. Based on Crane Wilber's play, the film is unfortunately overdosed with comic relief.

Featuring the director and star of *The Cabinet of Dr. Caligari* (Robert Wiene and Conrad Veidt), Austria's *The Hands of Orlac*, was the disappointing first adaptation of Maurice Renard's novel, later to be made in a superior version, *Mad Love* (1935). The silent was used as critics' evidence claiming scenario and set design caused *Caligari's* fame more than did Wiene's direction. Veidt plays a scientist whose hands are destroyed in an accident. Using a new grafting technique, they are replaced with a murderer's hands. When new homicides occur, we're led to believe the hands are forcing Orlac to kill. The story's power is ultimately stifled by a naturalistic copout ending.

Other science fiction films of 1925: Fox's *From Mars to Munich*, about a tipsy Martian's visit to a German brewery to sample the local lager; a self-explanatory Spanish picture directed and written by Manuel Noriega called *Madrid in the Year 2000*; *Our Heavenly Bodies*, a German tour of the solar system, previewing the universe's destruction much in the manner of modern planetarium shows; and Britain's *The Secret Kingdom*, about a machine that reads people's minds and inevitably destroys their lives.

Foreshadowing directly the *Frankenstein* pictures of James Whale and indirectly the many "mad doctor" films of the Thirties and Forties was M-G-M's *The Magician* (1926). It was produced and directed by Rex Ingram, who shot the picture at his personal Riviera studios and on location in Paris and Nice.

Ingram, maker of non–science fiction silents such as *The Four Horsemen of the Apocalypse, Scaramouche,* and *Mare Nostrum*, adapted *The Magician* from a 1908 story by Somerset Maugham. In both direction and pacing it is more than coincidentally similar to Universal's horror classics. It has the notoriety of containing the screen's first dwarf lab assistant, and there is even an angry mob with torches scene, without which no *Frankenstein* film would be complete.

Dr. Haddo (Paul Wegener of *Golem* fame), using maidens' heart blood and ancient documents, has created artificial life. He abducts the pretty blonde heroine (Alice Terry) to his castle laboratory, below which a symbolic furnace roars. The exterior miniature used for the castle tower is almost a duplicate for that used in *The Bride of Frankenstein* (1935). Using Svengali-like hypnosis, he surreally visualizes Hell in her mind. Harry Lachman, the production manager here, was influenced by Ingram's Hades in his own *Dante's Inferno* (1935).

After symbolically raping the heroine with induced hallucinations, he prepares to murder her in a wild lab experiment. Naturally the hero (Ivan Petrovich) arrives. Haddo and lab are destroyed in a holocaust of flame.

The picture, though precedent-setting, is not without flaws. Ingram's forte was visual depiction rather than literary adaptation. Though always interesting to look at, the scenario is vague, especially for a silent.

Fritz Lang's warning prophecy *Metropolis* was a major advancement in technical innovation, influence on Hollywood's spectacle films, and the biggest contribution to modern sf cinema from the silent era. The visually inventive German UFA production was inspired by Lang's 1924 arrival in New York Harbor during a visit to study Hollywood production methods. As he was travelling from post-war Berlin, Lang (1890–1976) was not allowed immediately to land, which gave him ample opportunity to gaze at the unique skyline's nocturnal fantasy. Lang saw merged beauty and oppression in the massive cityscape, felt as if he were visiting an alien universe, and thought about ways of conveying his alienation in cinema. Lang co-wrote the scenario with wife Thea von Harbou (1888–1954), a popular science fiction novelist. UFA was a progressive film company trying consciously to raise film's aesthetic standards in the process of creating German Expressionism.

The chugging factory of *Metropolis* (UFA, 1926).

Though Lang was still young when making *Metropolis*, he was none-theless worldly and experienced. Trained as an architect with a flair for graphic arts, he travelled worldwide before the war and earned money drawing caricatures, postcards and cartoons. Wounded in combat, Lieutenant Lang wrote his first scenario while mending in a German hospital.The product was *Hilde Warren and Death* (1917), with Lang himself playing the Grim Reaper.

The still-developing supercharged skills that produced Lang's initial efforts were derived from the early American and French serials. *The Spiders* (1919), *The Hindu Tombstone* and *Dr. Mabuse* (both 1922) combined a brisk visual style with a keen knowledge of popular fiction. All were intended as serials but chopped because of budget difficulties.

Of these, only *Mabuse* contained sf elements, though of the crime-melodrama variety. Mabuse, like Fu Manchu, ran a world-wide crime syndicate with Germanic efficiency. Primitve when compared to *Metropolis* (everything was), it is given highlights of sheer horror by Rudolph Klein-Rogge's performance in the lead.

While Lang made a name in German cinema, his wife was attaining success of her own writing futuristic novels. The couple had already meshed talent for *Mabuse* and the much-heralded fantasy *Siegfried* before *Metropolis* was made. Post-war Germany stimulated Lang's concern for social catastrophe, while his visit to New York — fleshed out by a maddening dash through Times Square — worked as a catalyst for his pessimistic prophecy.

Lang intended his film to take place in the year 2000, but the severely edited Paramount release the following year was advertised as a vision of a thousand years in the future. Since nothing with its scope or time frame had been done on film before, there were some closed-minded critics who felt it presumptuous — and seemed offended at being asked to accept another's mythology. A similar response was later caused by H.G. Wells' *Things to Come* (1936). Overall, reviews were glowing, filled with flattering comparisons between Lang's preview and Wells' novels.

The picture was a smash success — a necessity as far as UFA and producer Erich Pommer were concerned — as it was shot over a nine-month period and was by far the most expensive film made in Germany up to that time.

It is a shame that American audiences have only been able to see a fraction of the complete work. When Paramount assigned Channing Pollock (paying him $20,000 for his efforts) to edit and supply English-language titles, his first move was to cut the length. The 120-minute extravaganza (already chopped by 50 minutes in Germany) was thought by Twenties Hollywood to be wearisome. Removed were Lang's inventive titles. At one point in the German version, jagged impressionistic letters jump together from disarranged lettering flung into the frame, and at another a word appears to bleed.

The movie's scope, as would be the case with *Things to Come*, rendered it weak on human relationships — less than a flaw and more than compensated for by the strong visuals and political analogy. Pollack was smart enough to keep the film's strong points while cropping its weaknesses. The U.S. version, which runs a then-normal 70 minutes, includes all of the crowds, shock, and special effects, while its plot has been cropped till skeletal. Still, even seen complete, the film is as soulless as the society it depicts.

The story takes place in 2000 A.D. in the mythical German city of Metropolis. The city's industrial titan, Jon Frederson (Alfred Abel as the character known in the U.S. version as John Masterman), his son Freder Frederson (hero Gustav Fröhlich), and the rest of the city's wealthy live in luxurious tower-top penthouses, while the poor and oppressed yeoman live in muddled masses in the squalor below. Metropolis is introduced in a montage of chugging machines and sprawling urbanscape. Jon, ever-ascetic and benign in his responsibilities as the city's governor, dictates decisions to a team of eager assistants as his son competes in the local stadium or languorously plays in a garden with sparsely clad women supplied by his venerable chamberlain.

The fantastic sets were the work of Otto Hunte, Eric Kettlehut, and Karl Vollbrecht, while the special effects enabling characters and sets to interact were the work of Eugen Shuftan. Shuftan (originally Eugen Schuffan) was an innovator in the use of mirrors in filmmaking. Born in

Alfred Abel (left, as "Jon Frederson") in his *Metropolis* office (UFA, 1926).

1893, he, like Lang, studied architecture, painting, and cartooning before working in animated films. Three years before *Metropolis's* release he invented a new method of cinematic magic to become known as the Shuftan process. He combined the action of live actors with reflected images of model work or painted backdrops by removing selected areas of a mirror's reflective coating. Shuftan became an Oscar-winning Hollywood cinematographer for *The Hustler* (1961). Co-director of cinematography Karl Freund directed his own noteworthy pictures *The Mummy* (1932) and *Mad Love* (1935).

As young hearts are unaffected by caste, Freder falls in love with a beautiful working-class girl named Maria (heroine Brigitte Helm, b. 1906), the true focal point of the picture, who was considered an abomination of good taste by the boy's father. He meets the militant nurse as she and a group of ragamuffins invade his plush garden. "These are your brothers," Maria says before she and the children are forced out behind huge doors.

Freder asks his father to explain the street-level poverty, but Jon is evasive. The boy persuades an inquiry to gain him access to the lower levels; so dressed in the anonymous overalls of the workers, he descends into horrible catacombs pursuing love. It is a baroque dream of technology gone mad. Crumpled men become exhausted and collapse over vast machines.

Freder discovers Maria preaching the importance of mediation between labor and management in a subterranean church. She tells the story of the Tower of Babel, shown as a tilting cake of rock seething with bent subservients. Freder is impressed and unaware that his father and Rotwang (Jon's personal mad scientist, played with gusto by Rudolph Klein-Rogge [1889–1955] formerly *Mabuse*) are plotting to squelch the dissidence.

Klein-Rogge's performance makes Rotwang a memorable villian. His deformed and black-gloved right hand was later satirized by Peter Sellers as the title character in *Dr. Strangelove, or How I learned to Stop Worrying and Love the Bomb* (1964-British). Klein-Rogge sets a precedent here for a half century of cinema laden with Germanic evil. His gingerbread cottage at the roots of Metropolis' towers would be comical if it weren't for the pentagram — a symbol of satanic intent — above his remote-controlled door. Inside, the classic wizard has the power to create artificial life.

"We have made machines out of men," he profoundly exclaims. "Now I will make men out of Machines — a robot indistinguishable from a woman." Rotwang builds a robot double for Maria. Before the artificial woman's flesh is applied, she has the haunting face of a Mycaenean death mask, a domed head, and high round breasts. The robot oozes sensuality.

After kidnapping the ethereal heroine, the automated surrogate performs an erotic dance at a nightclub. The male crowd is worked into such a frenzy of desire that they riot. Unfortunately, the scene is so hot that censors frequently cut it. Helm's breasts, which naturally have the same charm as the robot's, are bare with the exception of pasties, and strings of beads cover her loins and inner thighs. She moves like a snake. The actress portrays a sexual animal as she writhes atop a hideous seven-headed statue. Men grope for her, fingers stretched, eyes filled with despair.

In the ensuing brouhaha the city's waterworks are smashed, causing the lower levels to be flood-ravaged. The real Maria escapes and is chased anxiously from niche to niche in the rising water. The villain and robot are destroyed — she by burning at the stake, her fake flesh melting to reveal her death mask face. Maria proves her courage by saving trapped toddlers. Thirty thousand extras were used for the mob scenes, 11,000 of which were asked to shave their heads. Freder gets the girl and Jon shakes hands with a burly foreman, striking a new labor-management understanding.

The hasty happy ending seems uncertain after the aspects of human nature displayed earlier. The permanence of the plot solution is in doubt and it is appropriate to call *Metropolis* pessimistic.

Though the cast is superb, it is the settings rather than the characterizations that immortalize *Metropolis*. The huge work areas are domed basements, curved rooms of automation. Above are airplane taxis while rail trains shoot off into vast distances at rocket speed.

Lang and von Harbou teamed again to make *The Woman in the Moon* (1929). In flight from harassing Nazis, Lang left his country and wife, ending up in Hollywood working on low-budget projects of little note.

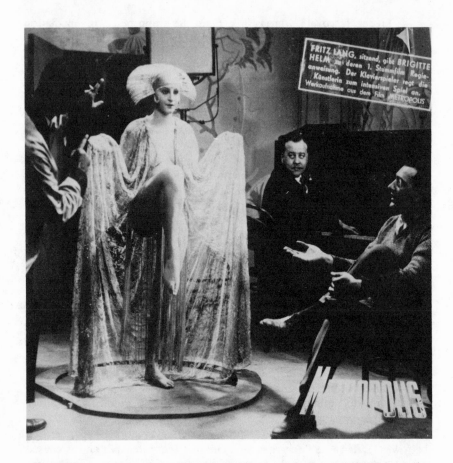

"Robots always point their toes," Fritz Lang (far right) reminds Brigitte Helm during a rehearsal for her erotic dance in *Metropolis* **(UFA/Paramount, 1926).**

Fox's *The Wizard* (1927) is a haunted-house thriller based on Gaston Leroux' 1912 story *Balaoo*. Previously filmed as *Balaoo the Demon Baboon* (1913), the story was originally straight horror with science fiction elements, but director Richard Rosson chose to instill it with extensive comic relief in the form of dumb detectives. Dr. Coriolos (Gustav von Seyffertitz) uses his created man-ape (George Kotsonaros) to murder those who framed his executed son. Though no prints of the film survive, contemporary reviews agree on the effectiveness of Frank Good's eerie cinematography.

Brigitte Helm returned in *At the Edge of the World* (1927), a German feature directed by Karl Grune that envisions a future war's destruction.

Also in Germany, Paul Wegener played the title role in *The Strange Case of Dr. Ramper* (1927), directed by Max Reichmann. An Arctic explorer, while trapped in the tundra, takes on the form of a prehistoric missing link.

Upon returning to civilization, he is forced to work as a sideshow freak, falls in love with his pretty trainer (Mary Johnson), gets rejected, has his normal intellect returned with the help of a scientist (Max Schreck, 1879–1936, most famous as the vampire in *Nosferatu* in 1922), and returns north to escape society's hypocrisies.

Wegener plays the scientist who uses artificial insemination to cross a prostitute with a murderer producing an evil offspring in Germany's *Alraune* (1928), written and directed by Henrik Galeen, an old friend of Wegener's from *The Golem*. The third version of Hans Heinz Ewer's controversial novel starred Brigitte Helm in the title role. Known in England as *Daughter of Destiny*, audiences there were confused when the film first appeared. All references to Alraune's conception were removed from their version by censors, leaving a confusing tale of a nasty girl who mistreats her foster father for no reason. Unlike the 1918 Hungarian version, Alraune changes from evil to good. German remakes in 1930 (with Helm) and 1952 followed.

Fritz Lang, criticized for his unscientific approach to the future in *Metropolis*, enlisted as technical advisors Germany's two outstanding missile experts Professors Hermann Oberth and Willy Ley, for his final silent *Woman in the Moon* (*Die Frau Im Mond*) (1928). The first portion, involving construction of a lunar-bound spaceship, was so reliably founded on contemporary astronautical theory that prints were later seized by Hitler — tipped off, no doubt, by Oberth, a contributor to the development of the V-1. Ley fled to America.

The second half, dealing with the lunar surface's exploration, is based on scientific conjecture and forgivably dated. The moon is given substantial atmosphere, caves full of gold, and mountaintops covered with snow.

Professor Manfeldt (Klaus Pohl), convinced that missile flight to the moon is possible, recruits young millionaire designer Helius (Willy Fritsch) to help. After construction, the team of astronauts is rounded out by scientist Windegger (Gustav von Wangenheim); his fiancée and the professor's secretary, Friede (Gerda Marcus); an undercover international trust agent (Fritz Rasp); and, at the last moment, a young stowaway (Gustl Stark-Gesettenbaur). Their mission is one of greed as Manfeldt believes the moon is made of solid gold. What follows is the screen's first countdown scene. When the rocket reaches the moon's sandy dunes, those aboard discover there are indeed large gold ore deposits there. The professor is killed by accident, the secret agent's identity is revealed, and Friede and Helius fall in love. As there is only oxygen left for two return passengers, Friede and Helius agree to stay. Windegger and the small stowaway return to Earth. Lang's next film was the classic *M* (1931), the launch of Peter Lorre's career.

Wrapping up the silent era: A villain uses Kappa rays to destroy aircraft in *Code of the Air* (1928) directed by James P. Hogan. A futuristic plane supplied with an ultrascientific fuel that gets 1,000 miles to the pint is the star of Universal's *The Sky Skidder* (1929) directed by Bruce Mitchell.

Sound

French Jules Verne (1828–1905) was the father of science fiction. The nineteenth century was a time of strides in scientific discovery, and if Verne's work is prophetic today, it is because of his intense research in keeping tabs on developing inventions. His detailed conception of the submarine *Nautilus* is indicative of his time's preoccupation. To measure his ingenuity, examine the condition of extant science when he wrote. Verne created the *Nautilus* 30 years before the first functional submarine.

Electricity, an important part of the *Nautilus*'s operation, was no more than a lab curiosity in the 1860's when Verne wrote *20,000 Leagues Under the Sea* and *Mysterious Island*.

After obtaining a law degree, as had his father, Verne began his literary career as a playwright. His work soon began to reflect his obsession with inventions, specifically those enabling exotic travel.

The first movie version of Jules Verne's *Mysterious Island* (1929), filmed in a two-color process by M-G-M, was the first science fiction picture with a soundtrack consisting solely of sound effects.

In typical Hollywood fashion, the scenario by Lucien Hubbard takes great license with Verne's novel. For example, Captain Nemo was inexplicably replaced as inventor of the futuristic submarine by Count Dakkar (Lionel Barrymore, 1879–1954). Hubbard also co-directed the film with Maurice Tournier and Benjamin Christiansen.

Dakkar has invented his underwater boat and inhabits the title island when monopolist Russians attack, driving hero and crew into the supposed safety of the sea's depths. While there, they discover a subaquatic community of tiny men and various terrors of the deep, including a giant octopus borrowed from Verne's *20,000 Leagues Under the Sea*. The special effects were provided by James Baseui, Louis H. Tolhurst, and Irving Ries.

Considering the 1929 antagonists' nationality, it is ironic that the first remake of *Mysterious Island* (1941) was produced by the Soviet Children's Film Studio. Designed for a juvenile audience, the Russian film, directed by Ev Pengiline and B.M. Chelintzev, tells of Captain Nemo aiding a group of youthful castaways.

Three other versions have been made. In 1950 Columbia adapted the subject matter into a serial directed by Spencer Gordon Bennett and produced by Sam Katzman. Again Verne's novel was freely adapted. Captain Nemo (Leonard Penn), using the *Nautilus*'s weaponry (including a device that enables him to walk through walls), battles Rulu (Karen Randle), a female Mercurian planning to conquer 1865 Earth with various ray guns.

The best version, by Columbia in 1961, told of Civil War prisoners who escape via hot air ballon, are blown off course by a thunderstorm, and land on the title island where they encounter oversized animals — compliments of the great Ray Harryhausen's special effects. Captain Nemo (Herbert Lom) shows up late in the screenplay (by John Prebble, Daniel Ullman and Crane Wilbur) in his *Nautilus* to help the castaways off the island where a volcano is ominously brewing. Cy Endfield directed the Charles H. Schneer production.

The most recent version, a French/Italian 1972 remake, starred Omar Sharif as Captain Nemo.

One of the most frightening prophecies was British-Gaumont's *High Treason* (1929), directed by Maurice Elvey, set in 1940. The L'Estrange Fawcett script, based on a play by Pemberton Billing, told of a world war between the Federated Atlantic States and the United States of Europe. Originally banned by U.S. censors after a limited run, the movie's most stunning scene shows a gas bombing of New York City. The film also envisions helicopter taxis, wall-sized TV screens, and an English Channel-spanning tunnel.

America flopped in its first attempt to make a big budget science fiction film. Fox's *Just Imagine*, directed by David Butler, was a 1930 musical set in 1980. Over $250,000 was spent on building an intricate model of New York City in the future. Too bad the songs of G.G. De Sylva, Ray Henderson, and Lew Brown were inane — as was the script.

As prophecy, *Just Imagine* took the collar. The characters have letters of the alphabet for first names and numbers for last. Prohibition is still in effect, although "bourbon tablets" can be acquired with ease. Babies come out of vending machines — quite a disappointment to the time-traveling hero — and a perfected TV spy system invades the privacy of young ladies' bedrooms. Only poor people cannot afford airplanes, which can land like helicopters on the tops of skyscrapers. The buildings in Manhattan are 200 stories high with rocket-powered elevators. The city is built on nine stacked levels. Doorbells of the future are rings of light.

With all of the budget blown on the NYC model, little money was left for the other effects in the film. When a rocketship takes off for Mars, it is clear that it is a model pulled on a string, and the ship's exhaust strikes heroine Maureen O'Sullivan (b. 1911) right in the face, yet leaves her unharmed with her hair mussed. The cuddly O'Sullivan later played Jane opposite Johnny Weismuller in *Tarzan* films.

The plot is the conventional boy meets girl, boy loses girl, and so on.

The acting still reflects the stagy mugging of the silent era. None of the songs ("I'm Only the Words," "Never Swat a Fly") have been remembered.

The first sound edition of Hans Heinz Ewers' novel *Alraune* was made in 1930 in Germany by UFA. Tepidly directed by Richard Oswald, it featured Brigitte Helm in a reprise to her role in the 1928 silent, again playing the product of artificial insemination, a cross between a prostitute and a murderer. The third of four film versions, this is the weakest. The last remake of *Alraune* (also known as *Unnatural*) was directed by Fritz Rotter in 1952 and starred Hildegard Knef in the title role. Erich von Stroheim played the scientist. Reversing the tale, the man is the evil character who exploits the innocent yet unnaturally-conceived girl. He shoots her dead at the climax and the film ends as the scientist walks through the fog to be hanged.

Another German 1930 remake was the plagiaristic *Der Anderer (The Other)*, based on a play by Paul Lindau. It stars Fritz Kortner as a scientist whose primal alter ego emerges after he drinks a potion. Does this sound familiar? The tale is known as *The Man Within*.

Sax Rohmer's insidious Oriental villain made his second sound film appearance in Paramount's *The Return of Dr. Fu Manchu*. Directed by Rowland V. Lee (1891–1975), who later directed *Son of Frankenstein* in 1939, it tells of Fu (Warner Oland, 1880–1938) and his new invention, a world-threatening serum that induces catalepsy. Rohmer's novel was scripted for the screen by Florence Ryerson and Lloyd Corrigan.

The Last Hour (1930) was an undistinguished British production directed by Walter Forde. A hijacking prince uses a death ray to steal airplane cargo. It disappeared soon after its release.

The usual mad-scientist-and-gorilla combination appeared in *The Horror* (1930), a Bud Pollard production, which suggested that its star *might* be Lon Chaney—then very ill—by using a look-alike actor and playing the resemblance to its fullest in advertisement posters.

The French contributed to the science fiction genre with *The End of the World* (1930), which is similar yet unrelated to the 1916 Danish silent with the same title, and not to be confused with the 1962 film also known as *Panic in Year Zero* (1977), or the loathsome 1977 Christopher Lee film. This picture, based on a novel by Camille Flammarion, depicts a comet's collision with the Earth.

Boris Karloff (1887–1969), the undisputed king of the horror films, was born William Henry Pratt in Dulwich, England, the son of a public official stationed in India. Karloff tried truck driving and farming before taking a job with a small British filmmaking company. When the Army refused his services during World War I because of a heart problem, Karloff went to Hollywood, changed his name, and scored a couple of supporting roles before getting his big break in 1931. He was signed by Universal Studios to play Frankenstein's monster in their classic adaptation of Mary Shelley's novel. Karloff was an actor for over sixty years and added a special magic to every role he played. He worked hard at his craft right up until his death.

Although the role that launched his career was mute, his unique vocal intonations gave him one of the most imitated voices in show business.

The role of Frankenstein's monster was originally offered to Bela Lugosi, who had been a hit in Universal's stagy adaptation of Bram Stoker's novel *Dracula* earlier in the year. After completing a screentest Lugosi turned down the role, his conceit not allowing him to play under such a heavy load of make-up in a nonspeaking part.

Karloff was not thrilled with the prospect either, but had not equalled Lugosi's success in acting. He agreed to play the part predominantly because of the steady $125-a-week salary. The movie grossed $14 million. Universal assigned British director James Whale (1886–1957) to make *Frankenstein* after Whale saw Lugosi's screentest and became interested in the project. Whale, in turn, hired Karloff to play the creature and cast British stage actor Colin Clive (1898–1937) in the title role. Interestingly, Lugosi did portray Frankenstein's monster – but not very well – in a later Universal B-picture sequel, *Frankenstein Meets the Wolf Man* (1943).

Make-up illusionist Jack Pierce (1889–1968) worked three hours a day with Karloff to develop his patented make-up, which was destined to become, along with Lon Chaney's *Phantom of the Opera* (1925), the most famous monster make-up in film history. The monster was 18 inches taller and 48 pounds heavier than the actor. Karloff's weight dropped from 175 to 155 during the rigorous shooting schedule.

Since Universal patented the make-up, no non-Universal *Frankenstein* movies contain monsters that resemble Karloff.

Pierce, after researching anatomy, surgery, criminology, and electrodynamics, discovered six ways a surgeon could cut a skull, and figured Henry Frankenstein (surgery not his forte) would choose the simplest. He would slice the skull straight across the top, hinge it, insert the brain, and clamp it shut. For this reason, Pierce gave his monster a flattopped box of a head. A big scar was dug across the creature's forehead, which was held together by two metal clamps. The metal studs protruding from the sides of the neck were inlets for electricity, although this fact was not revealed until the series' third entry *Son of ...* in 1939. The lizard eyes and false head were made of rubber. The face was coated with a blue-green greasepaint that photographed gray in black and white. Karloff's legs were stiffened with steel struts and he wore two pairs of pants and asphalt-spreader boots. His fingernails were blackened with shoe polish and his arms were made to appear longer by shortening the sleeves of the sheepskin jerkin that reached below the actor's waist.

The first step in the make-up's application was the layering of Karloff's eyelids with paraffin to weigh them down. Invisible wire clamps were fixed over the lips to pull the corners of the mouth out and down, The crown and overhanging brow, supposedly grafted from the head of another man, was attached in one piece. The face and neck were enlarged with flesh-like layers of cotton soaked in a special liquid preparation. The bolts were attached to the neck with cotton and glue—a technique which left Karloff's neck blemished with lingering scars.

Pierce, researching ancient and modern burial customs, learned that Egyptians had bound criminals head-to-toe before entombing them alive. When the body's blood became watery after death, it rushed to the extremities, causing abnormal growth and swelling in the arms, legs, hands, and feet. Pierce felt these deformities were suitable for a creation made from the cadavers of executed felons.

Pierce had entered show business after an unsuccessful stint as a professional baseball player. The diminutive shortstop was cut in the minor leagues in 1910 and was employed as a theater-manager/projectionist by Harry Culver, founder of Culver City. He worked for Young Deer, the American Indian film producer, until 1914 when he was contracted by Universal as assistant cameraman. He soon discovered his make-up skills and was employed in that capacity at Fox for a spell before returning to Universal to stay. Shelley's book tells of a well-meaning scientist who suffers great anguish when he tampers in God's domain by creating a living human being. The monster speaks articulate English and suffers greatly because of his abnormality; he only kills when driven by hate and rejection. In the screenplay, written by Robert Florey, Garret Fort, and Francis Edwards Faragoh, and adapted by Florey and John L. Balderston from the play by Peggy Webling, the monster is given a murderer's brain and is mute, though he does speak a few words in the immediate sequel, *The Bride of Frankenstein* (1935), and then again in the third sequel, *The Ghost of Frankenstein* (1942). In spite of the differences between the film and the book, the cinematography of Arthur Edeson, who shot the film in stark black and white, and the spooky settings of Herman Rosse, give the picture a Gothic flavor true to the novel. Shelley's theme remains hauntingly intact.

Karloff is magnificent as the walking dead, his childlike reactions to a brand new world and his own grotesque form giving the role a depth not apparent in the script. According to Karloff, the monster's pathetic hand gestures were copied from Lon Chaney's in *The Trap* (1922), although there are elements of *The Golem* and *Caligari* in his portrayal as well.

If the crisp dialogue and terse performances seem cliché-ridden by today's standards, it is only because of *Frankenstein*'s enveloping influence on both horror and science fiction films to follow.

The movie begins with a warning to impressionable audiences from Carl Laemmle, Jr., then the president of Universal, delivered from a single spotlight on a darkened soundstage by actor Edward Van Sloan: "We are about to unfold the story of Frankenstein, a man of science who sought to create life after his own image without reckoning on God. It is one of the strangest stories ever told. It deals with the two great mysteries of creation, life and death. I think it will thrill you. It may shock you. It may even *horrify* you!"

With this unsettling message under their belts, the audience is swept off to a gloomy night somewhere in Central Europe where a man is being buried in a medieval cemetery. Gravestones protrude from knolls at odd angles. Lurking in the shadows are Dr. Henry Frankenstein, a chemical galvanist, and his hunchbacked assistant, Fritz (the marvelous character actor Dwight Frye, 1899–1943), formerly the insect-eating Renfield in Universal's *Dracula*.

They wait for the solemn ceremony and the grave-diggers' labor to be completed. Henry is tall, thin and pale. Fritz is dwarfish and bounces about with an insectlike agility, aided by a gnarled walking stick. Alone at last, the doctor throws his coat to the dirt and the two begin to dig up the fresh corpse. In the background, the cloaked figure of the Grim Reaper looks on, holding a shepherd's crook. Henry is wild-eyed as he and Fritz struggle to lift the coffin from the grave. He pats the coffin as if comforting it and says, "He's just resting ... waiting for a new life to come!"

In a spine-chilling attempt to secure a brain for Henry's creation, Fritz, knife in teeth, climbs up a gallows to cut down a recently hanged man. Henry is disgusted when he finds the cadaver's neck broken, rendering the brain useless for his experiment. (One wonders why they searched a gallows for an unbroken neck.) The scientist orders Fritz to go to nearby Goldstadt Medical College to steal the preserved brain on display there. In the emptied lecture hall where Henry's former teacher, the distinguished professor of anatomy Dr. Waldman (Edward Van Sloan, 1882–1964, the vampire-hunting Van Helsing in *Dracula*), has just completed teaching an evening class, Fritz discovers two brains: a normal brain and the abnormal brain of a psychopathic killer. When the bungling hunchback drops the normal brain, he panics and grabs the other one before scurrying out a window.

Henry's pretty fiancée Elizabeth (Mae Clarke, 1910, best remembered as the recipient of James Cagney's grapefruit in *Public Enemy*) hasn't seen Henry since he began to conduct mysterious experiments in an abandoned windmill at the edge of town. She and friend Victor Morris (John Boles) worry about Henry, their concern fed by his raving letters. There is an odd assumption of platonicism between Elizabeth and Victor. She considers him a brotherly "dear," yet his crush is evident and his flirtations almost incestuous. Elizabeth and Victor visit Dr. Waldman, who agrees to accompany them on a visit to the mill to investigate.

They pick a lousy night to pay their call. Not only is there a raging thunder and lightning storm underway, but Henry is just about to bring his completed man to life. At first Henry orders Fritz to send the visitors away, but upon reconsideration decides to let them observe his grandest scientific discovery.

"Quite a scene, heh?" Frankenstein cackles when his sanity is questioned. "One man crazy ... three very sane spectators."

The assembled body is ceremoniously raised to the roof into the stormy night. Henry has discovered the life ray beyond the ultraviolet. Inside his impressive laboratory dials are turned and switches are thrown. His

Dwight Frye is bent in more ways than one as the dwarfish insect Fritz in *Frankenstein* (Universal, 1931).

elaborate equipment begins to crackle as if with anticipation. The fascinating electronic effects in the animation scene were the work of special effects man Ken Strickfaden. When the monster is struck directly by a lightning bolt, he is lowered. There is an excruciating moment of suspense before one of the monster's hands moves.

"*It's alive!*" Henry screams, nearly bursting with a mad pride.

At this point in the original screenplay Henry said, "In the name of

God, now I know what it feels like to be God!" But the line was cut by censors for being blasphemous, causing a noticeable jump in the film.

Later, Henry's father Baron Frankenstein (played for comic relief by blustery character actor Frederick Kerr) thinks this talk of bringing life to the dead is "stuff and nonsense." He is convinced his son is involved with another woman.

Back at the mill we see the monster, now standing upright with his back to the camera. He turns slowly and we get our first glimpse of his horrible face. The impact of his scene has been diluted by the fame of Pierce's make-up job, but was truly frightening to unprepared theatergoers.

Henry behaves like a proud father when his ugly creation displays an ability to obey simple commands for a concerned Dr. Waldman, but his euphoria is short-lived. The monster panics at the sight of a flaming torch and has to be bound in chains in a dungeon cell. Learning of the creature's fire phobia, Fritz becomes a cruel tormentor, torturing the frightened beast until he gets a little too close and is hanged to death. Here again censors made a cut. We no longer actually see the monster murder the sadistic hunchback. Instead viewers see a long shot of Waldman and Frankenstein from above and hear Fritz's death scream. In this case, the unseen murder is more effective. When Frankenstein and Waldman arrive in the cell, Fritz is hanging from his neck by a rope, casting a ghastly shadow on the dingy wall behind him. The creature is free of his chains and growling like an untamed animal. Henry manages to knock out his creation with a hypodermic needle, but not before Waldman has been choked into unconsciousness.

Baron Frankenstein arrives at the spooky mill to take the shaken Henry home, while a fully recovered Waldman promises to painlessly destroy the monster. Before the anatomy professor can keep his promise, the creature wakes and strangles him to death. The monster is loose!

Believing their nightmare over, the Frankenstein family prepares for Henry and Elizabeth's wedding. The monster runs into the young daughter of a woodsman who introduces herself to the mute as Maria. She is unafraid in her innocence, and the monster is soothed by her friendship. For the first time he twists his black lips into a crooked smile. Maria tosses daisies into a pond where they float and look like boats. She shares the flowers with the monster so he can play also. When the creature runs out of daisies he tosses the little girl into the pond thinking that she—like the flowers—will float. The scene of the little girl's drowning was cut by censors who thought it too vivid. In its current form the film moves awkwardly away from the pond as the smiling monster reaches out to grab Maria. Later, the horror of the murder is revealed as we see Maria's zombie-eyed father (Forrester Harvey) carrying the little girl's soggy corpse through the shocked town.

On the day of her wedding, Elizabeth worries about Dr. Waldman's tardiness. The monster, seeking his creator, sneaks into Elizabeth's room and frightens her. He leaves her unharmed, fleeing at the sound of her screams. A crowd gathers around Frankenstein Castle, furious about the murder of the child. Henry comes to the awful realization that his creation is still very much alive and obviously more dangerous than ever. Feeling responsible, Henry leaves Elizabeth in Victor's hands and joins a search party. The angry mob scene soon became a Universal trademark; none of the company's films in the Thirties and Forties was complete without a raging vigilante group.

Appropriately, it is Henry who finds the murderer. The monster shows little affection for the man who gave him life and knocks Henry cold. Frankenstein is gathered up under the monster's arm and dragged to the top of the windmill, the site of the creature's "birth." The mob arrives just in time to see the monster hurl his "father" from the top of the mill. Henry grossly strikes one of the mill's vanes before plummeting to the earth. The townspeople set the mill ablaze in the climax. The monster snarls in terror and agony as the flames lick upward, finally consuming the structure, and presumably the walking corpse. The climactic fire was created by Universal special effects wizard John P. Fulton, who won acclaim for his work on *The Invisible Man* (1933) which was also directed by James Whale.

In a cheery denoument (later cut to segue with the sequel) Baron Frankenstein drinks a glass of wine with his maids while Henry sleeps peacefully, Elizabeth at his side. The trailer has been restored to some TV prints.

As we all know, the monster was not really killed in the fire and was to make many more film appearances during his lengthy cinematic career. In spite of this film's success at the box office, it was four years before Universal made the first the best of many sequels, *The Bride of Frankenstein*, again directed by Whale and starring Clive and Karloff.

At the time of *Frankenstein*'s initial release near the end of 1931, a few prints were made with a green tint—the theory being that green was the symbolic color of horror—but the normal black and white prints, highlighting the starkly eerie settings, were the more popular.

Karloff received sacks of fan mail after the picture's release. This surprised Universal, which had sent him home after shooting and did not invite him to the gala premiere. Most of the letters came from children who, more than adults, showed great compassion and insight into the monster's character, understanding him to be bewildered and afraid, a victim of something beyond his control.

Frankenstein's pacing and self-seriousness make it joyous entertainment even today, long after its shock value has faded.

Dr. X, produced by First National and released by Warner Brothers in 1932, was the first science fiction film to be shot in the modern color process, although it is currently shown exclusively in black and white. It was also the first time that actress Fay Wray (B. 1907) ever screamed before a camera, launching the career of a great pair of lungs.

With a stress on shadows and angular images, director Michael Curtiz (1888-1962) tells of a police commissioner (Robert Warwick), a detective (Robert Halloran), and a wisecracking reporter (Lee Tracy) who investigate a series of full-moon cannibal murders. Their search takes them to the scientific academy of respected Dr. Xavier (Lionel Atwill, 1885–1946), whose daughter Joan (Wray) has narrowly escaped falling victim to the cloaked flesheater. The academy is an appropriately spooky old mansion on the "cliffs of Long Island," complete with a laboratory, secret panels, and a cluster of weird suspects.

The murderer turns out to be a one-armed scientist named Dr. Wells (Preston Foster, 1900–1970), creator of a new arm and face for himself with his recently invented synthetic flesh. The good-natured thrills are best illustrated by a scene in which Wells unscrews his artificial arm in front of our shocked heroes. He dies when the reporter torches him with a kerosene lamp. Although marred by excessive comic relief, *Dr. X* stands the test of time.

Fredric March (1897–1975) became the only actor to win an Academy Award as a movie monster for his title roles in the first talkie version of *Dr. Jekyll and Mr. Hyde* (1932). The Paramount film has seldom been seen since its debut fifty years ago. There are several reasons for this. M-G-M bought the property from Paramount to avoid a re-release that might compete with their 1941 version starring Spencer Tracy. Even after copyright and legal problems cleared up, the film did not resurface. March's Hyde characterization resembles a less-than-flattering Negro stereotype, rendering the film unsuitable for a racially sensitive era.

Though dated (March's performance now seems highly theatrical) the direction of Rouben Mamoulian (b. 1897) and cinematography of Karl Struss create an erotic intensity seldom seen in American films. Scenes in which Hyde lustfully paws strumpet Miriam Hopkins while taunting her with thinly-veiled lewd suggestions, caused censor troubles at the time of its release in England.

Especially impressive are make-up magician Wally Westmore's transformation scenes, done without the stop-motion techniques later made famous in Universal's *The Wolf Man* (1941). Enhanced by the sound of an amplified heartbeat, the effect was achieved through use of infra-red film, subtle changes in lighting, and special make-up visible in some light and not in others. This gives the impression that the actor's face is actually changing before our eyes. The same technique was used again by Westmore in *The Man from Half-Moon Street* (1944) for the rapid aging of actor Nils Asther. It is the rich quality of the visuals in this version of the Stevenson classic, rather than the performances, that make it a standout.

As the film opens, Dr. Henry Jekyll's theories on human psyche polarization are being scorned by colleague Dr. Lanyon (Holmes Herbert). After performing the experiment on himself, Jekyll/Hyde finds himself battling over his feeling for two women, one innocent (Rose Hobart) and one promiscuous (Hopkins). The sexy dance hall singer Ivy Pierson does not appear in the novel. She was introduced in the script of the Barrymore silent.

Uglier than ever, Hyde murders the father of Jekyll's fiancée and is tracked down by London police and shot.

Fredric March tells Miriam Hopkins she can run but she can't hyde in the racially offensive version of *Dr. Jekyll and Mr. Hyde* **(Paramount, 1932).**

German writer Curt Siodmak (b. 1902) became obsessed with transcontinental travel in the Thirties, perhaps predicting his own flight to America in escape from the Nazis. He wrote three films concerning the subject. Two predicted a railroad tunnel beneath the Atlantic, and a third, the best of the three, evisioned a huge platform in the middle of the ocean where planes could refuel and pilots could rest. The latter film was *F.P. 1 Does Not Answer* (*F.P. 1 Antwortet Nicht*) (1932), produced by Erich Pommer and directed by Karl Hartl.

Most of the film takes place on the platform, actually a borrowed floating drydock 1,500 feet long and 400 feet wide. In spite of its vagueness regarding nationalities during accidents and sabotage attempts, the script is intelligent. The concept was not so silly before the jet age.

Three versions were shot simultaneously in English, German, and French, co-produced by Fox, UFA and Gaumont. Adaptation of Siodmak's German dialogue into English was by Robert Stevenson and Peter McFarland.

The film's weak point is its wearisome attention to an uninteresting love triangle. An egotistical pilot (Hans Alber) and his designer friend convince a shipyard to build the F.P. 1 (Floating Platform). The sister of the shipyard owners (Sybille Schmitz) falls for the aviator, but he leaves her to fly nonstop around the world, Berlin to Berlin. He crash lands in Australia and doesn't return for two and a half years, by which time the girl has switched her affections to the designer and construction of the platform has been completed. The designer gets the girl, they survive a sabotage attempt, and the pilot shrugs his shoulders, promptly joining an expedition to capture a South American condor. Young Peter Lorre also has a bit part but isn't given much to do.

Brigitte Helm, heroine of *Metropolis*, starred as Antinea, Queen of Atlantis, a subterranean civilization beneath the North African desert, in *L'Atlantide* (1932), a German production based on the popular 1919 novel by Pierre Benoit. It was originally filmed as a 1921 French silent. Antinea seduces men to their palace doom, gruesomely displaying their stuffed corpses in her "trophy room." The sound version is by far the better of the two, predominantly because of Helm's catty performance. The movie was shot simultaneously in French, German, and English, with separate casts. Helm alone appeared in all three.

Twentieth Century–Fox released *Chandu the Magician* in 1932 with Edmund Lowe portraying the crimefighter who can dematerialize and materialize at will. Based on a popular radio show, the picture has Chandu battling a madman and his world-threatening ray. Directed by William Cameron Menzies (who directed *Things to Come* in 1936) and Marcel Varnel, the disappointng lower-berth feature co-starred Bela Lugosi, who later played the illusionist in the 1934 serial *Chandu on the Magic Island*.

Sax Rohmer (1886–1959) adapted his own novels for M-G-M's *The Mask of Fu Manchu* (1932) starring Boris Karloff in the title role. Charles Brabin and Charles Vidor directed. The screenplay combined a number of incidents from the writer's string of exotic thrillers, but Rohmer (also known as A.S. Ward), who claimed Fu was based on a real Limehouse gangster, never got a chance to see the picture as he was in Egypt during its short-lived exhibition. Equipped with death ray and mind-controlling drugs, Fu battles Scotland Yard investigator Nayland Smith (Lewis Stone) while searching for Genghis Khan's magic mask. The mask's owner, legend has it, is destined to rule the world. Karloff is the epitome of insidiousness in the title role. It co-starred a pre-*Thin Man* and quite adorable Myrna Loy.

The greatest monster in the history of film is *King Kong* (1933), made by RKO Radio Pictures, jointly produced and directed by Merian C. Cooper (1893–1973) and Ernest B. Schoedsack (1893–1979). Cooper was in Africa behaving not unlike the filmmaker in this picture when he came up with the idea for this classic tale of beauty and the beast. Returning to Hollywood, Cooper discussed his idea with RKO's vice-president in charge of production, David O. Selznick, who hired Cooper to make the movie. Cooper studied the works of Willis H. O'Brien, maker of *The Dinosaur and the Missing Link* (1917) and creator of the special effects for *The Lost World* (1925). He was so impressed that he hired O'Brien to do his effects for him. Models averaging 16 inches in height were used for the stop-motion animation. The film took a full year to make and cost $650,000, an extraordinary figure for the time.

In most cases live actors performed in front of a rear-projection of the moving models, but a full-sized torso and hand of Kong were built for some of the closeups with Fay Wray. The bust of Kong was twenty feet high and was covered with bear hides. The models used were the most sophisticated ever built. During the planning stages of the film O'Brien drew up several sketches of Kong from which Marcel Delgado (1900–1976) sculpted a dozen trial models of the ape. Six identical models of Kong were made for the actual shooting; so several sets of table-top work could be filmed at the same time. The models were the first to utilize metal armatures with ball and socket joints, which allowed them to be moved into practically limitless positions, all anatomically correct. Kong's flesh was made of rubber and covered with rabbit fur.

Like *Frankentstein* two years earlier, *King Kong* was hit by multiple censor cuts. There is a scene in which the ape, still on his island, shakes men from a log bridging an abyss, sending them plunging to their deaths. In the original version a giant spider came along to devour the men at the bottom of the canyon, but the scene was cut because of excessive gruesomeness.

In an attempt to tone down the gore in a shot of Kong killing a prehistoric monster by snapping its jaw, the studio changed the pictorial timing of the entire film to make it darker, even though the layered special effects had made it darker than the normal movie anyway. To soften the vividness of the torn dinosaur flesh, the studio destroyed thousands of dollars worth of intricate set detail, which shall forever more be in shadows. Detail in the huge wall built by natives to protect themselves from the ape, as well as much of the realism in Kong's New York City scenes, have been darkened into oblivion.

As the film opens, filmmaker Carl Denham (Robert Armstrong, 1893–1976) is about to set off to a jungle island to make his next adventure documentary. His producer insists that Denham put a heroine in this movie, since pretty girls mean money at the box office. At first Denham protests that the jungle is no place for a woman but finally concedes and sets off into the Manhattan night to discover a star. He finds her in front of a fruit stand trying to steal food. It is the Depression and pretty Ann Darrow (Wray) is down on her luck. It doesn't take much convincing before she is aboard *The Venture* on her way to Skull Island with an all-male crew.

On board are the crusty Captain Englehorn (Frank Reicher, 1875–1965) and handsome Jack Driscoll (Bruce Cabot, 1904–1972), with whom Ann falls in love. "I thought you hated women," she says when Jack begins to flirt with her.

"Yeah, but you're not women," Jack replies. On the island they discover the natives restricting themselves to a small peninsula; they have built a huge wall to keep monsters out. As Denham and his crew go ashore to make friends, they interrupt a sacred ceremony. A native woman is about to become Kong's "bride." The island residents aren't nearly as friendly as Denham had anticipated and take a liking to Ann, as they have never seen a blonde before. At night, back on the ship, natives sneak aboard and kidnap Ann so she can be Kong's gift. She is bound and left outside the wall.

At this point, Kong makes his first appearance. Even by today's sophisticated standards, this is awesome filmmaking. The ape seems real; the hours of special effects work put in by O'Brien and his crew show. Kong pulls Ann from her bondage and carries her screaming into the jungle, where he has to battle a tyrannosaurus rex and a pterodactyl to protect her. Since there is no Mrs. Kong, the ape is lonely and develops a huge crush on the diminutive blonde. The film crew and sailors give chase but most are wiped out by Kong before Jack rescues Ann. Denham uses gas bombs to capture Kong but not before the oversized ape mashes some natives between his teeth and toes.

The setting switches back to Manhattan where Kong is about to make his Broadway debut as "The Eighth Wonder of the World." As skeptical New Yorkers file into the theater, Denham is talking to the "boys in the press," describing the bravery of Driscoll and Darrow. Denham tells the boys to play up the beauty and the beast angle as the reporters snap photos and scribble in pads. The curtain goes up and Kong gets his first glimpse of his love since he was torn from his habitat. The monster is chained with his arms over his head and he is looking nervous. His tension turns to rage when the reporters flash lightbulbs in his face. Kong has no trouble snapping the steel that binds him, and the panicking crowd rushes for the exits.

The ape storms into the streets in search of Ann. He tears an elevated train from its rail and drops it to the ground. After pulling one unfortunate woman out of a window by mistake and dropping her coldly to the street,

Kong amazingly finds Ann's window. He pulls her out into the night before anyone can respond to her healthy screams. Confused and disoriented, Kong seeks the highest place he can find. With Ann in his first, he begins to climb what was then the world's tallest building.

The Air Force is called in and attacks the giant ape at the Empire State Building's peak. Seeing his danger, he gently sets Ann down on the observatory deck where she is at once pulled to safety by Driscoll.

Kong manages to pluck one of the fighter planes out of the air, sending craft and pilot to a fiery finish. But in the end the machine gun fire gets to be too much for the beast and he topples to his death, striking the side of the skyscraper on his way down.

As a crowd of curiosity seekers gather around the prone figure of the simian, Denham delivers his immortal line to a policeman: "T'was beauty that killed the beast." The dialogue may seem a little corny by today's standards, but the pace is fast and action-packed.

If ever there has been a film that didn't need a sequel, it was *King Kong*. At least director Ernest Schoedsack was smart enough to change the scope for *Son of Kong* (also 1933). Its quick release betrays its shoddy make-up. Instead of trying to match the original's epic proportions, the sequel is a whimsical fantasy, with most of the comedy provided by the title animated ape.

The premise raises a major question: If Kong had no mate, how did he muster a son? Surely Kong's crush on Ann Darrow was not consummated. Dependant on audience belief in the Hollywood stork, Kong, Jr. is a cuddly albino who understands English and is less than half as big as his old man.

Carl Denham, broke after botching his last big show, convinces Captain Englehorn back to Skull Island in search of treasure. Robert Armstrong and Frank Reicher repeat their original roles. Helen Mack provides the skirt as a caberet singer whose act resembles that of Tiny Tim. She tags along after her father is murdered. After a crew mutiny forces our heroes to beach on Skull Island in a smaller boat than expected, they find baby Kong, and there is a tender moment as the girl uses the hem of her slip to bandage the ape's wounded finger.

Then they face a natural menace. A volcano is about to blow. Little Kong saves Denham, sacrificing his own life. The ape holds Denham above the rising water in an upturned paw long enough for Mack to come to the rescue in a lifeboat.

As would be expected, the movie is most interesting for Willis O'Brien's effects. With the exception of model work for a disaster film, *The Last Days of Pompeii* (1935), directed by Schoedsack, a series of setbacks (including the war) prevented O'Brien from completing another animation feature until *Mighty Joe Young* (1949). O'Brien's life was marred with personal tragedy just before the release of *Son of Kong* when his estranged wife murdered his two sons.

In the exciting finale of *The Invisible Man* (1933), Jack Griffin,

rendered murderously insane by the same drug that caused his transparency, is trapped inside a barn by angry British policemen and townspeople. For obvious reasons he has been forced to move about the countryside naked; now the weather has turned against him. It is brutally cold and snow has begun to fall. When the barn is set ablaze, the invisible killer is forced into the winter night. Like magic, we see his footprints appearing in the snow, seemingly out of nowhere, until he is mortally wounded by gunfire. In a film filled with amazing special effects, this is the scene most apt to boggle the minds of the audience. The scene was shot very practically, without the use of trick photography. To achieve the effect, a small ditch was dug in the earth and then covered with a piece of wood in which appropriately placed footprints had been cut out. The footprint cut-outs—actually shoeprints to be made by a barefoot man—were replaced in the board and held in place by pegs. Each peg was attached to a rope. After the board had been covered by a blanket of artificial snow, the ropes were pulled one by one. The cut-outs fell out of the board, making it appear as if the footprints were mysteriously forming in the otherwise smooth white surface. This, along with the other more complex effects in the film, was the work of celluloid magician John P. Fulton.

Fulton was born in 1902 in Nebraska, where he worked as a young man painting backdrops for vaudeville. When his family moved to California in 1914, Fulton's father Fitch, not wanting his son involved in show business, insisted John study electrical engineering. Ironically, Fitch Fulton became a film-industry artist himself and painted 200 backdrops for *Gone with the Wind*. Undeterred by his father's early attitude, John took a job as assistant cameraman for comedian Lloyd Hamilton's film troupe in 1923. Though his first job entailed moving heavy equipment, John learned his craft quickly and by 1930 was winning acclaim as a cinematographer. Soon thereafter, Fulton developed his special effect techniques in the trick photography studios of Frank Williams. He got a job with Universal Studios and worked on *Waterloo Bridge* (1931) and *Frankenstein* (1931), both directed by James Whale, as well as John Ford's *Air Mail* (1932), before being assigned by Whale the task of making Claude Rains invisible.

The shots of Jack Griffin completely naked were relatively easy to film. Objects he handled were manipulated expertly by fine wires. The partially-clad scenes presented problems, since unfilled apparel would not move naturally. To solve this, Fulton walled and floored a sound stage in black velvet to be non-reflective, and dressed a stuntman head-to-toe in black, including gloves and headgear resembling a diver's helmet. The stuntman wore Griffin's clothes over this. When these shots were juxtaposed through sophisticated processing techniques with the desired setting, it appeared as if the invisible man were actually moving among the other characters.

Opposite: Publicity shot of *King Kong* (RKO, 1933) atop a circumcised Empire State Building.

Because of the intricate timing involved, many scenes had to be filmed repeatedly before results were correct. Even then, 4000 feet of film—about 64,000 frames—received individual hand treatment. Fulton's eye for perfection is apparent, especially when Griffin lights a cigarette held between invisible lips.

In a piece of pure hokum, Universal press releases attempted to make a great mystery of the effects process, saying only that they were optical illusions through the use of small mirrors.

At film's end, the dying man regains his visibility. We look straight down at the death bed, first seeing only the depression in his pillow and the shape of the sheets over his unseen form. Slowly a suggestion of bone structure appears, followed by a full skeleton. We see traces of flesh, then skin, and finally the man himself. The pillow was made of plaster and the sheets of papier-mache. A series of long slow dissolves were used to create the illusion, blending shots of a real skeleton with those of increasingly complete dummies, until we see the still form of Claude Rains (1889–1967).

Director James Whale originally offered the title role to Boris Karloff, whom he had befriended while directing *Frankenstein*. Karloff turned the job down when Universal refused to let him stay visible until the end of the movie. Although Rains is unseen until his character's death, the role launched his brilliant career. This parallels the Universal incident two years before when Bela Lugosi refused to play the Frankenstein monster and Karloff's stardom was born. It's hard to feel sorry for Karloff because of this career choice, as he returned to England instead to make the critically acclaimed British-Gaumont horror film *The Ghoul*.

Whale insisted that Rains get the part despite the 44-year-old actor's failing of his screentest. Rains had never made a film before, but the director knew the voice of Jack Griffin when he heard it.

Because of his invisibility, Rains used his versatile vocal capabilities to create an aura of malignant madness. Jack Griffin wails: "Suddenly I realized the power I held, the power to rule, to make the world grovel at my feet! Power to walk into the gold vaults of nations and into the secrets of kings, into the holy of holies. Power to make monsters run squealing in terror at the touch of my invisible finger. Even the moon is frightened by me!" When he discusses his power-hungry plans with former friend and colleague Kemp (William Harrigan), he says, "We will start with a reign of terror ... murders of great men, murders of little men, just to show we make no distinction." Rains' frenzied phrasing is perfect, and his job was made easier by a literate script written by R.C. Sheriff, filled to the brim with quotable lines.

Whale infused black humor in H.G. Wells' stylistic fantasy in the form of sight gags. The invisible man frightens townspeople by stripping off his clothes as he is chased. At one point he steals and rides off on a bicycle (belonging to Oscar-winning character actor Walter Brennan) that seems to be pedaling itself.

The story begins when the chemist, already invisible, arrives at the

Una O'Connor confronts the inventor of the see-through body (Claude Rains) in *The Invisible Man* (Universal, 1933).

Lion's Head Inn in the little town of Ipping looking for a room where he can have absolute privacy. His face is covered with bandages and he is wearing dark goggles. He has taken a drug called monocane, known to cause both bleaching and insanity in lab animals. Griffin knows that he has to find an antidote quickly and return to visibility before his sanity begins to deteriorate, a process which seems to be well underway. The chemical was developed by Dr. Cranley (Henry Travers), father of Jack's fiancée Flora. His intended is worried about Jack, since he disappeared without a trace.

The Lion's Head is run by old biddy Jenny Hall (portrayed superbly by mousy Una O'Connor, 1880-1959, who later played a similar role in *Bride of Frankenstein*). Already suspicious because of Griffin's bandages, Jenny barges into Jack's room without knocking, causing him to throw a temper tantrum. When she sends her husband upstairs to eject the guest, Griffin, with a fine sense of the dramatic, removes his artificial nose, goggles, and bandages, to reveal his transparency.

"E's all eaten away," a constable (E.E. Clive) says with both jaw and

walrus mustache drooping. Clive also appeared in *Bride of Frankenstein*, delivering the blustering line, "Monsters indeed!"

Griffin escapes with ease, kills a different cop, murders Kemp, and robs both a train and a bank before finally being cornered in the barn on a fateful snowy night.

Rains was convinced that the movie was going to be a disastrous failure and left Hollywood after shooting's completion. To his surprise, *The Invisible Man* was a smash with both critics and public. Hailed for its fine acting and technical ingenuity, 80,000 persons saw the picture at New York City's Roxy in one four-day period. It is surprising that the film's first sequel, *The Invisible Man Returns*, directed by Joe May and starring Vincent Price, was not made until 1940.

Science fiction's most gruesome synthesis with horror came in Paramount's *Island of Lost Souls* (1933), directed by Erle C. Kenton (1896–1980, who later directed *Ghost of Frankenstein*). A mad scientist, banished from civilization for unorthodox experiments, tries to speed up the evolutionary process by transforming animals into human beings by using horribly painful vivisection. The monsters—the scientist's mistakes that populate his tropical island—are tortured, pathetic creatures. Subject to a massive advertising campaign and released at the height of Universal's horror boom, it was a comparative financial failure and thought by audiences to be a breach of good taste.

Though based on H.G. Wells' novel *The Island of Dr. Moreau*, Wells outspokenly denounced the film, feeling it was a travesty of his intent. Yet the *Grand Guignol* luridity it depicts has made it a horror classic in recent times. In England, along with Tod Browning's *Freaks* (1932), *Island of Lost Souls* was banned by censors and not seen until the 1960's.

Filmed on location on Catalina Island, it stars Charles Laughton (1899–1962) as a surprisingly effeminate Dr. Moreau. Dressed in a three-piece white suit and wearing a pointy beard, Laughton's movements are affected. He seems a nonchalant, almost blasé maniac.

Also appearing in a disappointingly small role is Bela Lugosi (1882–1956) as a hairy-faced apeman. Despite Lugosi's good performance, it's hard to believe less than a year had passed since he declined portraying Frankenstein's monster because of feature-obscuring make-up.

The film's most famous line was Moreau's first usage of a popular cliché, "The natives are restless tonight."

Most erotic and offensive to censors were scenes in which Moreau attempted to mate his most successful specimen, a beautiful Panther Woman (Kathleen Burke), with the stranded hero (Richard Arlen, 1898–1976). Overt implications of bestial intent were not permissible, and Burke made no bones about motivation while portraying the mutation. The cat was in heat.

Opposite: Charles Laughton, as Dr. Moreau, cheers up a manimal slave on the *Island of Lost Souls* (Paramount, 1933).

The Panther Woman's beauty is the island's exception. Moreau's least successful experiments are formless monstrosities kept in laboratory cages. The intermediate cases are mobile and act as the doctor's slaves. Moreau, whip in hand, leads his mutant subservients through a primitive recital of his rules, paraphrasing the song of the monkey people in Rudyard Kipling's *The Jungle Book*.

"What is the law?" Moreau asks.

"Not to spill the blood. That is the law. Are we not men?" the mutants (led by Lugosi) reply. This last ironic query was recently popularized by the new-wave rock group Devo.

Breaking of the law means a session in the "House of Pain," where the vivisections are performed. Inevitably the creatures turn on their master. As the hero and his pretty fiancée (Leila Hyams, b. 1905) escape the island, the sadistic scientist is strapped to the operating table. His death screams end the picture.

Wells' story was remade as *The Island of Dr. Moreau* (1977) with Burt Lancaster as the scientist, Michael York as the hero, and Barbara Carrera as the lusty feline. Don Taylor directed.

German filmmaker Kurt Bernhardt explored the possibilities of connecting Germany to North America in *The Tunnel* (1933). Scripted by Curt Siodmak and based on a novel by Bernard Kellerman, it explained the tunnel was being built to "promote world peace," an ironic goal considering the historical events to follow. With well-done special effects and weak plot, it examines the trials of excavators as they burrow beneath the Atlantic, suffering cave-ins, floods, and volcanic eruptions. The associate producer was killed in an accident during shooting. Released simultaneously in German and French, Paul Hartmann was the hero of the German version while Jean Gabin played the French lead.

The Tunnel was remade in England as *The Trans-Atlantic Tunnel* (1935). At first simply called *The Tunnel*, the name was lengthened to avoid confusion with the original, only two years its elder. It was directed by Maurice Elvey, and like its predecessor was scripted by Curt Siodmak, who had already fled Germany after reading the writing on the wall.

In a futuristic world where television phones have been invented, young engineer McAllen (Richard Dix) has one goal in life: to connect England and America by tunnel, thus establishing a "permanent peace between the English-speaking peoples." He realizes his dream with the help of Lloyd (C. Aubrey Smith), England's richest man.

Though the tunnel is completed by the end of the picture, after a generation of digging, the project takes its toll on McAllen. His wife (Madge Evans) goes blind working as an underground nurse and his son (Leslie Banks, 1890–1952) is killed by a volcanic explosion.

In Majestic's B-feature, *The Vampire Bat* (1933), directed by Frank R. Strayer, Lionel Atwill plays a crazed chemist who murders townsfolk and sucks them dry searching for a medically revolutionary blood substitute.

Despite Phil Goldstone's skid-row production, stark gloomy photography and fine corny performances by the principles make this an above average chiller. This was the first of many mad scientists Atwill played expertly over the next decade.

Four stars go to Dwight Frye as red-herring Herman Glieg, a twitchy, stammering, dim-witted servant who keeps bats in his pocket and—though harmless—believes himself to be a vampire. Like Lenny in Steinbeck's *Of Mice and Men*, Herman strokes his fanged pets until they are dead. Believed to be the murderer by all, Herman takes his own life rather than face a mob of angry locals. Chased to a cliff's edge, he jumps to evade the lynching rope.

With Herman dead, heroine Ruth (Fay Wray) is bound and gagged in Atwill's laboratory where artificial life is grown. She is about to become a source for plasma when hero Carl Brechschneider (Melvyn Douglas) bursts in and saves her. With a name like that you can be sure that this was a pre-war hero.

The movie is enhanced by the subtle yet effective Freudian dialogue, illustrated by a discussion of the "vile penetration" of each victim's neck.

The year 1933 produced three other minor science fiction efforts. In a whimsical British featurette (50 minutes), *I'm an Explosive* by George Smith Productions, a small boy drinks a liquid bomb. The film's adults spend the rest of the picture fearing a boom.

The Last Man on Earth (1924) was remade in England as *It's Good To Be Alive* directed by Alfred Werker. It tells of a near-future plague that has wiped out the world's males. Order in the surviving matriarchy is disrupted when a single man (Paul Roulien) is discovered alive and healthy.

British-Gaumont's *The Man They Couldn't Arrest*, co-written and directed by T. Hays Hunter, features the inventor of an electronic eavesdropping device able to tune in on conversations from afar.

From a story remarkably similar to Sir Arthur Conan Doyle's *The Lost World* came Great Britain's *The Secret of the Loch* (1934) directed by Milton Rosmer (formerly an actor). The script, involving a search for the Loch Ness Monster by a scientist, his daughter, and her journalist suitor, was written by Billie Bristown and Charles Bennett, the latter most famous for scripting early Hitchcock thrillers.

With horror booming, 1934 offered only four other minor films with science fiction elements. Based loosely on an Edgar Wallace mystery, *Return of the Terror* was a mild Warner Brothers thriller. Boosted by an excellent cast of Mary Astor, Lyle Talbot, and J. Carrol Naish, the now-familiar plot concerns the inventor of a deadly x-ray device, unjustly imprisoned, who uses his weapon to wreak revenge on those who framed him once released.

In a Hal Roach M-G-M two-reel comedy, a scientist invents a ray that causes its targets to lose their inhibitions. The short was entitled *Another Wild Idea* and was both directed by and starred Charley Chase (1893-1940), a dapper mustached American most famous for his roles as harried husbands.

A British short, *The Inventors*, produced by Al Christie for Educational

Films, showed the assemblage from old car parts of a being much like the *Frankenstein* monster. Based on a story by William Watson and Sig Herzig, it starred Chase Taylor and Bud Hulik as grease-monkey scientists. In Britain's *The Birth of a Robot*, a seven-minute exercise in stop-motion photography, the directorial team of Humphrey Jennings and Len Lye envision the first few minutes in the life of an automated man.

The Bride of Frankenstein (1935) is one of the greatest horror films ever made; Universal was never this good again. The first sequel stands easily as an equal beside the original, and in some facets surpasses *Frankenstein*. The lavish production, tenderly hammy performances, and rousing Franz Waxman score capture Gothic horror's intrinsic sadness with intensity.

Before releasing the sequel, the studio clipped the happy ending from *Frankenstein*, so that it faded out on a shot of the blazing mill. The original ending was returned in 1957, when the film was released to television, and currently both versions can be seen.

The preface takes place on a stormy night in the Geneva home of Mary Shelley (Elsa Lanchester, b. 1902, now widow of Charles Laughton), where her husband, Percy Bysshe Shelley, and friend Lord Byron are asking the demure young woman for an encore to her masterwork. Mary proclaims that her monster was not destroyed in the mill fire and the story begins with no passage of time. The angry mob has dispersed. The mill smolders, creating a fantastically spooky scene, the stuff of nightmares. Henry Frankenstein (Colin Clive again, as pale and thin as remembered) has been badly injured but not killed by his terrible fall. Carried home, he regains consciousness to see his pretty fiancée, Elizabeth (18-year-old Valerie Hobson).

The father of the drowned little girl, now played by a different actor, and his shuddering wife linger after the others have gone. He insists on seeing the corpse of the creature. When he crawls into the watery mill basement he discovers the monster alive and angry. Boris Karloff had put on some weight in four years. Gone are the skeletal face and deep-underscored eye sockets. Horribly scarred by the fire, and with most of his hair burned away, this is a decidedly healthier, crueller creature. The father's neck is snapped. His wife investigates and clutches the monster's hand, thinking it is her husband's, and is likewise pulled to her death.

With the rest of the town unaware of the monster's survival, Henry is visited by a demonic physician named Praetorius (Ernest Thesiger, 1879–1961, a superior comic grotesque) who, like Henry, has created human life. Since Praetorius is unable to animate full-sized people, his glass-enclosed homunculi are doll-like and playfully costumed. Praetorius proposes a team effort, but Henry refuses. His first attempt at tampering in God's domain nearly cost him his life.

The monster stumbles away from his supposed pyre, frightening an eccentric shepherdess (played for comic relief by mousy Una O'Connor in a role very similar to the once she played in *The Invisible Man*). He is wounded by hunters before hearing the soothing sound of a violin. Following the music, he meets a blind hermit (Australian-born O.P. Heggie, 1879-1936) who assumes he is a mute and accepts him as a fellow unfortunate. The creature is taught friendship and affection, learning to enjoy smoke and drink. He even speaks a few words before the touching camaraderie is interrupted by firing hunters (among them John Carradine, b. 1906) who inadvertently burn down the hermit's shack. The monster staggers through the gloomy countryside until captured by a mob of angry townspeople, tied to a cross and thrown into the dungeon. Though some may find the Christian symbolism heavy-handed, it is especially ironic after the morality of the creature's rapid domestication.

Karloff bound becomes a snarling animal. He soon escapes and there is a poignant moment as he—realizing he is supposed to be dead—seeks refuge in a cemetery catacomb. The underground chamber is occupied by Praetorius and his grave-robbing henchman Karl (Dwight Frye). As usual, Frye is a scene-stealer with his brilliant integration of evil and naiveté.

Sensitive British censors once again managed to get splicing knives on the product, removing a Thesiger scene felt to portray necrophilic tendencies.

Praetorius kidnaps Elizabeth and blackmails Henry into helping him create a mate for the pathetic creature. The following laboratory scenes (the work of electrical effects master Ken Strickfaden) are the most spectacular ever filmed, enhanced by Waxman's climactic score. The woman's body (Lanchester once again) has been constructed and kites are flown above the lab as a thunderstorm brews.

Lanchester found her experiences on the set terrifying. It took three days to film her scenes, and for most of this time she was bound head-to-toe in gauze, propped up on the set unable to move or talk. She had to be fed by her dresser and one can only imagine the other inconveniences. She managed to keep her sanity despite the strain, but this was not the case with a stand-in similarly bound to a slab. Stricken with claustrophobia after orders to be silent, she screamed hysterically until her gauze was removed.

In *Frankenstein*, Henry's creation was lifted to the roof of the mill and rejuvenation achieved through direct lightning strike. In a classic example of progress, the electricity in *Bride* is brought down into the lab by wire for the female's vitalization.

The woman's make-up is patterned after ancient representations of the Egyptian goddess Nefertiti, while her robot-like head movements are reminiscent of Brigitte Helm's as the robot in *Metropolis* (1926).

When the rejuvenated woman sees her abnormal mate, she hisses like a snake and screams in terror as the monster desperately tries to comfort her by patting her hand. Heartbroken, the creature decides that suicide is the answer. First allowing his creator and Elizabeth to escape, he pulls a switch that blows up himself, his mate, and Praetorius.

Peter Lorre (right) made his Hollywood debut as the super-sadistic, smarmy Dr. Gogol in Karl Freund's *Mad Love* **(M-G-M, 1935).**

Karloff would return to portray the Frankenstein monster for the third and final time in *Son of ...* (1939), the last time Universal could translate Gothic horror adequately into an A-picture. This signalled the beginning of a studio slide that continued into the Forties, each picture in the series being a little shoddier and pulpier than the one preceding it.

Maurice Renard's *The Hands of Orlac* was produced for the second time in 1935 as M-G-M's *Mad Love* starring Hungarian-born Peter Lorre (1904–1964) in his first American film. He plays the movie's scientific deviate. This and Universal's *The Mummy* (1932, with Karloff) were German cinematographer Karl Freund's only directorial credits. Later lured from retirement by Desi Arnaz, Freund revamped TV technique with the three-camera system in the early Fifties.

A famous French concert pianist, Stephen Orlac (Colin Clive), his hands destroyed in a train wreck, meets perverted scientist Dr. Gogol (Lorre), who volunteers to help Orlac using his new surgical procedure. Orlac agrees, unaware that Gogol collects other men's wives and desires Madame Orlac (Frances Drake). Gogol grafts the hands of a guillotined murderer (Edward Brophy) onto Orlac's wrists, and though Orlac struggles to regain his musical skills, he finds that he can throw knives with unerring accuracy. The film's most frightening segment shows sadistic Gogol—disguised in dark cloak, black glasses, broad-brimmed hat, neck brace, and artificial metal arms— driving Orlac crazy by posing as Rollo, the executed killer living again through Gogol's medical genius, in search of his hands.

In the chilling climax, Orlac saves his wife from an unspeakable fate at Gogol's hands by using his new knife-throwing skill. Ted Healy heads up the supporting cast as the familiar wise-mouthed reporter.

The rich overtones of sado-masochism are established in the opening sequence. Gogol attends a performance of the *Grand Guignol*, where Mrs. Orlac stars as an unfaithful wife bound and branded. Lorre expresses sick satisfaction, thus establishing his motivation and ominously foreshadowing the conclusion.

Working from a terse script by P.J. Wolfson and John L. Balderston (adaptor for *Frankenstein*), Freund examined the mental deterioration of both Orlac and Gogol, using his photographic expertise to communicate their nightmarish worlds. The 1925 German silent known in America as *The Hands of Orlac* starred Conrad Veidt as the title character. Directed by Robert Wiene in a gloomy milieu and overacted by Veidt, it is alienating and difficult to grasp. The most recent edition, *The Hands of Orlac* (1959), is a British production starring Mel Ferrer as the pianist and Christopher Lee as the doctor. It is antiseptic compared to *Mad Love*, flat and actionless in its attempt to be civilized.

Anyone who believes science fiction's exploitation of sex and violence began with the new freedom of the Sixties will be shocked to learn that *Maniac* (1935) exists. Its inclusion of frontal nudity, simulated rape, and a cat's on-screen mutilation forced it quickly into stag film status. It was perhaps at one time known as *The Sex Maniac*. Produced by the unknown Hollywood Producers and Directors Company, and directed by Dwain Esper, the skidrow effort told of mad scientist Dr. Marsholtz (Horace Carpenter) injecting assistant Maxwell (Bill Woods) with a psycho-killer serum. With the exception of one stretch of lonely dirt road, the entire picture was shot in one house. Most of the cast is college-aged. This is a genuinely sick movie and should be avoided by anyone who likes cats.

Wiley Post, the one-eyed pilot who died in a plane crash with Will Rogers, co-starred with Ralph Bellamy in Columbia's quickie *Air Hawks* (1935) about secret agents and a ray gun that konks out airplane engines.

Germany's 1935 feature, *The Master of the World*, is set in the future when machines have made human labor obsolete. Directed by Harry Piel, the film's future technology has affected the weaponry. George Muehlen-Schulte's script includes death rays. Known in Germany poetically as *Der Herrn der Welt*, the film starred Walter Janssen and Sybille Schmitz.

When the cathode ray tube was science fiction, Imperial made *Murder by Television* (1935) starring Bela Lugosi as two brothers, one a genius inventor, the other a homicidal maniac. Fuzzily directed by Clifford Sanforth, the potboiler is best noted for its boob-tube effects, compliments of technical supervisor Henry Spitz and TV technician Milton M. Stern. The bad brother uses his sibling's expertise to build an insidious weapon. A phone call triggers a death ray mounted in a television camera.

In *Once in a New Moon* (1935), a British-Fox self-effacing political satire directed by Anthony Kimmins, an approaching star's gravity yanks the Essex village of Upper Shrimpton off the Earth and into orbit someplace beyond the moon. The change in habitat forces the local squire to impose a conservative government.

Stage actress Helen Gahagan performed her only film role in the first sound version of *She* (1935), produced by Merian C. Cooper and adapted from H. Rider Haggard's novel. A 500-year-old queen, kept youthful by a "Flame of Immortality," rules of the lost Siberian kingdom Kor. When an explorer (Randolph Scott) discovers her land, she believes him a reincarnation of an old lover. The film co-starred Nigel Bruce (1895–1953, Watson to Basil Rathbone's Sherlock Holmes). There had been four silent versions of *She* and the subject was gruesomely remade again in 1964 by Hammer, with Ursula Andress as the queen.

In Columbia's *Superspeed* (1935), directed by Lambert Hillyer, an inventor perfects a rapid transport device.

H.G. Wells (1866–1946) was born the son of a shopkeeper and a servant in a London suburb. Though his parents wanted him to be a tailor, the boy had a love for science and won a scholarship to the Normal School of Science in London, where he studied Darwinism under biologist Thomas Henry Huxley. The theory of evolution turned Wells' head to the future—and the possibilities implied by man's inevitable mental development. After a short-lived teaching career was squelched by health problems, Wells became a writer. By the time he was 27 he had published the short prophecies "The Man of the Year Million," and "The Advent of the Flying Man." Two years later, in 1895, Wells wrote *The Time Machine* and launched his career. His influence on science fiction to follow, both in print and on film, had been unparalleled. Only Jules Verne approaches his impact on the genre. Wells showed an unprecedented ability to fantasize the future in three dimensions while using believable tales to communicate his allegories.

Including *The Time Machine*, which was made into a George Pal film in 1960 (the 1978 film-for-TV of the same title had nothing to do with Wells), six of his major works were filmed. They were, in the order that he wrote them: *The Island of Dr. Moreau* (1896), made into *Island of Lost Souls* (1932), and then again with Wells' title in 1977; *The Invisible Man* (1897), filmed by Universal in 1933 and spawning a slew of sequels; *The War of the Worlds* (1898), also filmed exceptionally by George Pal in 1953, but adapted most stunningly by Orson Wells for radio in 1938; *The First Men in the*

Moon (1901), which suffered whimsical but forgivable modifications at the hands of Georges Méliès in 1902; *The Food of the Gods and How It Came to Earth* (1904), the first part of which allegedly became an awful Marjoe Gortner picture in 1976; and *The Shape of Things to Come* (1933), from which Wells himself wrote the screenplay to history's best-filmed future, *Things to Come* (1936). Wells wrote one other screenplay, *The Man Who Could Work Miracles* (1935), but his forecast was his cinematic masterpiece. He was omnipresent during filming, making sure the scenery, costuming, and acting motivation remained strictly to his detailed specifications.

Of course, Wells' nitpicking presence would have been a nuisance without the spendthrift generosity of producer Alexander Korda. The film, which ran 130 minutes in Great Britain and 113 minutes in America, cost $1.4 million, by far the most ever spent on a British picture. Korda, a Hungarian with the Midas touch, had no trouble finding backers. His short Hollywood stint had produced *The Private Life of Helen of Troy*, a successful silent. Moving his career to England, against normal migration paths, he produced *The Private Life of Henry VIII*, which turned Charles Laughton into a star. Perhaps only he could have secured the funds to manifest Wells' vision.

Korda assigned William Cameron Menzies (1896–1957) to direct. Menzies was a former children's book illustrator, a pictorial thinker, and pre-sketched all scenes to prevent wasting screen space. Menzies, born in Scotland, entered film first as an art director. He worked in a minor capacity on the Douglas Fairbanks version of *The Thief of Bagdad* and later directed the Korda remake.

Korda put his brother Vincent in charge of set design and assigned Lajos Brio, the pen behind *The Private Life of Henry VIII*, to help Wells with the script.

The sets for *Things to Come* would have to be intricate functioning models of ultra-modern architecture and technology. Korda employed American technician Ned Mann to head his special effects department. It was Mann who built the New York City model so realistically reduced to rubble in RKO's *Deluge*. Mann built his models large enough to look real when filmed from any distance or angle—a necessity considering Menzie's love for full-blown panorama. Among the difficult effects Mann conquered were a huge "Space Gun" for the film's finale, giant digging machines, hangars filled with biplanes, and—for the montage spanning 1976 and 2036—automated building centers reconstructing the ruins of ravaged metropoli.

Mann was teamed in the special effects department with Harry Zeck, who had invented the split-screen technique, used meticulously in the film.

The superb original score for the film was composed by Arthur Bliss, who was later knighted and became personal composer to Queen Elizabeth II. Instead of writing two or three themes to be repeated throughout, as was common, Bliss wrote individually styled pieces for each sequence. The score, which ranges from *ballet mécanique* to churchly chorus, is still available on record and receives occasional airplay on classical music radio stations.

It is Christmas 1936 in the city of Everytown, a thinly disguised London. Two families, the Passworthys and the Cabals, whose histories we will follow, are gathered together for their celebration when World War II breaks out unexpectedly. Through scraps of newspaper in the wind we follow the war's increasing destruction until "the Wandering Sickness," a man-made plague, halts civilization.

The scene advances to 1976 where the ruins of Everytown remain, reduced to a peasant village in the film's parallel to Piccadilly Circus. Tribes battle over limited fuel supplies. One group is led by "Rudolph the Boss" (Ralph Richardson, 1902-1983), who battles "the Hill People." Their primitive war is interrupted by the arrival of a strange aircraft and pilot John Cabal (Raymond Massey, b. 1896) dressed in black with a huge fishbowl helmet. He is a visitor from the Iraqi-based "Wings Over the World" organization, the planet's surviving base of technology. Before Rudolph can kill Cabal and steal his plane for battle, Cabal's friends fly over and drop glass "peace gas" bottles, anesthetizing all into alliance. The world is united and progress once again begins.

Again the film jumps a generation, by montage, to 2036, where Everytown has been built into Utopia. To save energy—this many years before the word ecology was invented—the city has been constructed into a mountain's side. Despite seclusion necessitated by limited sunshine and contaminated air, it is beautiful, with glass towers, massive open spaces, and winding bridges and walkways. The time's only controversy concerns manned travel to the moon via the recently invented space gun. The lifesize model built for the film, though expensive, was no more than a scientifically silly cannon. The physical impossibility of such a flight is glaring compared to the careful logic Wells built around it.

Raymond Passworthy (Edward Chapman) and Oswald Cabal (Massey again) have had their son and daughter respectively chosen to be the first astronauts, but the flight does not go off without a hitch. Luddite sculptor Theotocopulos (Cedric Hardwicke, 1893-1964) incites a mob to destroy the gun, but they fail and the pair launch lunar-bound at film's end.

If one must criticize the film—and many have—the major complaint is that the characters are too strictly allegorical, more the abstractions of a morality play than real people, even more so than in *Metropolis*. There is little sympathy in this film; yet, to depict a more personal story would have been to prohibitively narrow Wells' scope. Its rigor and power as a logic-oriented prophecy are unmatched. No mushy scenes were necessary.

Between *Things to Come* in 1936 and 1950 there were few cinematic attempts at prophecy. Space travel was nonexistent at the movies except in juvenile serials. During the war even the chapterplay kiddie shows scrapped their extraterrestrial adventures in favor of anti-Axis morale builders. With the atom bomb and Sputnik still well in the future, mankind's fear of technology was internalized into the laboratory, repeatedly deriving its scientifically impossible menace from variations of the horrible man-made

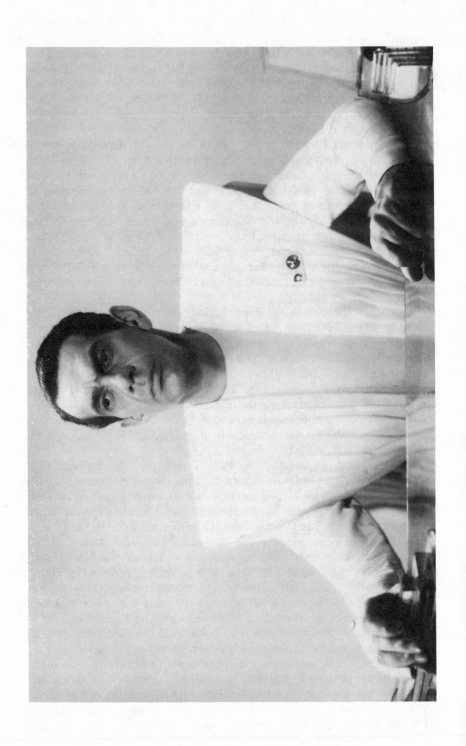

monster. Just as the Fifties were dominated by permutations of Wells and Verne, the Forties offered endless adaptations of Shelley and Stevenson. Either a mad scientist (Karloff, Zucco, Atwill, or Carradine) was turning himself into a gruesome psycho-killer, or he was using his new medical discovery to transform some other chap. Some sought revenge against those who had wronged them and inevitably found it before meeting their demise. Others, in their warped way, had the benefit of mankind in mind.

The mad scientist films were B-features, either heading matinee bills or booked second to more elaborate productions in the larger first-run houses. As was true of serials, studios reused production teams and actors, releasing similar pictures in quick succession. Because the B-features seldom ran much longer than an hour—compared to the serials five times as long made with the same or less money—an intelligent product was possible. Creative filmmakers occasionally overcame forced haste and the shoestring format, birthing the posthumously appreciated *film noir*. As a rule, the B-features were head and shoulders above the serials in quality and rarely reused footage, a common and necessary practice in chapterplays.

Whatever the insane doctor's motive, it was essential that the mad scientist and/or monster created be identified with by the audience. Unlike *Island of Lost Souls* or *Murders On the Rue Morgue*, the Forties relied on technology gone wrong rather than intrinsic evil to derive their antagonist. *Frankenstein* and *King Kong* proved monster sympathy added depth to audience reaction, whereas serials were almost exclusively clear-cut battles between good and evil. White and black hats merged into shades of gray in the Forties' B-feature.

For example, in *The Monster and the Girl* (1941), the only real hero in the film commits seven murders, while the male representative of good, who lives and gets the girl, is seventh down on the cast list and has limited on-screen time before the final reel. The hero spends the second half of the picture with his brain encased in a gorilla's head. We forgive his crimes because his victims are white slavers, seducers of his sister, and those who framed him for murder.

In *The Man in Half-Moon Street* (1944), the hero is a mass murderer without conscience. Still, he seeks eternal youth, something all want. His morals have folded under a difficult temptation. Here is the key: by forcing us into the murderer's mind—much as Lang did in *M*—the programmer directors of the Forties raised consciousness of human dilemma. Part of us feared a monster would get us, yet a troubling part feared the monster was in us trying to get out. Though this psychologically effective technique has been exploited by modern slasher films, such as the *Friday the 13th* series, a subjective camera placing us in the shoes of a sadistic killer cannot match illuminating plot hooks offering understanding of the murderer's motivation.

Opposite: Raymond Massey and his extraordinary nostrils in *Things to Come* (London/United Artists, 1936).

Michael Curtiz, later to direct *The Charge of the Light Brigade* and *Casablanca*, directed Karloff in Warner Brother's *The Walking Dead* (1936), a science fiction thriller with a plot to become increasingly familiar over the next decade. Karloff plays a low-key lead. It is a quietly effective and strangely disquieting film. An ex-con (Karloff) is framed for the murder of his convicting judge by a gang of thugs, executed, and brought back to life through a vague process by a scientist (Edmund Gwenn, 1875-1959, most famous as Kris Kringle in *Miracle on 34th Street*). In the lab sequence Karloff's make-up, aided by Hal Mohr's cinematography, is contrived to make him greatly resemble the Frankenstein monster. Naturally, the walking corpse seeks vengeance but doesn't actually have to commit murders. His ghostly appearance from the grave causes each thug to bring about his own death. The hero finally re-enters eternal sleep, describing the death he has known and seeking to refind his "peace."

Karloff returned to his native England in the mid-Thirities to make a trio of pictures for Gaumont, *The Ghoul, Juggernaut*, and *The Man Who Lived Again* (1936). Only the latter contained science fiction elements. Also known as *The Man Who Changed His Mind* and later re-released as *The Brain Snatcher*, it was directed by Robert Stevenson (b. 1905, who later directed *Mary Poppins* and other Disney pictures). The imaginative script, centered on physical and mental ailment, was written by John L. Balderston, the pen behind Universal's *Dracula*, and Sidney Gilliat, a wit who wrote for Hitchcock during this same period.

Karloff plays Dr. Laurience, a scientist experimenting, like the protagonist in *The Fly* (1958), with a method to dissolve, transmit and reassemble matter. Specifically, he seeks to move brains from one body to another. After a successful monkey experiment, he switches to humans, transmitting the mind of his dying assistant (Donald Calthrop, in a memorable study of a paralytic) into a corrupt financial wizard (Frank Collier), a character particularly boo-worthy during the Depression. The rich man dies while Laurience's assistant lives on his healthy body. Also terminal, the doctor switches bodies with the rich man's son (John Loder), investigator of his father's death and suitor to Laurience's heartthrob aide (Anna Lee). By the final scene everyone has his head together and Laurience has been buried, along with his notes.

Karloff and Lugosi were teamed in *The Invisible Ray* (1936), a Universal feature that warned, "The scientific dreams of today may very well become the scientific fact of tommorow." With special effects supplied by John Fulton, it told of a scientist cursed with the touch of death after a exposure to an unknown isotope. Crisply directed by Lambert Hillyer (b. 1889, who directed Universal's *Dracula's Daughter* the same year), its message merely brushes the surface of radioactivity's menace.

Dr. Janus Rukh (Karloff, in a compelling study of a tortured soul), travels to Africa in search of a fallen meteor, which he discovers glowing with Radium X. Soon Rukh, too, is luminous, and no one wants to shake hands with him. Like *the Invisible Man*, his affliction causes increasing madness. Outfitting himself in lead, he works on a temporary antidote with Dr. Benet (Lugosi) until the colleague succumbs to his now-murderous intent. Experimenting with a machine that follows light beams through time and space, he investigates Radium X's cosmic origins. When he learns he has been cuckolded and his Radium X experiments are rejected by a scientific congress, he goes on a murder spree. His mother (Violet Kemble) finally puts an end to his reign of terror by destroying the essential antidote, thus vaporizing the glowing scientist.

The concept of reducing human beings to doll size, later used in *Dr. Cyclops* (1939) and *The Incredible Shrinking Man* (1957), was originated in M-G-M's *The Devil Doll* (1936), directed by Tod Browning and based on Abraham Merritt's novel *Burn Witch Burn*—not to be confused with *Devil Doll*, a 1964 remake of *Dead of Night*, and *Burn Witch Burn*, the American title of the 1962 British production *Night of the Eagle*.

Browning (1882–1962) gained both fame and controversy with *Dracula* (1931) and *Freaks* (1932). *The Devil Doll* was his second-to-last film and seemed as much influenced by his twice-made *The Unholy Three* (1925, 1930) and *The Count of Monte Cristo* as by Merritt's novel.

Lionel Barrymore stars as a financier unjustly imprisoned for twenty years who escapes from Devil's Island with a scientist friend (Henry B. Walthall, 1878–1936). He hopes to avenge his frame-up and is haunted by the realization that his daughter (Maureen O'Sullivan) has matured thinking him a murderer.

In his hideout the scientist demonstrates the ability to shrink animals, explaining his misguided intentions: With the world made small, only one-tenth of the food supply will be needed to feed everyone.

When the scientist dies of natural causes, Barrymore employs his invention to shrink two of his three enemies to six inches, absurdly impersonating an old lady to lure the thugs. Before the final antagonist can be diminished he confesses and Barrymore walks off screen to an implied suicide; the Production Code forbade suicide as a plot solution.

The first sound version featuring the animated clay man, *Le Golem* (1936), was a Czech production filmed in Prague. Known in Britain as *The Legend of Prague*, it was directed by Julien Duvivier and was essentially a vehicle for Harry Baur (1881–1943) as Emperor Rudolph II, a dabbler in the black arts. He headed a cast composed of French and Jewish players. Baur went to Germany in 1942 to star in a musical, where it was discovered he was a Jew. He was executed in a concentration camp.

Throughout, Duvivier explores the use of an off-angle, subjective camera. Though its attempt to intrigue becomes tiresome, it does portray a more human clay slave than any of the silent versions. Rabbi Jacob was played by Charles Dent while Ferdinand Hart played the monster.

The best scene shows the golem moving through Rudolph's palace ballroom like a juggernaut, tension mounting as the horrified crowd parts.

The clay character appeared in another Czech film known in England as *The Emperor's Baker* (1951), a comedy. There was a French version of the original story in 1966, and Roddy MacDowell starred in *It* (also 1966), using the rejuvenated golem to kill his boss and kidnap Jill Haworth. He is killed in the finale by a nuclear bomb, as the pointy-headed golem walks through the mushroom cloud into the sea, ending his cinematic career.

Buster Keaton starred in a Fox short, *The Chemist* (1936), produced by Al Christie, as the inventor of a human shrinker-enlarger potion.

Puritan's *Ghost Patrol* (1936), directed on skid row by Sam Newfield (1900–1964), starred Tim McCoy as an intrepid adventurer in search of a radium-tube anti-aircraft weapon, while harassed by typical potboiler gangsters.

The Columbia feature, *Panic On the Air* (1936), starred Lew Ayres and was directed by D. Ross Lederman. Here, an electronic invention plucks radio waves from the air, thus halting all broadcast.

Young Dean Jagger (b. 1903) plays an American scientist able to enliven the dead in *Revolt of the Zombies* (1936), a Medallion production directed by Victor Halperin. Almost unwatchable due to ineptness, Jagger goes on a recruiting mission, thinking an army of corpses would make a perfect war machine.

Jimmie Allen, from the Thirties radio show *The Air Adventures of Jimmie Allen*, played himself in Paramount's *Sky Parade* (1936), directed by Otho Lovering. The film unveiled the world's first automated airplane operated from below.

In Columbia's *Trapped by Television* (1936), directed by Del Lord, an inventor (Lyle Talbot, b. 1904) comes up with a new cathode ray tube (special effects by Roy Davidson) enabling police to monitor the underworld. Mary Astor co-stars as his lonely wife, who wonders why hubby spends so much time in his laboratory.

Karloff fans might find the master's role in Universal's *Night Key* (1937), directed by Lloyd Corrigan, a bit gentle for their taste. He plays Professor David Mallory, a kindly inventor who, though going blind, has invented an invisible-beam detecting device that renders the current system obsolete and the burglary of business establishments practically impossible. His daughter Jean (Jean Rogers) is thrilled, thinking that the new invention will provide her father with the money he so desperately needs for a sight-saving operation. Their happiness is halted when villain Steve Ranger (Samuel S. Hinds) of Ranger Detecting Service steals the professor's security system and installs it himself — not knowing Mallory has a "key" to turn his system off. Mallory begins an odd crime wave, breaking into store after store without stealing anything, so Ranger's clients will stop using the stolen invention. When smarmy elements learn of the key, "The Kid" (Alan Baxter) forces Mallory to help him steal. The professor sabotages one heist and the crooks barely get away. The Kid kidnaps Jean, but in the end Mallory's honesty and ingenuity win out.

A tame thriller. Though Karloff's performance adds class to the production, it is actionless. The special effects, which are few, were done by John Fulton.

Four other films containing science fiction elements were released in 1937: In director Donald Carter's British featurette (38 minutes) *The Gap*, starring Patric Curwen, the horrible not-so-distant future was manifested. It was a pseudodocumentary of an air raid on London.

Paramount's B-feature, *The Girl from Scotland Yard*, starred Karen Morley as a pretty detective stalking a murderer whose arsenal includes a machine that emits lethal radio waves. It is based on characters created by Edgar Wallace.

Anna Lee got a chance to perform in the future in British-Gaumont's thriller *Non-Stop New York* directed by Robert Stevenson. The comely lass starred as the unfortunate witness to a murder and is forced to hide from death ray killers aboard a then-impossible trans-Atlantic commercial airliner.

India's 1937 science fiction entry was *Zambo*, over two and a half hours long. It is about a kindly scientist who turns a gorilla into a man, creating an Indian version of Tarzan. The Indians also produced *Professor Waman* (1938) about a scientist who learns to master nature.

There were two other science fiction films in 1938, one a bland detective story and the other a kiddie comedy.

In Paramount's *Arrest Bulldog Drummond*, John Howard has the title role, lethargically battling the ray gun destroyer of huge munitions caches. James Hogan directed the Stuart Palmer script, adapted from H.C. (Sapper) McNeile's novel, *The Final Court*.

The title betrays the quality in Warner Brother's *Shh! The Octopus*, a lowbrow comedy whose evildoer possesses both a death ray and the mechanized title creature. The forgettable Allen Jenkins and Hugh Herbert star as wacky private dicks.

Bela Lugosi steals the show in Universal's *Son of Frankenstein* (1939). He plays a shepherd/graverobber whose survival of a hanging attempt leaves him warped in both body and mind. Lugosi's portrayal rivals his performance as Dracula as the greatest of his career. At one point Ygor smiles with glee as he raps his knuckles against his grossly bent and enlarged neck, producing the sound of hollow wood. He plays his flute sweetly as he sends the monster out to do his killing.

Universal, having lost money the previous four years, paid Lugosi only $500 a week for his chores after signing the other principles to lucrative deals. To add insult to injury, studio executives instructed that all of his scenes be shot in the same week. Angered, director Rowland V. Lee expanded Ygor's part on the set and saw to it that Lugosi was kept busy during the entire shooting schedule.

Make-up artist Jack Pierce had his hands full, creating both Ygor and the Frankenstein monster daily. Lugosi's make-up alone took four hours to

A decidedly healthier, crueller creature: Jack Pierce's masterwork on Karloff in *The Bride of Frankenstein* (Universal, 1935).

apply. It consisted of a rubber broken-neck piece attached by a strap under the arm, shaggily cut and glued yak hair, and a set of snaggle teeth.

This was Karloff's third and final performance as the monster. It has been estimated that Karloff spent over 900 hours under the painful load of greasepaint and rubber. Though frustrated over a script that reduced the intricacy of his role, Karloff adds his own special empathy, making his performance shine over all imitators. Once again Pierce's make-up had to be altered noticeably to compensate for the actor's rapidly aging face. He was 51.

Also superb is Lionel Atwill as local police Inspector Krogh, who wears a movable artificial arm — when he was a boy, his real one was torn off by the monster. He uses his real arm to twist the other into the desired position, giving his movements an eye-catching quirk, later satirized in Mel Brooks' *Young Frankenstein* (1974).

On the con side, the overplayed performance of Basil Rathbone (1892–1967) as the wimpy Wolf, the son of Henry and Elizabeth Frankenstein, is nothing short of annoying. Colin Clive had died consumptive and alcoholic in 1937. A large oil portrait of Clive is displayed prominently in this picture's castle. Inexplicably, a "von" has been added to Wolf's name. Audiences are left unappeased when the impotent sniveler emerges in the end as the hero.

Also irritating is a snotty, whining performance by Donnie Lanagan as Peter, Wolf's son. The boy's voice sends fingernails-on-blackboard shivers down the spine. An unfortunate casting decision.

The story opens with Wolf and his family travelling to the castle of his father. American-educated, Wolf watches the scenery getting gloomier as he approaches his new home. Once in town, he can't understand why everyone isn't glad to see them. Inspector Krogh has to convince Wolf that the townspeople are angry with him, the memories of his father's creation still vivid in their minds. Wolf is quickly inspired to continue his father's work when he finds a letter from Henry addressed to him in the library.

Jack Otterson's psychological castle interiors truly set the mood for the horrible deeds they hide. The tall ceilings and oddly spiraling staircase are reminiscent of the surrealistic sets that gave the German silent classic, *The Cabinet of Dr. Caligari* (1919), its dreamlike quality. They are an orderly assemblage of geometrical masses to give an aura of Gothic horror without getting in action's way.

The location of the castle, however, offers a continuity problem. In the first two pictures Frankenstein's castle was in the center of the village, but here it has been moved to the side of a mountain over a mile outside town. The costumes and scenery were originally designed for color photography but the film was shot in black and white after color tests resulted in the distortion of Karloff's make-up.

Exploring the family tomb, Wolf discovers Ygor caring for his father's comatose monster. Ygor has been killing off the jurors who convicted him and is pleased when Wolf agrees to give the monster new life. The shepherd is anxious to have the monster complete his work for him.

The creature is rejuvenated and begins to kill for Ygor, squeezing the necks of jurors until their hearts burst. Realizing that the monster is once again on the loose, townsfolk mob the castle. Ygor attacks Wolf and the doctor shoots him dead. As Wolf runs to inform the inspector of the shooting, the monster wails agonizingly over the fallen form of his friend and, seeking revenge, kidnaps small Peter. The boy is carried to the castle's basement where there is an open boiling sulphur pit. Wolf and Krogh charge in with guns drawn. The monster gently puts the boy down and tears the inspector's artificial arm off. (Again?) Wolf swings from a rope like a swashbuckler, kicking the monster into the pit where he is parboiled.

But not to his death. The creature had many film appearances left in his career. Next stop was *The Ghost of Frankenstein* (1942) with Lon Chaney, Jr. given his sole opportunity to play the monster.

A bald, bespectacled Peruvian scientist uses radium rays to reduce people to 13 inches tall in Paramount's *Dr. Cyclops* (1939). Director Ernest B. Schoedsack returned to science fiction/horror after seven years working on western programmers. The casual pacing makes it hard to believe *Dr. Cyclops* was directed by the same man who made *King Kong*.

Dr. Cyclops was only the second science fiction film to be made in modern color, the first being *Dr. X* (1932). Green is the color most commonly associated with fear, yet pervasive greens here, both in the lab and prevalent jungle scenes, give it a cheesy feel — as if Dorothy Lamour were about to make her entrance in a sarong. This, along with a jolly score, squelch any thrills the exotic setting and sadistic menace might have induced. Even shock scenes, like a battle between the six little people and a house cat, could have been handled better.

Special effects artist Farciot Alexander Edouart (1895–1980) used rear projection, including both large and tiny screens, to visualize shrunken characters. Though Edouart received an Oscar nomination for his effects, similar illusions were handled better in Tod Browning's *The Devil Doll* (1936), and later in *The Incredible Shrinking Man* (1957).

The title villain (Albert Dekker, 1904–1968, a fine stage actor) is by far the most interesting person in the picture, in spite of his skullcap's betraying rubber shine. He delivers the film's best line when he lifts his pet cat from the floor and says, "These mice are not for you. At least not yet."

Hero Thomas Coley is worth only a yawn and heroine Janice Logan — though appropriately demure — leaves much to be desired in the scream department.

Dekker worked in movies right up until his death and ended his career in Japan where he appeared in *Gammera the Invincible* (1966).

Between 1939 and 1941, Karloff moved from Universal to Columbia where he made four science fiction B-features. *The Man They Could Not Hang* (1939), *The Man with Nine Lives* (1940), *Before I Hang* (1940), and *The Devil Commands* (1941) were all filmed in a few months. All were produced by Wallace MacDonald and featured Karloff as a doctor whose downfall comes from his pseudoscientific dabblings. The last, and most skimpily produced, is the most notable.

Rarely has such a rich studio produced such a threadbare look. The budget for *The Devil Commands* was lower per minute than the contemporary serials. Since it was the last of the four to be filmed, MacDonald had run out of money. Still, a tight script and imaginative (to say the least) direction pull it through.

Director Edward Dmytryk was not given the funds to create realistic sets, so he effectively substituted darkness and shadows to create an eerie surrealism. The film looks as if it were filmed in a bizarrely illuminated garage. The most expensive set, the laboratory, consisted of an electronically wired kitchen table, straight-backed chairs, four coffin-like boxes with dials on them, and bare walls laden with stark shadows. Audience acceptance equalled that of off-Broadway theatergoers.

A scientist (Karloff), trying to record human thought waves, stumbles upon a way to communicate with the dead. World War II, with its inevitable bereavements, induced a spate of media on communication with the departed. The film's major flaw is an absurd past-tense narration by the scientist's daughter which is supposed to create an aura of doom.

The scientist learns to animate the dead and uses his zombies to operate his laboratory machinery. In an unsatisfying climax, Karloff's tiny lab blows up when angered villagers storm his house. It is clear that the precious set was unharmed in the staged explosion. The scientist escapes unscathed and proclaims, "There are things that human beings have no right to know."

The other three films in Karloff's Columbia quartet were directed by Nick Grindé (b. 1893), who, though working with more money, produced a less interesting product than Dmytryk.

In *Before I Hang*, co-starring Edward Van Sloan, Karloff plays Dr. John Garth who, after being imprisoned for euthanasia, attempts to develop a youth serum. The potion backfires and he is transformed into a psycho-killer.

Karloff plays Dr. Leon Karvall in *The Man with Nine Lives*, blandly written by Karl Brown. The uninspired tale tells of a scientist seeking a cancer cure who steals terminal patients from a hospital and places them under suspended animation in his secret laboratory. Karvall then freezes himself for ten years until he and his patients are discovered by a billiant young doctor (hero Roger Pryor). Though his cure is proclaimed a success, Karvall remains coldly pursued by local police for kidnapping.

In *The Man They Could Not Hang* Karloff portrays the benevolent inventor of an artificial heart, which he hopes will save many lives. When one of his patients dies accidentally during an operation, he is executed for murder. He is reanimated by his own invention and goes on a murder spree, slaying his convicting jurors. Victoriously, he proves his invention functional by retrieving his daughter from death before expiring again with his secret.

Humphrey Bogart (1899–1957) was being punished by Jack Warner when cast in *The Return of Dr. X* (1939) as a notorious child-killer resuscitated from the dead. Languid, with pallid face, sunken cheeks and horn-rimmed glasses, Bogart (as Charles Quesne) goes on a homicidal rampage for human blood. His performance is about all of worth to be found in this half-hearted pseudo-sequel.

Directed by Vincent Sherman, it featured Wayne Morris as a fast-talking newspaperman with an offensively tipped hat brim, Rosemary Lane as a buxom nurse (whose blood is apparently particularly delicious), and John Litel as the doctor whose array of lab equipment animates Quesne. Lya Lys portrays a macabre dancer who, like Quesne, dies but does not die.

The best and funniest scene involves the reporter and his intern friend (Dennis Morgan), who go to the cemetary to exhume Quesne's body. Removing the casket, they leave the hole to be filled by a grumpy cemetery watchman.

The title is purposefully misleading. Warner Brothers wanted moviegoers to think this a sequel to *Dr. X* (1932), named after Lionel Atwill's character Dr. Xavier. The only doctor in the "sequel" (Litel) is named Flegg.

Stock footage from the 1909 silent *Dante's Inferno* was abused in *Hellevision* (1939), a Roadshow Attractions production about a scientist's latest invention: a cathode ray tube that can pick up transmissions from Hades.

The possibility of television in homes was getting a lot of press in 1939 (though the war would delay its development) and interest was reflected in cinematic output. In Paramount's 1939 thriller, *Television Spy*, directed by Edward Dmytryk (*The Devil Commands*), secret agents battled over a wall-sized TV unit capable of broadcasting nationwide.

The dangers of science were explored in Columbia's *Hidden Power* (1939), directed by Lewis Collins. It stars Jack Holt as a chemist who, while seeking a pain-killer, accidentally invents a potentially deadly explosive.

The poverty-row Monogram Film Company adapted Hal Forrest's comic strip "Tailspin Tommy" into *Sky Pirates* (1939). Scientists invent an automated bomber plane capable of dropping explosive cargo from as high as 30,000 feet. Jason Robards, Sr. plays intrepid airman Tommy, and the supporting cast includes Milburn Stone.

Supposedly based on a story by Jack London and predictably lurid was *Torture Ship* (1939), which borrowed heavily from the gruesome appeal of *Island of Lost Souls*. A product of the Producer's Releasing Corporation, noted for their bad cinema, the film stars Irving Pichel as a doctor "curing" convicts of criminal tendencies with gland injections. His floating laboratory is populated with grotesque "mistakes."

Also released in 1939 was Columbia's *The World of 1960*, a nine-minute pseudo-documentary.

Schizophrenia via transplantation of brain tissue provides the science fiction element in Universal's intelligent thriller *Black Friday* (1940), scripted by Curt Siodmak and Eric Taylor, and tersely directed by Arthur Lubin.

In state prison, Dr. Ernest Sovac (Boris Karloff) awaits the electric chair as a priest prays solemnly. Sovac slips notes to a reporter before walking the longest mile, and the story is told in flashback.

Dr. George Kingsley (Stanley Ridges) is an absent-minded but kindly college professor and teacher to Sovac's daughter Jean (Anne Gwynne).

During a jolly visit to the university, Sovac expresses his gratitude for Kingsley's special attention to his daughter, but their pleasant world is shattered when they blunder into an armed robbery. A horrible car crash ensues. Both gangster Red Cannon and Kingsley are badly injured. The thug is paralyzed and dying while the professor has severe brain damage. Sovac rides along in the ambulance and quickly determines that the only way to save the teacher's life is to perform a "brain transplantation" between the two—an operation which Ernest has successfully administered to animals but knows is illegal. The gangster dies during the operation while Kingsley makes a miraculous recovery. When Sovac learns the thug died knowing the whereabouts of $500 thousand, he wonders if Kingsley retains this knowledge, since the teacher is intermittently displaying the criminal's harsh personality traits. Sovac takes his patient to New York, hoping Red's environs will help his personality emerge. Kingsley is introduced to Red's dance hall-strumpet girlfriend Sonny Rodgers (Anne Nagel) and forced to live in Red's frequented midtown hotel. Hypnosis is a catalyst for the *déjà vu*. Red, living inside Kingsley's body, immediately sets out to kill the members of his gang who betrayed him. Sovac realizes that he has created a monster but is reluctant to stop it until he gets the money.

Bela Lugosi has a small role as Red's crooked colleague Eric Marney, murdered by suffocation in a locked closet. At the film's release, the Universal publicity department announced Lugosi was hypnotized for the death scene to believe he was actually suffocating.

For the first time Karloff and Lugosi worked together in a film in which neither of them were asked to wear feature-altering make-up. The occasionally tense co-workers kept things light on the set by loudly pretending not to recognize one another, and then chiding the other on his "frightening looks."

After all thugs and Sonny are dead, the gangster is dormant. Kingsley returns to his teaching job and behaves normally until he panics at a police siren. Ernest is forced to kill "Red" when the gangster tries to strangle Jean.

Though Karloff is technically the star of the film, the best performance is by Ridges. Without make-up, Ridges changes appearance drastically with his Jekyll-Hyde-like transformation. He is equally effective as the docile professor and sneering gangster.

In the grandest style of Willis O'Brien, United Artists released *One Million B.C.* in 1940. Though the screen credits list the directors as producer Hal Roach and his son, this journey into the past was actually directed by D.W. Griffith. The story is told visually, like a silent, making the film seem much older than it actually is. The naiveté of the silent approach gives the film a charm that would have been missing had it been more sophisticated and enhances indentification with the childlike discoveries being made by the cave people characters. Despite this, Griffith was reportedly upset when Roach substituted for English dialogue with grunting cave syllables.

The dinosaurs were lizards projected onto a rear screen to look enormous. The technique, now associated with shoddier productions and considered inferior to stop-motion animation, was more than adequate before the forced artificiality of painted panoramic backdrops. The effects, by Roy Seawright, Frank William Young, Fred Knoth, Danny Hall, and Jack Shaw, had stunning moments. Lon Chaney, Jr., in his first feature science fiction performance, skinnier and made up beyond recognition, is gored realistically by a horned prehistoric beast. Near the conclusion, a running woman is engulfed by a flowing river of molten lava. But it was the extended toothful grapple of two lizards that was reused by later features such as *Tarzan's Desert Mystery* (1943). The effects team won an Oscar nomination for their efforts.

The fully orchestrated score, composed by Werner R. Heyman, occasionally seems too full-blown for the accompanying visual; he purposefully lacked delicacy to bring out Griffith's dated look.

The male lead is Victor Mature (b. 1915) — all muscles, black hair and teeth — brutishly stomping in front of elaborate sets. The heroine is Carole Landis, whose blonde mop bounces as she squirrelishly scurries.

The film, also known as *Man and His Mate*, concerns the trials of two primitive tribes begrudgingly sharing a neighborhood while defending against lizard and mastodon attacks. They are the Rock People, of which Chaney and Mature are members, and Landis' Shell People, more advanced in having invented the spear and learned to share food. By the end, love between the couple unites the tribes. The climax comes when a nearby volcano erupts on cue and Mature saves Landis before she becomes lizard chow. After slaying the beast, he walks into the new dawn with his mate and child.

Universal's *The Invisible Man Returns* (1940), their first sequel to the original, was scripted by Curt Siodmak and Lester Cole, directed by Joe May, and starred unknown Vincent Price (b. 1911) as the title transparency. It was too directly derivative; audiences felt they had seen the gimmicks before. This in no way criticizes Price's performance or John Fulton's topnotch effects. Price is no Claude Rains, but he gives the role a distinguished intensity that predicted his stardom.

Innocent Sir Geoffrey Radcliffe (Price), two hours from execution for the murder of his brother Michael, is visited by friend Dr. Frank Griffin (John Sutton), brother of the original invisible man. Griffin injects Radcliffe with the invisibility serum, and the prisoner escapes to find the real murderer. He cannot dawdle, for he must solve the mystery before the serum drives him mad. Meanwhile Griffin works on an antidote.

Radcliffe escapes the police repeatedly, and makes his girlfriend (Nan Grey) faint by removing his bandages. Once, his location is revealed by a Scotland Yard inspector's cigar smoke. He is a raving lunatic by the time the derelict who testified against him reveals Richard Cobb (Cedric Hardwicke) as the murderer. Cobb is cornered in a mining shaft and comes to a nasty end, falling from an underground train. Luckily, he confesses his crime to Scotland Yard before he dies.

Not knowing his name is cleared, Radcliffe runs insanely through a cornfield stealing clothes from a scarecrow. He stumbles home cold and sick. Griffin administers a transfusion of pure blood, which turns out to be the antidote. Sanity returns with Radcliffe's visibility; so he and Helen can live happily ever after. The plot was reused in 1962 in a Spanish film called *H.G. Wells' New Invisible Man*, with Arturo de Cordova as the unjustly accused murderer made invisible to prove his innocence.

Two other minor science fiction films were produced in 1940. In Monogram's screen adaptation of Laurie York Erskine's novel *Renfrew—Ride the Sky*, called *Sky Bandits*, Royal Canadian Mounted Police aviator Renfrew (James Newell) battles nasty scientists and their death rays. Phil Goldstone produced, Ralph Staub directed, and Goldstone adapted Erskine's book for film.

In *The Invisible Killer*, a Producer's Releasing Corporation quickie which had nothing to do with *The Invisible Man*, sound waves are the title menace. They are diabolically used as instruments of murder.

The Monster and the Girl, an ugly misogynistic 1941 Paramount release, takes so many bizarre plot twists that one has to wonder about the attention span of Stuart Anthony, the writer. Though it contains scenes of a rather bland doctor (George Zucco, 1886-1960) transplanting the brain of an executed prisoner (Philip Terry) into the head of a gorilla, the first half of the film depicts the cruel seduction of a virgin (Ellen Drew) into a prostitution ring and the framing of her vengeance-seeking brother for murder. Never before had the villains been so sadistic and the heroes so dull. Good guys move only their lips while villains both move their lips and wiggle their eyebrows.

When pretty Susan Webster (Drew) meets sad-eyed but seemingly kindly Larry Reed (Robert Paige) on an unemployment line and marries him only days later, she should have paid closer attention to the sleazy company he kept. Susan wakes up the morning after her wedding night, stretches languorously and beams with her new womanhood. Just then a mustached thug enters the room. "There is no Larry. Never has been. Never will be." After being slapped around for a long time, Susan realizes that she is a spoiled woman in need of work. When loving brother Scott pokes around, he is quickly framed for murder, tried, convicted, and sentenced to the chair. Susan tries to testify in his defense but her testimony is disregarded by the court, who considers her a "woman not worthy of trust."

The science fiction is gotten out of the way hurriedly. In less than five minutes Zucco arrives on death row and arranges to use Scott's brain. Scott is executed, transported to a familiarly spooky mansion; Zucco performs the transplant in a sparsely-equipped soundstage laboratory, and the gorilla escapes to kill. First the D.A. gets it. One by one the gang of pimps begin to drop. As the coroner puts it, each corpse is found with "no abrasions, no bruises, but every bone in the body broken."

Gang leader Bruhl (Paul Lucas) kidnaps Susan, giving the remaining sadists a chance to slap her around some more, thinking she knows the killer's identity.

The leading man apparently is snide reporter Sam Daniels (Rod Cameron, who doesn't even move his lips very much and is seventh in the cast credits, below many of the gangsters). He exclusively considers Susan a real human being despite her past and gets to shoot the ape dead in the final scene, after the gorilla has successfully wiped out the bad guys.

Some argue that the true hero is Susan's dog Skipper, who even appears in scenes where he doesn't belong. The small dog befriends the ape, instinctively knowing it is really his master. The final shot shows a very sad Skipper on the sidewalk outside the building where the ape lies dead.

Universal gave Lon Chaney, Jr. (1906–1973) his first starring role in an science fiction feature in *Man-Made Monster* (1941), directed by George Waggner. Though only moderately successful at the box office, Universal cast Chaney in *The Wolf Man* the same year, which was to become the studio's largest annual grosser.

Man-Made Monster (also known as *The Atomic Monster* and *The Electric Man*), bore an uncanny likeness to Universal's *The Invisible Ray* (1936) and was originally intended as a Karloff-Lugosi vehicle. Chaney survives a lethal dose of electricity after his bus crashes into a power tower, killing the other passengers. Following a stint as the glowing "Electric Man" in a sideshow, he becomes the lethal tool of opportunistic Dr. Rigas (Lionel Atwill). Framed on a murder charge, the attempted electrocution not only doesn't kill him, but escalates his problem into high-voltage monsterdom. Forced to wear a rubber suit, he kills Rigas when the doctor tries to electrify heroine Anne Nagel (1912–1966).

Besides his glow, Chaney's condition is visualized through increasing use of black eye make-up. He weaves across the countryside, falling afoul of a juiced barbed-wire fence that tears his insulated clothing and draws his life away. Special effects were by John Fulton.

Rigas' laboratory is clean and efficient, devoid of the Gothic cobwebs found in Henry Frankenstein's work area. Atwill is at his best as Rigas, chortling lechery, strapping the helpless heroine to his operating table.

Not counting plagiarisms, *Dr. Jekyll and Mr. Hyde* was filmed for the eleventh time in 1941 in M-G-M with Spencer Tracy (1900–1967) playing the lead. Directed and produced by Victor Fleming (1883–1949), who made *Gone with the Wind*, the film borrows many scenes from the 1932 Paramount *Jekyll*, but nonetheless falls way short of its immediate predecessor. Perhaps believing the Barrymore myth, Tracy used a minimum of make-up to play Hyde. With the exception of a pair of bushy eyebrows and suckable teeth, Tracy's face was unaltered, leaving the actor to rely on facial expressions to communicate his polarization of good and evil. Rather than becoming the lewd menace that March and Barrymore had achieved, Tracy's Hyde was more of a mischievous libertine and less successful.

John Lee Mahin's script is dreary and bogged down with multiple

Lionel Atwill takes it to the max as Dr. Rigas in *Man-Made Monster* (Universal, 1941).

dream sequences, yet the film is almost saved by the casting against type of its female leads. The usually demure and innocent Ingrid Bergman (in her favorite role) plays Ivy Pierson, the sexy, promiscuous dance hall girl — a foil for Jekyll's wicked alter ego — while vampish Lana Turner wears a halo as Jekyll's virginal fiancée.

Not counting a meeting with Abbott and Costello, Stevenson's personification of the psyche did not appear on screen again for twenty years. The next was Hammer's *The Two Faces of Dr. Jekyll* starring Paul Massie and directed by Terrence Fisher. It was a 1961 attempt to exploit the plot's erotic potential, causing unintentional humor. Even further bastardizing the book was *Dr. Jekyll and Sister Hyde* (1972), also by Hammer, in which Ralph Bates transforms into beautiful Martine Bestwick after drinking the formaldehyde.

The writers of *The Invisible Man* screenplay, Curt Siodmak and Joe May, penned the story for *The Invisible Woman* (1941), a light film whose object was to amuse rather than frighten. Both Siodmak and May (whose real name was Joseph Mandel) were self-exiled major influences on the German film industry before the war. Despite the creaky screenplay, which relied on comic gimmickry standardized in the *Topper* series, the special effects of John Fulton (for which he received yet another Oscar nomination) and John Barrymore's performance make this enjoyable viewing. Barrymore takes to slapstick as if to the manner born, both arch and gleeful, groping with his hands and making mirthful clucking noises while puffing out his cheeks.

Professor Gibbs (Barrymore) invents a machine rendering fashion model Kitty Carroll (Virginia Bruce) invisible. Foreign spies stumble upon the discovery and seek both the invention and the girl.

In Monogram's *King of the Zombies* (1941), a Nazi doctor (George Zucco) living on a tropical island learns to revive the dead. Only Dick Purcell can stop him from boosting the Axis effort with an army of marching corpses. Mantan Moreland's rolling eyes and chattering teeth at every sign of a "spook" was once considered comic relief, but would now be considered tastelessly racist.

The Ghost of Frankenstein (1941), the fast-paced fourth entry in Universal's series and immediate sequel to *Son of…* (1939), starred Lon Chaney, Jr., as the monster. For the first time, Karloff did not play the role. Chaney, fresh from his previous year's success in *The Wolf Man*, donned eighteen-pound boots to play a stiffer, shallower version of the monster. Though Chaney does not give the beast Karloff's depth (and it is unfair to compare), he *is* menacing—this enhanced by ground-up camera angles to emphasize his height—and handled the part better than either Bela Lugosi or Glenn Strange to follow.

Chaney was difficult on the set, usually inebriated for his afternoon schedules. The actor was cranky and prone to getting lost. His scenes had to be delayed for a week when Chaney opened gashes in his forehead tearing off Jack Pierce's rubber headpiece in aggravation.

If the entries in this series are to be thought of as parts of a whole, this picture is filled with glaring inconsistencies. For example, the villagers grinning happily at the end of *Son* are filled with hunger and despair at this film's opening. Ygor (with Lugosi, thankfully, repeating his brilliant characterization), who had his belly pumped full of lead in *Son*, now shows no effects from his wounds. At least two members of the town council killed by the monster in the previous film are once again alive. Still, this is the last of the series to produce a genuine member of the Frankenstein family as the mad scientist. Universal assigned Erle C. Kenton (*Island of Lost Souls*) to direct.

The monster, thought dead after a plunge into the Frankenstein Castle sulphur pit, is rejuvenated when directly struck by a bolt of lightning. Joined again by Ygor, the chalky monster is taken to the hometown of another of Henry and Elizabeth Frankenstein's sons, Ludwig (Cedric Hardwicke). Also a doctor, Ludwig hopes to turn the killer monster into a model citizen by replacing his abnormal brain. Proving himself both inept and easily duped, Frankenstein puts Ygor's brain into the monster, bungles the operation, and renders the creature blind.

Mute in *Frankenstein*, able to speak in *Bride*, speechless in *Son*, the monster once again gains vocal capabilities with the shepherd's brain in his head. He fell silent after this picture and never uttered another word.

Dwight Frye is reduced to a bit role here but is still effective as he heads Universal's obligatory angry-mob scene, urging the destruction of Frankenstein Castle. Frye's career had plummeted terribly. His job before this was in a nudie stag film, playing a wide-eyed voyeur. He was dead two years later.

Playing Frankenstein's wicked assistant was Lionel Atwill, who was likewise finding it increasingly difficult to get work; his career was in the process of being ruined by a sex scandal. Evelyn Ankers (b. 1918) played Dr. Frankenstein's wife.

The monster brings about his own death by fire when he knocks over flammable chemicals in the lab. This is the most vivid death scene in the series as we see the creature's face blistering away. Not surprisingly, the death of the man-made creation was only an illusion. He was to rise next in *Frankenstein Meets the Wolf Man* (1943).

Self-exiled German Curt Siodmak got his chance to write a screenplay replete with anti-Nazi propaganda for Universal's *The Invisible Agent* (1942), starring dandy Jon Hall (b. 1913) as the hero and Peter Lorre and Cedric Hardwicke as insidious Axis spies. Though the dialogue was inane, it was well within the spirit of wartime kiddiefare, and John Fulton's special effects were again good enough for Oscar nomination.

Frank Raymond (Hall), despite the name change, is supposedly the son of the original invisible man, whom we all know died a bachelor. Shortly after Pearl Harbor he volunteers his body and the remainder of Dad's invisibility serum to go on a secret mission in Germany. Transparent, Raymond parachutes into Berlin where he makes contact with a pretty secret agent (Ilona Massey). Through the girl, he learns from the head of the Secret Nazi Police (Hardwicke) of Hitler's plans for immediate attack on America. Obtaining a list of Axis agents operating in the United States from evil Japanese spy Ikito (Lorre), he is almost captured with a hook-lined silk net, but escapes injured. He rejoins the girl and successfully returns to England by stealing a German bomber.

In spite of its shaky premise, Universal's *The Night Monster* (1942), produced and directed by serial veteran Ford Beebe, is a genuinely chilling horror tale boosted by an excellent cast including Bela Lugosi, Lionel Atwill, and Ralph Morgan (1882–1956). Morgan plays an eccentric millionaire who, because of an unsuccessful operation, has had both of his legs amputated. Using scientific mind-control—this is the shaky part—the millionaire can make new legs appear on his body. As the film opens he has invited all of the bungling doctors to spend the night in his home, where they are murdered one by one. Lugosi and Atwill play victims.

Universal also made *The Mad Doctor of Market Street* (1942), a disappointment with Atwill as a doctor able to raise the dead. He declares himself the god of a South Sea island, thus conning the locals after fleeing Philadelphia to avoid a murder rap. Worshipping him as they do, the dark natives are more than willing to be used as human guinea pigs for his bizarre experiments.

Monogram, a subsidiary to Allied Artists, made three skid-row potboilers in 1942 with science fiction premises, two of them with Lugosi.

The Hungarian starred in *Black Dragons* (1942) as a plastic surgeon who agrees to change the faces on Japanese secret agents. The misuse of drugs also comes into play, transforming the surgically-altered Orientals into grotesque monsters.

It was clear that Lugosi did not take Monogram quickies too seriously in *The Corpse Vanishes* (1942), yet his hammy performance is the only saving grace to a vapid plot that has him as physician with a screw loose trying scientific means to reverse his wife's annoying aging process.

In *The Living Ghost*, starring James Dunn, a mad scientist's unusual experiment turns a successful businessman into a mongoloid.

The performance of J. Carrol Naish (1900–1973), as a monkey scientifically transformed into a human being, highlights Fox's *Dr. Renault's Secret* (1942), quickly paced (58 minutes) by director Harry Lachman (1886–1975). George Zucco is appropriately evil as the title scientist whose pathetic mutant brings about tragic results. Among the supporting cast was an excellent broken-nosed character actor, Mike Mazurki. This was the third adaptation of Gaston Leroux's novel *Balaoo*, the first two being *Balaoo, the Demon Baboon* (1913, French) and *The Wizard* (1927).

Young Craig Stevens, best known as TV's private eye *Peter Gunn*, starred in Warner Brothers' *The Hidden Hand* (1942), a flat drama set in a world where suspended animation is the ultimate weapon.

Scientifically-induced lycanthropia is the subject of *The Mad Monster* (1942), a Producer's Releasing Corporation shoestring feature starring George Zucco as Dr. Lorenzo Cameron, a well-meaning but bonkers physician who believes he can create a super-race of Anti-Nazi werewolves through blood transfusions. Glenn Strange, soon to be the Frankenstein monster, plays the doctor's assistant who ends up growing extra facial hair during the full moon. Pretty Anne Nagel heads up the supporting cast. Uneventful.

Monogram made *The Man with Two Lives* (1942), (not to be

confused with *The Man with Nine Lives* or *The Man Who Lived Twice*), a skid-row thriller starring Edward Norris as the victim of a fatal accident brought back to life by a kindly scientist. Unfortunately, when rejuvenated he has the personality of a gangster executed at the moment of his death.

The Universal horror series had degenerated to programmer status by the making of *Frankenstein Meets the Wolf Man* (1943), intended as a sequel to both *The Ghost of Frankenstein* (1942) and *The Wolf Man* (1941). Though it originated the oft-imitated "grappling monsters" theme, the mood and lighting here are far more cheerful than in any of the previous films in the series. Universal apparently thought that, with a world war raging, monsters needn't be as frightening. There is even an elaborate musical production number.

Bela Lugosi, who turned down an opportunity to play the Franken-stein monster twelve years before, accepted this time around; his ego was deflated by his waning career. His performance is clumsy but not entirely by his own fault. Since the monster had been blinded in *The Ghost of ...*, shooting began with the creature still sightless. While in production, the screenplay was altered to give the monster sight. Carelessly, the original footage was never re-shot, making Lugosi's blind stumbling seem ridiculous. The menace of Frankenstein's creation was further depleted by shrinking his height a foot so he would be eye-to-eye with Lon Chaney, Jr., who was repeating his role as the tortured lycanthrope.

In Curt Siodmak's original screenplay the monster spoke fluently, having Ygor's brain in his head. But all of the monster's dialogue was cut when Lugosi's Hungarian accent produced hysterics in the screening room. In some cases the soundtrack was erased so that the monster's lips move but no sound comes out. The actor's health was failing, and he was forced to get up at 2:30 A.M. to soak in a hot tub before each work day. A new, smaller headpiece was designed but Lugosi was prohibitively immobile inside the heavy costume. Many of the monster's scenes, including the monster's entrance caked in ice and the climactic wrestling match, were actually done by 41-year-old stuntman Eddie Parker.

The only representative of the Frankenstein family in the script is Baroness Elsa Frankenstein, the same character played by Evelyn Ankers in *The Ghost of ...* Here, the daughter of Ludwig and granddaughter of Henry is played by toothy blonde diva Ilona Massey (heroine of *Invisible Agent* the previous year). Massey is the only actor to give a Frankenstein an East European accent.

Far more screen time is dedicated to the story of Lawrence Talbot (Chaney), a nobleman who, after being attacked by a werewolf, turns into one himself whenever the moon is full. Talbot has been struck dead by a blow to the head from his father (played in *The Wolf Man* by Claude Rains) as this movie begins. The legend has it that a werewolf must be killed by someone who loves him.

Two graverobbers seeking jewelry make the mistake of digging up

Larry's coffin when the moon is full. When the moon's rays hit Talbot's body, he comes alive as a wolf and kills one of them before collapsing from the effects of his skull fracture.

For Chaney's transformation, Jack Pierce used stopmotion photography, adding yak hair a little at a time, shooting five to ten frames at each make-up stage. The already ornery actor was forced to stay immobile for 22 hours to produce a few seconds of film. Still, Chaney was happiest when playing Talbot, and he never played another fantastic role as well. His sad, hound-dog face is perfect for the character's hopelessness. Talbot is always touchingly sympathetic.

Larry wakes in a hospital and learns that his father has died of a broken heart, unable to deal with killing his son. Larry wants nothing more than to be really dead himself, since he knows that as long as the cursed blood runs in his veins he will kill. In a scene of stunning violence, the wolf man escapes from the hospital and is dark and shadowy as he tears the throat of a policeman. It is much too early in the film for the horror to peak.

Once well, Larry sets off to find Maleva, the gypsy woman whose son's bite infected him. She is spookily portrayed by Maria Ouspenskaya (1876–1949), repeating the role. Maleva tells Larry to go see Dr. Frankenstein, a man who possesses the knowledge of life and death. But when Talbot gets to the Frankenstein Castle he finds the doctor is dead, killed in a fire. Talbot instead finds a crackpot physician (British Patric Knowles, b. 1911, also repeating from *The Wolf Man*), Frankenstein's daughter, and the frozen body of the Frankenstein monster (making his debut 37 minutes into the picture). Larry convinces the doctor to drain his life-energy into the thawed creature so he can finally achieve peaceful death. Before this can be done, there is a full moon. Wolf and monster battle briefly (110 seconds) in the laboratory, trying in vain to strangle one another. No punches are thrown. Before a winner can be determined, a disgruntled townie (Rex Evans) blows up the dam upstream from the castle (both dam and castle are toy-like miniatures) and the title creatures are drowned.

Dwight Frye appears briefly again as a bespectacled local. Still he manages to deliver one of the best lines in the picture with, "Yes! A wolf! That's his cry!" After this movie, Frye was forced to make a living designing bombsights for the war effort and died of a heart attack at 44.

Universal was still giving Lionel Atwill work, here playing a benign blustering mayor. Soon after he completed shooting on *Frankenstein Meets the Wolf Man*, he was convicted of perjury at his own rape trial and banned by the Hays Office. Atwill finished his career making serials.

Edgar Rice Burroughs's ape man had been endlessly varied by 1943 when RKO produced *Tarzan's Desert Mystery* with Johnny Weismuller (b. 1904) in the lead and regular Johnny Sheffield as Boy. Tarzan and Boy travel across sand dunes instead of jungle in search of malaria-curing vegetation. On the way they battle Nazis and encounter huge grappling lizards, compliments of footage spliced from *One Million B.C.* (1940).

One of the worst Lugosi vehicles of the Forties was Monogram's *The Ape Man* (1943), also known as *Lock Your Doors*. Based on Karl Brown's story "They Creep in the Dark," this Sam Katzman production was directed by William "One-Shot" Beaudine (1890-1970), who earned his nickname because of his dislike for reshooting, often printing obviously botched scenes. Because of this shoddy yet spendthrift attitude, the director found steady work from the silent era until he made *Billy the Kid versus Dracula* (1966). He once made a film for Hygenic Productions called *Mom and Dad* about an unwed mother. At the end of the black and white film, he attached a live birth in full color. Beaudine's ham acting trademark is left on all performers. Here, Lugosi is a scientist who self-injects a simian serum and becomes homicidal. Beaudine believed thespian techniques peaked before talkies and encouraged the use of the broad gestures and wild expressions that comically date his work. Lugosi hides in a cellar and sprouts a forehead rug, going outside only to obtain spinal fluid for an antidote.

Monogram and Sam Katzman produced a pseudo-sequel called *Return of the Ape Man* (1944), also starring Lugosi but with no other connection to the original. Directed by Philip Rosen, Lugosi plays Professor Dexter, who along with Professor Gilmore (John Carradine) has discovered a way of reviving the dead. They test out their formula on a prehistoric ape (played by George Zucco and Frank Moran) found preserved in ice. When complications arise, Dexter murders Gilmore and transplants his brain in the missing link's body. Lugosi further accumulates audience sympathy by blow-torching the beast's face as discipline. Naturally the ape escapes, becomes violent, murders a couple of people, and turns on his creator so both can be destroyed in a budget-conscious lab fire.

John Carradine plays a scientist changing a female orangutan into a beautiful woman (a beauty contest winner billed as Acquanetta, b. 1921) in Universal's fun *Captive Wild Woman* (1943) directed by Edward Dmytryk. Milburn Stone plays an animal trainer, though his action scenes are carefully edited footage of Clyde Beatty from *The Big Cage*. The film was popular enough to warrant two sequels. Acquanetta repeated her role as former ape Paula Dupree in *Jungle Woman* (1944). Though killed at the end of *Captive Wild Woman*, she is rejuvenated by scientist J. Carrol Naish. Directed by Reginald LeBorg, the film ends with the woman's second demise. But, as any Frankenstein fan will tell you, a good monster is hard to kill. The ape woman returned for the third and last time in *Jungle Captive* (1945), directed by Harold Young. Vicki Lane plays the girl to Otto Kruger's mad scientist, with acromegalic Rondo "The Creeper" Hatton (1894-1946) heading up the supporting cast. This time the girl's plans to win the heart of hero Robert Shayne (b. 1905, best known as Inspector Henderson in TV's *The Adventures of Superman*) are hampered by her slow regression, reminiscent of the troubles of Lota the Panther Woman in *Island of Lost Souls*.

In a classic case of self-plagiarism, Monogram released *Revenge of the Zombies* (1943) directed by Steve Sekely, a film remarkable similar to their *King of the Zombies* (1941). Here, Carradine plays the Nazi scientist attempting creation of a zombie army after discovering the secret of life. Robert Lowery is the hero, Gale Storm the heroine, and, as in the previous picture, Mantan Moreland provides the now racially offensive comic relief. In the conclusion, the scientist's fickle wife (Veda Ann Borg, 1915–1973), a fetching member of the walking dead, turns the army of zombies on her husband.

Universal was more successful with *The Mad Ghoul* (1943). George Zucco played the unscrupulous scientist. Directed by James Hogan, Zucco invents a "death-after-life" gas, which reduces its inhalor to shriveled subservience. This is the unhappy fate of actor David Bruce (1914–1976), who needs a fresh human heart every few days to stay alive. In between gruesome murders, the doctor flirts with his zombie's ex-girlfriend (Evelyn Ankers) and endangers her new boyfriend (Turhan Bey). It holds together despite Bruce's laughably simulated lobotomy.

Working under the theory that the more monsters the better, Universal made *House of Frankenstein* (1944), adding Karloff as a mad scientist, John Carradine in his initial portrayal of Count Dracula, and J. Carrol Naish as a homicidal hunchback to the already-teamed Wolf Man (Chaney) and Frankenstein monster (played for the first time by Glenn Strange, 1899–1973). This is actually two short pictures strung together: a Dracula movie and a sequel to *Frankenstein Meets the Wolf Man* (1943). Universal's desperation was clear. The original concept, known as *The Devil's Brood*, even crammed in *The Mummy*.

Karloff was suffering from back trouble and underweight during production, yet still found time to encourage Strange, who found himself in the biggest role of his career with little to do. Strange had been making westerns, serials, and low-grade horror films when he showed up in Jack Pierce's make-up studio to receive a facial scar, impressing the artist with his size and strength. His choice for the part was economical, as Strange was an unknown, and Universal was already straining their salary budget with a multi-star billing.

Naish, twice Oscar-nominated for best supporting roles, studied the role of bent Daniel by living in an L.A. boarding house with a hunchbacked derelict, an indulgent study of mannerisms no doubt rare during the studio system's most automated period.

Recently escaped from jail where he was put away for conducting illegal experiments on human cadavers *a la* Dr. Frankenstein, Dr. Neimann (Karloff) and his assistant Daniel cross paths with a traveling sideshow run by Professor Brudon Lampini (George Zucco). The show boasts possession of Dracula's skeletal remains, which Lampini acquired in Transylvania, though none of Universal's *Dracula* pictures had given the count an East European demise. Neimann, seeking revenge against those who imprisoned him, orders Daniel to kill Lampini, assumes his identity, and travels to the town of Frankenstein where he promises Daniel an upright body using Henry

Frankenstein's notebooks. Neimann rejuvenates Dracula and promises him shelter from the sun if he'll suck a few enemy necks. Dracula keeps his end of the bargain, killing the local burgomaster and avoiding the police inspector (Lionel Atwill), but is reduced to bones when Neimann tosses his coffin over a cliff into destroying sunshine.

In the town of Frankenstein, Daniel falls in love with a remarkable pretty gypsy girl named Alonka (Elena Verdugo in a brunette wig, who later achieved fame as Nurse Consuelo on TV's *Marcus Welby, M.D.*). The hunchback prays that his new body will be attractive so the girl will be able to love him back.

In the ravaged Frankenstein Castle, flooded at the end of *Franken-stein Meets the Wolf Man*, Neimann finds the frozen remains of the grappling monsters. Keeping the man-made creature sedated, they ride out of town, the werewolf having returned to his normal state as Larry Talbot. Larry and Alonka instantly fall in love, leaving Dr. Neimann's deformed assistant out in the cold. Larry gives the girl a gun loaded with a silver bullet. When the inevitable full moon rises, Larry lopes across the countryside looking for someone to kill. Alonka pursues. The girl allows the wolf to strangle her before she shoots him so they can find eternal peace together.

With Neimann procrastinating and his love dead, Daniel becomes angry, yet realizes that rebellion would destroy his only chance of getting a healthy body. In frustration Daniel wakes the sleeping monster by beating it mercilessly with a strap. Furious, the monster breaks free of his stringent bondage and throws the hunchback through a window. Strange, overzealous in one of his few action scenes, threw Naish so hard he missed the carefully placed mattresses on the other side of the window. Luckily, Naish was not seriously injured, his fall cushioned by his rubber deformity.

With most of the cast already dead, angry townspeople gather around Neimann's new laboratory. The monster totes the mad scientist under his arm and comically carries him to the marshes where they sink together in quicksand brilliantly illuminated by burning swamp gas.

Strange is not to blame for the blundering in the finale. While carrying Karloff's double, he was struck in the back with an anxious extra's hurled torch, and almost fell down a flight of stairs. He was forced to gallop into the quicksand when backlot exploding swamp gas came too close, singing the hair of Karloff's double.

In spite of the cast's destruction, all three monsters were to return in the series' final entry, *House of Dracula* (1945). After the genius of *Frank-enstein* and *The Bride of Frankenstein*, this film emerges as a parody, a methodical assemblage of stock horror sequences.

John Fulton again provided the effects for Universal's *The Invisible Man's Revenge* (1944), which, though featuring a character named Griffin, avoids sequel status by having nothing to do with the previous films. With a credit that reads "suggested" by H.G. Wells' novel, Universal patterned their own lackluster revenge-is-sweet gangster film. To make matters worse they miscast wimpy Jon Hall (also the hero in *The Invisible Agent*) in the lead. It was produced and directed by Ford Beebe and edited by Saul A. Goodkind, recent graduates from Universal serials. The pair had directed *Buck Rogers* (1939) and Beebe directed the two *Flash Gordon* sequels. Because action was unessential, Beebe left it out all together. Snoozing is interrupted only by the effects and strong performances by heroine Evelyn Ankers, mad scientist John Carradine, and scheming villainess Gail Sondergaard (b. 1899). Sondergaard is best known as the acid-hurler in Claude Rains' version of *the Phantom of the Opera*, as well as her title roles in *Sherlock Holmes and The Spider Woman* (1944) and *The Spider Woman Strikes Back* (1946).

On a foggy London night, Robert Griffin, recent murderer of two interns during an insane asylum escape, has mailed himself into the city in a crate. After buying a new set of clothes, he visits Jasper and Irene, who've cheated him of diamonds discovered together on expedition. Irene (Sondergaard) drugs Griffin and has him thrown into the river to drown. Surviving, Griffin stumbles upon the home of Dr. Surée (Carradine), who befriends him and shows off his invisible parrot Methuselah and his transparent dog Brutus, visualized as a stiff leash and floating collar. Naturally Griffin insists on being injected, allowing Surée to wail on about his immortality before the new invisible lunatic takes a powder, seeking revenge. To complicate matters, Griffin is obsessed with Irene's daughter Julie (Evelyn Ankers), whom he knows only by her portrait on the wall.

The best effects in the film are reserved for the comic relief. Griffin puts powder on his face to prove his existence to a drunk and later helps his inebriated chum win at darts.

The morality of scientifically induced youth is examined in Paramount's rarely seen but effective *The Man in Half-Moon Street* (1944) directed by Ralph Murphy. The film, written by Charles Kenyon from an adaptation by Garret Fort of a play by Barré Lyndon, stars Nils Asther (b. 1897) as a London scientist who remains eternally young through periodic gland transplants.

Dr. Julien Karrell (Asther) becomes engaged to pretty London socialite Eve Brandon (Helen Walker) after painting her portrait. Over ninety years old, he's had young male glands inserted in his body at ten-year intervals by his endocrinologist friend Dr. Bruecken (Reinhold Schunzwl). In each case the unfortunate donor died. The next operation is due but Dr. Bruecken is too old to perform it. Karrell finds another doctor (Paul Cavanaugh), who botches his operation. Eloping, Karrell and Eve are on a train to Paris when he feels himself growing old. Running away so Eve can't see, he ages visibly, turns gray, withers, and dies.

The make-up effects for the final scene were done by Wally Westmore, the same man who transformed Fredric March's Jekyll into Hyde. As in the March film, subtle changes in lighting were used to make already-applied make-up become visible.

Asther was a Swedish film star, but his success was limited in Hollywood.

When viewed today he has a strong screen presence. He is handsome and evokes sympathy despite his character's immorality. Unfortunately, his European accent is not distinctly Scandinavian, making his likeability impossible in the war era. The character has a zest for life and seems exactly the sort who would be seeking immortality. He repeatedly throws champagne glasses into the fireplace. After being kissed by him, Eve says with dreamy eyes, "You're not *all* scientist, are you?"

Other lines from the pen of Kenyon stand out. When the aging doctor tells Karrell he can no longer operate he gazes downward at swollen knuckles and mutters, "Not so agile now." Later he warns Karrell against marriage, "Men like us must always walk alone." When Scotland Yard arrives at Karrell's house the hero quips, "If you are looking for *corpus delecti*, there is always the cellar."

But the best piece of dialogue comes at film's end after the hero is dead. Eve walks alone, realizing the truth about her man's past.

"Are you going, miss?" a porter asks.

"Sometime," she replies.

The film was turgidly remade in 1959 as *The Man Who Could Cheat Death*, a Hammer production directed by Terrence Fisher with Anton Diffring as the doctor in search of eternal life. The remake also starred Christopher Lee and Hazel Court.

Though Curt Siodmak was one of Hollywood's busiest scriptwriters during the war, he had nothing to do with the initial adaptation of his most famous novel, *Donovan's Brain*. The film was Republic's *The Lady and the Monster* (1944), the first of three versions, all featuring the same story. It was directed by George Sherman and written by Dane Lussier and Frederick Kohner. The cast included Vera Ralston, a former Czech skating star, Richard Arlen and Austrian actor/director Erich von Stroheim (1885–1957).

After financial wizard W.H. Donovan is killed in a desert plane crash, his undamaged brain is removed by a scientist to a nearby lab. The brain is preserved in a glass tank and turns out to be so powerful it takes over the wills of those around it, forcing others to carry out evil plans.

The film was remade in 1953 as *Donovan's Brain*, directed by comedy-short veteran Felix Feist and adapted from Siodmak's novel by Feist and Hugh Broke. Lew Ayres plays the scientist who keeps the man's brain alive.

The most recent version is Britain's *The Brain* (1963), directed by former Oscar-winning cameraman Freddie Francis.

The Producer's Releasing Corporation made *The Monster Maker* (1944) directed by Sam Newfield. It starred the usually great J. Carroll Naish as a scientist who, while experimenting with glandular research, learns to induce acromegaly. When a concert pianist (Ralph Morgan) refuses to allow the scientist to marry his daughter (Wanda McKay), he gets injected with the dreaded serum. Before long his hands are too big to play the piano and his face has developed grotesque lumps of putty. Even at the programmer level this is a weak effort. Glenn Strange headed the supporting cast.

When quickie producer Sam Katzman and director William Beaudine got together for Monogram to make *The Voodoo Man* (1944), it was no surprise that the product was shoddy. Even a great cast, including Bela Lugosi, John Carradine and George Zucco, couldn't salvage this pulp, considered campy even in its day. Lugosi plays a scientist who tries to save his catatonic wife by performing gruesome experiments on innocent young girls.

Universal's follow-up to *House of Frankenstein* was *House of Dracula* (1945), which again put their menagerie of monsters in a single package, thus diluting the effectiveness of all. Only Lon Chaney, Jr., touching as ever as the ursine Larry Talbot, manages to retain his role's original dignity.

Dr. Franz Edelman (Onslow Stevens, 1902–1977, a serial veteran) believes he can "cure" the Wolf Man, Dracula, and the Frankenstein monster throuh purely scientific means. In an interesting twist on horror norms, his lab assistant is beautiful brunette Nina (Jane Adams), who's sadly deformed with a humped back. She and Daniel both have been promised a healthy body.

John Carradine again plays Dracula with a distinguished British accent, but his only major function is to bite the scientist, driving him to madness and death.

Frankenstein's monster plays an even smaller supporting role. Again portrayed by Glenn Strange (who later played the part in Universal's comedy *Abbott and Costello Meet Frankenstein* in 1948), the monster spends most of the film strapped to an operation table. Shots of the monster in a dream sequence were clips of Chaney from *The Ghost of ...*, and Eddie Parker in ... *Meets the Wolf Man*. When finally loosed near the end of the film, he is a mindless murderer. Strange would later gain success on TV, playing the barkeep at Kitty's saloon on *Gunsmoke*.

Applause for creepiness above and beyond the call of duty goes to Skelton Knaggs (1911–1955) as Edelmann's servant Ziegfried, who has his throat torn away by the vampirized scientist.

There is no doubt that Talbot is the hero. Not only is he cured by film's end, but he also wins the heart of the heroine (Martha O'Driscoll).

Lionel Atwill made his last feature performance here as Inspector Holtz. With only months to live, Atwill had just become the father of Lionel, Jr., by his fourth wife.

In *The White Gorilla* (1945), made by the independent studio Weiss Global Enterprises, Ray "Crash" Corrigan (star of Republic's serial *Undersea Kingdom*) plays a hunter on African safari in search of the treasure-laden "cave of the cyclops," where he battles tiger-men and the title creature. Corrigan gets to be the hero when the missing link whisks away heroine Allison (Lorraine Miller, former star of the Ziegfeld Follies).

The Producer's Releasing Corporation and director Sam Newfield filmed a similar lightweight product in 1945. *White Pongo* (borrowing more than a little from *King Kong* and known for a short time as *The Challenge of*

King Kong) is an oversized albino ape. Maris Wrixon plays the obligatory screaming skirt and Richard Fraser saves her when she finds herself wrapped in hairy arms.

Weiss Global Enterprises followed up *The White Gorilla* with *The Devil Monster* (1946), starring Barry Norton as a sailor searching the South Pacific for a lost friend while battling the oversized tentacles of an undersea "devilfish."

Director William Beaudine, Monogram Films, and John Carradine teamed for more mad scientist drivel in *Face of Marble* (1946). Experiments drawing animals and people back from the dead inevitably lead to Carradine's demise.

One of the silliest "serious" films ever to be made was the Producer Releasing Corporation's *The Flying Serpent* (1946), reminiscent in texture to serials at their worst and a must-see for bad cinema buffs. George Zucco plays the homicidal captor of the Aztec bird-god Quetzalcoatl. He uses the monster to repeatedly kill after placing a huge feather on each intended victim. The bird moves awkwardly on visible wires. Both acting and score are laughable. It's no wonder that director Sam Newfield had his name listed in the screen credits as Sherman Scott. The monster reappeared in *Q* (1982).

Gail Sondergaard, the villainess in *Sherlock Holmes and the Spider Woman*, recreated her role in *The Spider Woman Strikes Back* (1946) directed by Arthur Lubin. Co-starring pretty Brenda Joyce and ugly Rondo Hatton, it features a plant that feeds on debutante plasma.

Republic's less-than-convincing *Valley of the Zombies* (1946), directed by Philip Ford, has a misleading title. There is only one zombie, Ian Keith, a scientist resurrected from the dead who survives with transfusions from unwilling donors. Incredibly stupid police fill the rest of the 56 minutes.

Silly special effects plus a contrived script mar the independently produced *Unknown Island* (1948), directed by Jack Bernard. The worn plot concerns a Pacific Island expedition endangered by an assortment of unreal prehistoric monsters and a man in a monkey suit two stories tall.

Muscle-flexing beachcomber Ted Osbourne (Richard Denning) and his cocky, rich fiancée Carol Lane (Virginia Grey) are in Singapore to charter a ship. They want to investigate the strange animals Osbourne saw on a secluded island as a fighter pilot during WW II. Grizzled Captain Tanowski (Barton MacLane) assures his aid, thinking Miss Lane might be fun on a long cruise because she is the sort of woman who goes on expedition in spike heels and a tight dress. To navigate, the captain kidnaps handsome but drunken John Fairbands (Philip Reed), whose life was broken when he saw friends "chewed up" on the same island.

The native crew mutinies once aware of their destination, but, in a classic example of Forties racism, the disturbance is quickly squelched by the white captain.

The island's fearsome occupants look like floats in a parade, plastic models of brontosauri mounted on wheels, drawn along by strings.

The cast camps ashore and is attacked the first day by a huge hairy beast. The monster is amazingly frightened away when a gun is pulled on him, yet never fired. Similarly, the girl is accosted by the captain who kisses her roughly but gets caught by Ted. The ex-pilot's thinking seems a bit askew. He is willing to "sacrifice men for the sake of science," but wants to leave the island immediately when his girl gets kissed. The captain insists that they stay until he captures a live dinosaur. By the end, natives die in the reefs trying to flee, the captain is eaten alive by the hairy beast, and Ted loses the pretty girl to a sober and heroic John.

Former Czech figure skater Vera Ralston starred as a leopard-wrestling Amazon with the secret to eternal youth in Republic's *Angel on the Amazon* (1948), an el cheapo programmer. In the climactic highlight of Ralston's acting career, things backfire and she becomes an old hag.

Ralph Byrd, star of the science fiction serials *Dick Tracy* (1937), *Dick Tracy's G-Men* (1939), and *Dick Tracy vs. Crime, Inc.* (1941), ended his master sleuth career in RKO's *Dick Tracy Meets Gruesome* (1948) directed by John Rawlins. Karloff played the villain, who schemed to become an underworld kingpin by turning all foes into human statues with paralyzing gas. Anne Gwynne led the supporting cast.

Britain's Hammer Films produced the first of a trilogy of futuristic secret agent films: *Dick Barton—Secret Agent* (1948), directed by Alfred Goulding, stars Don Stannard as he combats deranged Dr. Casper (George Ford), who plans to destroy England with a man-made plague. Stannard returned in *Dick Barton Strikes Back* (1949), directed by Godfrey Grayson, saving the world from the granddaddy of today's neutron bomb. There was also *Dick Barton at Bay* (1950), with the hero hampered by a scientist's death ray.

The terror of germ warfare was predicted in *Counterblast* (1948), a British production directed by Australian Paul L. Stein and written by British Jack Whittingham. The latter later co-scripted *Thunderball* (1965, British).

Dr. Karl Bruckner (Mervyn Johns) is a post-war Nazi scientist and POW escapee who murders an Australian bacteriologist to assume his identity at an Oxford research center. Surviving Nazis have created a germ plague to unleash on the world. Bruckner's mission is to discover a Germanic inoculation assuring the master race's survival. All goes well until his conscience gets the better of him. When colleagues become suspicious of his true identity, his superiors order him to murder his female assistant (Nova Pilbeam), but he instead kills a Nazi agent. Forced to flee the country and hiding in the hull of a ship for Rotterdam, the villain is killed symbolically by a fumigating gas.

Jack Pierce's patented Frankenstein make-up made its last appearance, applied by Wally's brother Bud Westmore, in *Abbott and Costello Meet Frankenstein* (1948), again on the face of Glenn Strange. The successful assimilation of horror and comedy had the notoriety of being only the second and last film with a Bela Lugosi Dracula. Lon Chaney, Jr.'s Wolf Man rounded out the monster line up.

Charlie Chan's sole science fiction entry came when the series was on its deathbed—William Beaudine's *The Feathered Serpent* (1948) by Monogram with Roland Winters as the Chinese crimebuster. The true star is Keye Luke (Kato in the *Green Hornet* serials) as Number One Son. Chan and sons battle a murderous flying snake.

The Creeper (1948)—not to be confused with the Rondo Hatton series—stars Onslow Stevens as a doctor whose injected serum transforms his victim into a catcreature murderer.

Director and producer Ernest B. Schoedsack, effects wizard Willis H. O'Brien, and actor Robert Armstrong, together in *King Kong* and *Son of Kong*, teamed again for *Mighty Joe Young* (1949). Naturally, the star is an oversized monkey.

Armstrong plays a Hollywood nightclub owner searching the jungle for animal oddities as stage attractions for his plush joint "The Golden Safari." A far cry from *King Kong*, it holds interest better than Kong's witless sequel. Though overly cutesy, it is more than redeemed by O'Brien's Oscar-winning effects. Though Young, at 12 feet, was the smallest of O'Brien's apes, his convincing relationship with a young girl (Terry Moore, b. 1929) is a tribute to the skilled animation.

When the nightclub owner discovers Terry and her pet, dollar signs flash in front of his eyes. His enthusiasm mounts when he learns the ape does tricks when the girl sings "Beautiful Dreamer."

Once stateside, Terry and the ape go show biz, but the pressure gets to Young. After a tug of war with human strong men (which he wins) and a brief victorious grapple with former heavyweight boxing champion Primo Carnera, he smashes the nightclub and escapes into the streets. Pursuing police are ordered to shoot him on sight. Luckily, our hairy hero passes a burning orphanage and redeems himself by risking his life to save the kids.

O'Brien was assisted during the three-year project by his heir to the throne of cinematic magicians, Ray Harryhausen (b. 1920). Harryhausen handled the animation for a charming scene of Young fed liquor by three drunks in a basement. Twenty-five assistants worked for O'Brien. Among them was sculptor Marcel Delgado, another veteran of the *Kong* pictures.

It was a successful return to form for O'Brien, whose career had been plagued with bad luck. He was to have made *The War Eagle*, a prehistoric tale of natives riding on the backs of turtles in a world full of dinosaurs until, after much pre-production planning, the project was scrubbed when producer Merian C. Cooper (*King Kong*) entered the service. The war scrapped O'Brien's next project *Gwangi* in 1942, to be about Texas mesa cowboys who encounter prehistoric monsters. Other O'Brien projects never to be realized were *El Toro Estrella* about bulls and giant South American reptiles and an adaptation of H.G. Wells' *The Food of the Gods* in which toxic feed mutates farm animals into giants.

Mighty Joe Young was the first fruit of O'Brien's genius in fourteen years. He went on to write the story for *The Beast of Hollow Mountain* (1956), handled the effects in *The Black Scorpion* (1957), and supervised animation for the British *Behemoth the Sea Monster* (1958) before his death in 1962.

Rounding out the science fiction features of the Forties: Bernard Knowles directed Britain's comedy *The Perfect Woman* (1949) about a scientist (Stanley Holloway) who builds a robot (Pamela Devis) in his niece's image (Patricia Roc), and then hires a playboy (Nigel Patrick) and his valet (Miles Malleson) to test his creation by posing her as the playboy's wife over-night in a luxury hotel. The fun ensues when the real niece, naturally enamored of the playboy, substitutes herself in the experiment and slapsticks her way through various compromising positions until discovered by a pin-prick test and replaced. When the test is repeated on the mechanical beauty, she short-circuits and blows into small pieces, to the dismay of the inventor who arrives just in time to see the debris.

Though achieving moderate success in England, it was greeted as a turkey in the U.S. despite a massive ad campaign exploiting the physical charms of Ms. Roc.

Serials

When a kid went to the movies on Saturday afternoon before 1950, he saw a cartoon, a comedy short, coming attractions, a serial, and a B-feature. The serial ran about 20 minutes and told a continuous story over 12 or 15 weeks—say, a summer. Each episode ended with a cliffhanger with the purely motivated hero or heroine left in dire danger. A gadget-oriented super-menace was no doubt responsible. The following week the hero or heroine escaped unscathed to continue the pursuit of justice over evil.

Because of their format, these were the most action-packed films ever made. They were neat-o. Many chapterplays featured one punchface session every eight minutes. Over 60 cliffhangers between 1915 and 1949 took place in the corny world of the scientifically impossible.

Serials averaged five hours in length and were alotted budgets lower than the 65-minute features they shared bills with, making them the shoddiest films ever produced by major studios. Yet because of their intended audience, few over the age of 14 can authoritatively criticize them.

With good guys in white and bad guys black, the entire world was at stake. Some insidious futuristic weapon, most commonly a "death ray," had fallen into the wrong hands. Each week the hero would escape doom by the skin of his teeth, and in the final chapter goodness would prevail.

Many serials mimicked mysteries by masking their villains (and in one case the hero), their surprise endings exposing the true identity. Inevitably the criminal was an unexpected minor character arbitrarily chosen by scriptwriters. Serials were never really mysteries. Villains in masks were just more interesting to look at, scarier.

During World War II, when villains were almost exclusively representatives of the Axis powers, the serial functioned as a security blanket. God was on our side, and everything was going to be all right.

It was the sameness of the chapterplays that provided their charm. They were filmed comic books filled with bad actors and the best stuntmen in Hollywood. Viewed today, they draw unintentional laughs and have camp appeal. But more than that, by assuming a total suspension of belief among their audiences, serial-makers created some fascinating surreal moments.

89

The charming miniature rocketships dangling from strings in *Flash Gordon* or *Buck Rogers* offer more interest than much of the multi-million dollar modern special effects that fill recent sterile Hollywood spaceoperas.

The first serial to incorporate science fiction elements into its theme was *The Exploits of Elaine* (1915). It appropriately starred the undisputed queen of the silent serials, Pearl White (1889–1938), who had become famous the year before as the heroine in *The Perils of Pauline*. Here, Elaine is menaced by archvillain The Clutching Hand, who possesses a death ray. In the tenth chapter Elaine is actually extinguished by the malefactor, but is revitalized by her scientist/detective friend Craig Kennedy with his "life current" — a method borrowed from Shelley. The Kennedy character returned in the 1936 stage and screen sound serial *The Clutching Hand*, with favorite Jack Mulhall playing the scientist sleuth.

White's work concentrated on mystery stories rather than out-and-out adventures, thus achieving success more slowly than her contemporaries. Yet her screen presence sustained her unsurpassed popularity throughout her career. the villain in *The Exploits of Elaine* was played by Sheldon Lewis, best known for the leads in a 1920 version of *Dr. Jekyll and Mr. Hyde.*

White returned as the heroine to Lewis' villain in *The Iron Claw* (1916), produced by Pathé. Once again Lewis terrorizes the tough but naive heroine with a death ray which, like an arsonist's dream, can set buildings ablaze from afar. All looks lost for White until the scapegrace contracts an aging virus in the climax and withers till dead.

Evildoers with ultrascientific weapons provided the science fiction in most silent serials. In 1920 pro-science daredevils battled villains over a new, improved supertank in *The Great Radium Mystery*. An atomic ray endangers the world in *The Invisible Ray* (1920), not to be confused with the Universal Karloff feature 16 years later. *Ray* was directed by Harry A. Pollard and produced by the short-lived Forham Amusement Corporation.

Robert F. Hill also directed Universal's *The Flaming Disk* (1920), starring film's first Tarzan, Elmo Lincoln (1889–1952). The film clashed good and evil over a recently invented lens that could reduce iron to dust.

In Universal's *The Diamond Queen* (1921), the conflict centered around an invention that produced diamonds artificially. Directed by Edward Kull, it was based on Jacques Futrelle's novel and remade as *The Diamond Master* (1929).

Pearl White made her final science fiiction appearance in *Plunder* (1923), a little known mystery about a girl harassed by a half-human, half-ape monster.

In *The Power God* (1925), which was produced by the obscure Vital Exchanges company, scientists invent a machine that creats endless energy without fuel. It was directed by and starred Ben Wilson.

Universal converted their setting to England for *Blake of Scotland Yard* (1927), directed by Robert F. Hill. Blake, a retired criminologist, seeks The Spider, who is attempting to abscond with a gold-making formula. The character Blake was to return in a non-science fiction sequel, *Ace of Scotland Yard* (1929), and then again in Sam Katzman's sound serial *Blake of Scotland Yard* (1937), to be discussed later.

Science fiction met the western for the first time in Vitaphone's *The Mystery of the Lost Ranch*, directed by Harry S. Webb and Tom Gibson. White hats skirmish black hats over a ray gun. The crossing of science fiction with westerns inevitably produced absurd results, most notably in *Phantom Empire* (1935) with Gene Autry.

John Wayne, not yet a star, appeared in the first science fiction talkie serial in 1932. The film was *Shadow of the Eagle* by Mascot. Wayne portrayed skywriting-aviator Craig McCoy who, along with buddy Nathan Gregory (Edward Hearn), battle The Phantom, inventor of an anti-aircraft ray gun.

The Phantom of the Air (1933) also concerned aviation in the not-so-distant future. The Universal cliffhanger starred Tom Tyler as a pilot hired by scientific engineer Thomas Edmunds (William Desmond), to test the "Contragrav," an invention that will revolutionize flight by overcoming gravity. The notorious chieftain of a smuggling ring Mort Crome (LeRoy Mason) yearns for the device's secret. In disguise as a soft-spoken pilot, Crome finds his larcenous efforts repeatedly thwarted by The Phantom, a remote-controlled airplane operated from Edmund's underground headquarters. Crome, now desperate, corners Edmunds in his workshop and tries to gain the secret by force. The scientist is forced to blow up his engineering lab with Crome in it. Edmunds escapes in the nick of time so he can be reunited in the denouement with the hero pilot and his pretty daughter Mary (Gloria Shea).

Type-cast Bela Lugosi was the sinister Professor Strang in the 1933 Mascot Master-Serial *Whispering Shadows*. Producer Nat Levine took advantage of Lugosi's bloodsucking image—given birth by his portrayal of the count two years before—by blatantly aping the cinematographic style of Karl Freund in *Dracula*. The picture is heavy with close-ups of Lugosi's hypnotic eyes, angular eyebrows, and furrowed brow.

Strang sculpts animated wax figures capable of moving and speaking like real people for his "House of Mystery." Each time a paraffin person is transported by radio-equipped truck, the driver is dispatched by one of The Whispering Shadow's henchmen. Neither the underworld, the law, nor the audience know the villain's identity, but each week we are led to believe it is Strang. The villain's electronically-altered voice and intonations greatly resemble Lugosi's, and it seems unlikely that he would star in a film as anything but the antagonist. The Whispering Shadow is an electronic genius who uses radio and television to project his voice and image to desired sites. He has X-ray vision and super-hearing and can electrocute opponents from afar with his radio-wave death ray. Among the ray's victims is henchman Kruger, who is about to reveal the mystery identity to the police.

Audiences were shocked when Lugosi's character emerged a red herring, and there are many who still think the film-makers were fibbing while making Strang innocent of wrongdoing. In the unfulfilling conclusion we learn the criminal was actually an unimportant janitor named Sparks (Karl Dane), who, until unmasked, provided bumbling comic relief. Though Lugosi played similar roles in other serials, he was always the villain from this point on. And there was no mystery about it. Audiences did not like being led on, and the studios responded to their dissatisfaction.

Director Robert F. Hill made a successful transition to sound with Screen Attractions' *Queen of the Jungle* (1935). White hunters battle African natives over a jungle idol whose eyes emit radium beams. The title character is a female Tarzan who mediates.

When massive lightning storms throw Earth into chaos, electrical engineer Bruce Gordon (Kane Richmond, 1906–1973), with the backing of the world's nations, develops a machine that traces the disturbance's source to Central Africa, in Krellberg Films' popular *The Lost City* (1935). Gordon, along with his friend Jerry (Eddie Fetherstone) and colleagues Colton and Reynolds (William Millman and Ralph Lewis), travel to the dark continent to investigate. Their trek leads them to the Magnetic Mountain, where nasty Zolok (William "Stage" Boyd) envisions conquering the world. Involuntarily aiding Zolok is Dr. Manyus (Joseph Swickert), his benevolence compromised by daughter Natcha's abduction (Claudia Dell). Zolok televises our heroes' approach while taking advantage of Manyus' "brain-reducer/body-enlarger" to create a cadre of brainless behemoths, a supposed conquering army. Zolok explains that he is the last of the master scientist race of Liquarians, and feels his destiny is an extension of "the electromagnetic tradition of (his) people."

The film also features the toothless and whiskered George "Gabby" Hayes as Butterfield, a grizzled trade-post operator aiding Richmond in his mission.

After Zolok's power-hunger drives him mad, he activates all of his electronic equipment simultaneously, causing a massive explosion. While good guys escape, *The Lost City* is blown to bits.

Gene Autry, "The Singing Cowboy", was cast as the star of Mascot's *Phantom Empire* (1935), concerning an ultrascientific subterranean civilization below the crooner's dude ranch. Contemporary publicity for the chapterplay claimed proudly that writer Wallace MacDonald conjured up the premise while gassed during a tooth extraction.

No doubt.

In 1933, when Autry was a popular country and western singer on a local Chicago radio station, he wrote a letter to Nat Levine, the boss of Mascot Studios, noting his growing Midwestern fame and looking for work in films. As the letter coincided with MacDonald's revelation, Levine summoned Autry and his radio troupe to Hollywood. The singing cowboy was put on the payroll at $100 a week. After a small part in a serial called *Mystery Mountain*, he was cast in the lead for *Phantom Empire*. Despite his lack of acting ability, the serial was a huge success. It established for Autry a career in film paired with his pal Lester Alvin "Smiley" Burnette.

Autry (as Autry) and young friends Frankie and Betsy (Frankie Darrow and Betsy King Ross), are warring against a gang out to steal his ranch for its rich radium mine. Chased, the crooks hide in the mine caves beneath the ranch and discover the gates to the metallic metropolis Murania 10,000 feet below the surface. Gene's pursuit leads him into the city where he is promptly captured by local Muranians, led by beautiful Queen Tiha (Dorothy Christi) and sadistic Prime Minister Argo (Wheeler Oakman). The local men possess superhuman strength and their weapons are more destructive than anything found on the surface. They also have an army of robots, which appear to be stuntmen clumsily walking inside stovepipes with silver private eye hats on their heads.

Fortunately for Autry and company a Muranian revolution breaks out, and they escape via elevator to the surface. Murania is destroyed by its own death ray.

The U.S. Marine Corps battled The Tiger Shark, an evildoer destroying American military aircraft with his radio gravity gun, in *The Fighting Marines* (1935), directed by B. Reeves "Breezy" Eason.

Heroes Colonel Bennett (Robert Warwick), Corporal Lawrence (Grant Withers), and Sergeant McGowan (Adrian Morris) try to establish a landing field on Halfway Island, only to have their efforts squelched by The Tiger Shark's repeated sabotage. When the Marines engage the villain in a gun battle inside his cave headquarters in the finale, an errant bullet finds a misplaced bottle of nitroglycerin. Leaving Marines unharmed, the explosion annihilates both terrorist, and gravity gun.

Flash Gordon, science fiction serials' premiere hero, was cartoonist Alex Raymond's creation. The King Features Syndicate newspaper strip made its debut nationwide on January 7, 1934. Being a sensation, it took only two years for Universal to adapt Flash to the screen. Hollywood was shocked when Universal announced their allocated budget of over $1 million to produce the 13-episode chapterplay *Flash Gordon* (1936).

Flash, a blonde Yale graduate and famous polo player, along with friend Dale Arden, are taken to the planet Mongo in a rocket by Dr. Alexis Zarkov (Irish character actor Frank Shannon) as Earth faces total destruction from the approaching globe. There they meet evil Emperor Ming, tyrant of Mongo, who hates Flash and takes a lustful liking to Dale. At Ming's side is Princess Aura, hopelessly enamored of our hero.

In the comic strip Dale Arden was a brunette. For the serial, dark-haired Jean Rogers dyed her hair blonde, as Universal reasoned audiences would associate blondes with good and brunettes with evil. For the same reason, Princess Aura had darker hair in the serial than in the comic strip.

Actor Larry "Buster" Crabbe also had to lighten his hair for the part, a facet of his role that made him ill-at-ease on the set. Crabbe donned a cap between takes, complaining that men whistled when he removed it.

Despite the big budget, the studio went out of its way to save money during production. The windmill that served as the monster's birthplace in *Frankenstein* (1931) ends up on Mongo. The statue of the alien planet's "Great God Tao" was previously used as an Egyptian deity in *The Mummy*. Rocketships for *Flash* were borrowed from Fox's *Just Imagine* (1930). These ships were to appear again in *Buck Rogers* (1939). Shots of Earth seen by Zarkov's telescope on Mongo were clipped from *The Invisible Ray* (also 1936). Yards of silent newsreel footage showed massive destruction. A dance sequence — erotically attired women writhing for Ming's amusement — was spliced from *The Midnight Sun* (1927). Instead of composing an original score for the serial, as was done for projects with comparatively minuscule budgets, Universal assembled bits and pieces from previous scores to compile the piecemeal soundtrack. Strains from *The Invisible Man* (1933), *Werewolf of London* (1935), *The Bride of Frankenstein* (1935) and *The Invisible Ray* were joined with selections from Tchaikovsky's *Romeo and Juliet* to complete the score.

Further money was saved by shooting almost exclusively on interior soundstages or on back lots. The limited location filming was done in Griffith Park's Bronson Canyon, a bowl-like quarry carved out of rock for mineral mining. With 250-foot walls and several cave mouths, it was quite suitable for Mongo.

The script was written by co-director Frederick Stephani, George H. Plympton, Basil Dickey and Ella O'Neill. They remained faithful to Raymond's story line presented both in the comic strip and reprinted in the Whitman Publishing Company's "Big Little Books," such as *Flash Gordon on the Planet Mongo, Flash Gordon and the Monsters of Mongo*, and *Flash Gordon and the Tournaments of Mongo*. Such respectful adaptation was rare in serials. According to film historians Jim Harmon and Donald F. Glut in their book *The Great Movie Serials*, "Raymond's comic strip was virtually a movie storyboard for whole sequences and the costumes, which Hollywood's Western Costume Company fashioned with the most meticulously accurate detail." One major difference between the strip and serial was the Mongonians' skincolor. In the strip they were Oriental yellow, but no mention of this pigmentation appears in the film. Later the aliens were presented as Caucasians in the newspapers as well.

Buster Crabbe (b. 1907 as Clarence Linden Crabbe) was an Olympic swimming gold medalist and began in movies working as Joel McCrea's double in RKO's *The Most Dangerous Game* (1932). His first starring role came in Paramount's *King of the Jungle* (1933). He portrayed Kaspa the Lion Man in overt mimicry of Tarzan. He did play the famous ape man in a Principal chapterplay, *Tarzan the Fearless* (1933), but it is for his roles as space-heroes Flash Gordon and Buck Rogers that he is remembered today.

Mongo is hurtling toward Earth and imminent destruction is causing world panic. Flash and Dale are on a airplane struggling through atmospheric disturbances when they go into a tailspin and bail out in the nick of

Buster Crabbe as *Flash Gordon* (Universal, 1936), greased in Ming's static room. Can certain death be far away?

time. Landing by parachute near the lab of Dr. Zarkov (whose name is Hans in the comic strip and Alexis here), they are shown the scientist's missile which he hopes to pilot to Mongo and then prevent the catastrophic collision. Game and red-blooded, Flash and Dale accompany him on his journey. They land, evade the deadly breath of giant iguanas, and are captured by heavily-armored Officer Torch (Earl Asham) and two robot soldiers who hold them at bay with scientifically-advanced rifles. They are taken to Ming, played with virtuoso villainy by Charles Middleton (1879–1949).

Ming is completely bald. His Fu Manchu mustache droops on either side of his thin-lipped mouth. His beard is pointy. His head is mounted on a black and white collar rising well above his shiny scalp in the rear.

His daughter Aura (Priscilla Lawson with shaved eyebrows pencilled into arches) falls for Flash at first glance—a common malady among screen villainesses—but will kill him if she can't have him for herself.

Mongo is a combination of the futuristic and the primitive. Though their technology is advanced, their Hollywood costumes resemble those of the Roman Empire. Mongonian soldiers, despite their superior arsenal, would prefer to draw swords for battle.

Ming, deciding Dale will be his wife, drugs the girl into subservience. Flash is hurled into the "Arena of Death" for Ming's entertainment, where he fisticuffs a trio of fanged subhumans. In the comic strip these characters were red apes. Flash is saved from doom by Aura, who sees such sport as waste of good flesh. Dr. Zarkov convinces Ming it is wiser to preserve Earth so it can be conquered, setting up the framework for 12 more episodes of adventure.

Complications, of course. Ming's empire is attacked by Mongonian dissidents known as The Lion Men. In the comic strip the feline warriors had tails, but here are relieved of the embarrassing appendage. Their leader is King Thun (James Pierce), whose gyro ships pepper Ming's palace with fire. After evading Aura's seductive nails and escaping from a giant reptile pit, Flash battles Thun and subdues him. Realizing their common enemy, they join forces and head to save Dale. First they must battle Ming's army and survive the "tunnel of terror," the residence of a dinosaur monster with lobster claws (Glenn Strange). The monster is about to super-pinch Flash when Thun zaps him with his ray gun.

Before the serial was through, Flash was forced to defeat a menagerie of grotesque monsters. When he is captured by The Shark Men, led by evil King Kala (Duke York, Jr.), he is thrown in a tank with the tentacled Octosac. Flash encounters winged Hawkmen who live in the Sky City, a floating community supported by light rays. During Ming's "Tournament of Death," Flash battles a horned hairy ape, the Sacred Orangapoid (Ray "Crash" Corrigan, soon to be a serial star in his own right). Again he is saved by lovesick Aura, whose spear impales the beast.

In the conclusion, Flash has again been captured and sent to the firing squad. Luckily, Zarkov has used his feigned allegiance with Ming to build an invisibility ray that works on Flash before shots are fired. Thun and his Lion Men vanquish Ming's forces and besiege his castle. The emperor, a coward in the face of peril, flees to the "Sacred Palace of the Great God Tao," from which no man returns, to take his own life.

Prince Barin (Richard Alexander, best known for his roles as heavies), whose father was usurped by Ming, reclaims his throne in the denouement. Beside him is Aura, his new love. Barin is a powerful man wearing dragon-emblazoned chest armor and a flowing cloak. Flash, Dale, and Zarkov return to Earth, their mission complete.

Of course, Ming was not dead at all. He and Flash were to meet twice again in sequels, *Flash Gordon's Trip to Mars* (1939) and *Flash Gordon Conquers the Universe* (1940), both to be discussed later.

Lugosi returned to a more comfortable villain role in Sam Katzman's Victory serial, *Shadow of Chinatown* (1934), as a crazed Eurasian scientist whose cross-breeding leads him to hate both Caucasians and Orientals. Dr. Victor Poten wars against good with a sun-ray amplification beam, an odorless death gas, and an army of Oriental slaves headed by an idol-like robot. He assists beautiful European importing firm representative Sonya Rokoff (Luana Walters), who is assigned to eliminate Chinese competition by sabotaging Chinatown touristless.

Contemporary publicity posters for *Shadow of Chinatown* took advantage of Lugosi's *Dracula* image, painting him in profile, stare hypnotically, hands in mid-mesmeric gesture.

Engaging the antagonist to death's brink is Martin Andrew (Herman Brix, 1909, later called Bruce Bennett), a novelist and aficionado of Oriental communities, and Joan Whiting (Joan Barclay), a pretty newspaperwoman recently promoted from the society page to reporter.

The serial features a false denouement and surprise ending. The villain is presumed dead, his car having plunged off a cliff into murky ocean, and the young writer and his friends celebrate their victory at a Chinese merchants' banquet held in their honor. One of the waiters is Poten in disguise. Martin discovers the waiter's identity before his wine can be poisoned, and the mad scientist is dragged away to face the law.

The solution of the cliffhanger at the beginning of each week's episode offered a problem to overworked scriptwriters. Chapter after chapter they had to conjure a fresh way to prevent certain death. Most frequently there was a clingable limb just over the cliff's edge, or the hero was revealed to have leaped from his horse a fraction of a second before the dive. Sometimes, however, studios were forced to cheat by altering cliffhanger footage. In other words, an audience eager to learn how their hero survived the fall they had seen him take would groan with disappointment as they watched the following segment open with the hero pulling up just short of the cliff and never falling at all.

Such was the case with Republic's second serial, *Undersea Kingdom* (1936). In one episode Ray "Crash" Corrigan (1907-1976, here playing himself) is tied to the front of a juggernaut by a young, thin Lon Chaney, Jr., rammed through a closed gate and apparently crushed. We see the gate smash violently. In the disappointing solution, the gates open just in time to allow the juggernaut unharmed passage.

The plot of *Undersea Kingdom* is similar to *Flash Gordon*, the source of the menace coming from the Lost Continent of Atlantis rather than an alien planet. Atlantis, encased under a glass bubble, is at war. The White Robes (obviously the good guys) combat Black Robes led by tyrannical Unga Khan (Monte Blue). After conquering the undersea world, Khan plans to use

his disintegrating machine to gain control of the entire surface civilization. Noting the unprecedented earthquakes rocking the planet's crust, brilliant American scientist Professor Norton (C. Montague Shaw) constructs a rocket-powered submarine to search for Atlantis, the determined source of the disturbances. Accompanying him are Corrigan, athlete and naval officer, and tenacious reporter Diana Compton (Lois Wilde).

Atlantis, like Mongo, is both barbaric and scientifically advanced. While there Corrigan confronts a robot army, sword-wielding Roman soldiers, and an assortment of ray guns before defeating Khan and putting an end to his power-hungry plans.

Universal adapted Eddie Rickenbacker's comic strip, *Ace Drummond*, in 1936 with John King as the hero. Jean Rogers, fresh from her fame as Dale Arden, co-starred as Ace battled The Dragon, a ray-gun-toting mystery villain who sends his messages with prayer-wheels and almost crushes our hero in a room with closing walls.

Silent serial hero *Blake of Scotland Yard* returned in 1937 in a Sam Katzman/Victory Films production. Blake (Herbert Rawlinson) was now a retired Scotland Yard C.I.D. inspector, and his name had been changed from Angus to Sir James. He has financed young inventor Jerry Sheehan (Ralph Byrd, to be Dick Tracy for the first time that year) to create and perfect a death ray. The weapon is sought by the masked and cloaked Scorpion, whose right hand resembles a lobster claw. Sheehan collaborates on the weapon's invention with Blake's pretty niece Hope Mason (Joan Barclay). Hope, Sheehan, and Blake spend equal time getting into trouble, the film-makers using European settings to create exceptionally chilling cliffhangers. Sheehan is mugged and thrown into Parisian sewers. Blake is similarly tossed into the Thames.

In the conclusion, The Scorpion is unmasked as Blake's supposed friend, mild-mannered Dr. Marshall. He is caught stealing the death ray from a safe, discovering the weapon so electrically charged he can't let go.

Chester Gould's comic strip *Dick Tracy* made its debut for the Chicago Tribune-New York Times Syndicate on Columbus Day, 1931. Because of its sharp-nosed sleuth, freakshow criminals, and science fiction crime-busting gadgetry, it became an instant success. Republic converted Tracy to film in 1937 in *Dick Tracy*, directed by Ray Taylor and Alan James. The chapterplay was popular enough to spawn three sequels: *Dick Tracy Returns* (1938), *Dick Tracy's G-Men* (1939), and *Dick Tracy vs. Crime, Inc.* (1941).

Though the filmmakers made no effort to make actor Ralph Byrd (1909–1952) look like Tracy, they did muster a villain in par with Gould's grotesqueries—The Spider, a meanie with an oversized domehead sparsely rimmed with hair and a single eyebrow all the way across his forehead.

Opposite: A bearded Bela Lugosi focuses his sun-ray amplification beam in *Shadow of Chinatown* (Victory, 1936).

The Spider kidnaps Tracy's brother Gordon and transforms him into a zombie with a secret gland operation on his brain. Two actors were used to play Gordon Tracy. Richard Beach played normal Gordon, while Carleton Young was the post-operative slave.

The super-sleuth finally tracks down the master criminal and returns his brother to normal despite repeated attacks from "The Flying Wing," The Spider's super-scientific airplane equipped with a death ray.

Serial producers knew the low mean age of their audience. Taking advantage of their product's youth appeal they began to cast youngsters in leading roles — assuming correctly that the cliffhanger's addictive value was in direct proportion to audience identification. Such was the case in Universal's *Radio Patrol* (1937), directed by Ford Beebe and Cliff Smith, based on comic strip characters created by Eddie Sullivan and Charlie Schmidt.

Radio Patrol starred pre-teen hero Pinky Adams (pugnosed Mickey Rentschler), the son of a recently murdered inventor, who alone knows his father's formula for flexible-yet-bulletproof steel. Pursued by his father's killers, Pinky is aided by radio cop Pat O'Hara (Grant Withers) and comely Molly Selkirk (Catherine Hughes). The boy keeps mum and bares the leader of the crooks as Wellington, the owner of the local steel mill.

Lugosi was at his villainous best in Republic's *S.O.S. Coast Guard* (1937), directed by William Witney and Alan James. Lugosi plays Boroff (an odd abbreviation of his chief screen competitor, Boris Karloff), a crazed chemist who invents a disintegrating gas from raw "arnatite." He plans to supply the fictional country of Morovania with the chemical warfare weapon. Assisting him is giant mute Thorg (iron-thewed Richard Alexander, Prince Barin in *Flash Gordon*). Battling Boroff is Coast Guard Officer Terry Kent (Ralph Byrd, a very busy actor), reporter Jean Norman (Maxine Doyle), and her cameraman Snapper McGee (Lee Ford).

It is not the heroes who bring about Boroff's demise, but Thorg. Wounded by Boroff's bullet, the lumbering hulk snaps his master's neck.

Lugosi made only one serial after this. Two years later he starred in *The Phantom Creeps*, ending the only chapterplay career of villainy in which the actor regularly received top billing.

The Spider magazine first hit the stands in 1933. It was filled with pulp fiction and was an attempt to capitalize on the popularity of radio's *The Shadow*. The Spider, like The Shadow, wore a cloak and hat and battled arch-fiends while keeping his real identity a secret. The magazine was the work of novelist and war correspondent Norvell Page, writing under the pseudonym Grant Stockbridge.

The film version, Columbia's *The Spider's Web* (1938), had to water

Opposite: Flash (Buster Crabbe, left), Dale (Jean Rogers), Dr. Zarkov (Frank Shannon), Happy (Donald Kerr) and Prince Barin (Richard Alexander) pose for an album cover before confronting Ming's stronghold in *Flash Gordon's Trip to Mars* (Universal, 1938).

down the texture of the pulp fiction for approval by the Motion Picture Production Code. The steamy magazine depicted a lusty hero who sought to kill as many criminals as possible, much in the manner of Mickey Spillane's cold war mysteries. The serial, directed by Ray Taylor and James W. Horne, featured a hero closer to the limits of the law.

The Spider (Warren Hull wearing a full-head black mask with a webbed design) was actually brilliant criminologist Richard Wentworth. During his escapades, Wentworth also found occasion to pose as Blinky McQuade, a dim underworld figure with sensitive ears. The villain was The Octopus, who wore a KKK-like robe and spoke with an electronic voice.

Ira Meredith played Nita Van Sloan, The Spider's *very* close sleuthing girlfriend. In the magazine Nita and Richard were lovers and clairvoyant enough for their actions to be interchangeable. Their relationship was toned down for the movies in every sense.

The Octopus, seeking destruction of U.S. transportation systems, tried to squelch The Spider with a ray gun and a gas-filled room, monitoring his movements with a television spy system. In the conclusion The Spider shoots The Octopus dead and removes his hood, revealing the arch-villain as insignificant banker Chase (Charles C. Wilson), in retrospect an embarrassing choice of character name.

In 1938 Orson Wells terrified America with his Halloween presentation of H.G. Wells' *War of the Worlds*. For this reason Universal changed the setting for their second space epic in *Flash Gordon's Trip to Mars*. It featured the original cast: Buster Crabbe as Flash, Jean Rogers as Dale, Charles Middleton as Ming, and Frank Shannon as Zarkov. Added for comic relief was rocketship stowaway newspaper reporter Happy Hapgood (Donald Kerr). Directed by Ford Beebe and Robert F. Hill, it was based on Alex Raymond's "Big Little Book" version of his comic strip, *Flash Gordon and the Witch Queen of Mongo*.

Flash, Dale and Zarkov are rocketing to Mars to learn what evil force is sucking the nitrogen from Earth's atmosphere and discover Ming, presumed dead, alive and responsible for their woes. He is altering the air with a tremendous nitrogen lamp.

On Mars, Flash befriends a race of clay people led by Clayface (C. Montague Shaw), turned into human mud pies by the magic spell of beautiful Queen Azura (Beatrice Roberts), Ming's ally. Predictably, Azura develops a huge crush on Flash.

Fifteen chapters later Ming is once again presumably destroyed when he is thrown into his own disintegration machine.

According to Jim Harmon and Donald F. Glut in their book *The Great Movie Serials*, "*Flash Gordon's Trip to Mars*, though only two years later than its predecessor, seems surprisingly modern when viewed today. While *Flash Gordon* remains somewhat primitive in style and production values despite its appeal, the Martian adventure appears as though it could have been filmed recently." This statement might be colored with nostalgia, but the special effects for the sequel do hold greater aesthetic appeal than the original's. Queen Azura's huge squadron of "Stratosleds" carried powerful bombs, while a secret "rocket subway" connected the Queen's palace with the underground home of the clay people. People on Mars were able to walk high above their city, seemingly defying gravity with the use of glowing "light bridges."

The picture was re-released in feature form as *Space Soldiers' Trip to Mars*. Flash and Ming were to battle one more time for Universal in *Flash Gordon Conquers the Universe* two years later.

Crabbe took time out from his Flash Gordon chores to portray *Buck Rogers* (1939), directed by Ford Beebe and Saul A. Goodkind. Rogers, a 20th Century man who fights oppression in the far future, was a character created by Philip Nowlan in his novels *Armageddon 2419* (1928) and *The Airlords of Han* (1929). Buck, along with teenage pal Buddy Wade, were popularized in a comic strip by Nowlan and Dick Calkins that ran from 1929 to 1967. In the film, Rogers is a dirigible pilot whose craft crashes in 1938. He and Buddy are preserved in suspended animation by gas that fills their cabin until they awaken 500 years later.

When Buddy (pug-nosed and eager Jackie Moran) learns he is not in the 20th Century anymore, he exclaims, "Five thousand years! That makes me old enough to be my own great-grandfather!"

The pair quickly learn that the world is not as they left it, having been conquered by a Hitler-like tyrant named Killer Kane. Rogers and Wade are given refuge in The Hidden City, a pocket of freedom from Kane's rule. They adapt to their new surroundings within seconds. Without any training—after all Buck is a pilot and an *American*—Buck and Buddy take charge and head a fleet of space ships to run Killer Kane's air blockade. One must buy the premise to enjoy the film; there is no room for question in the hero's omnipotence.

The model space ships look like clothes irons with sparks flying from their tails. They are cute, if not convincing, and make the sound of an electric razor. The strings that hold the crafts, though invisible, are frequently betrayed by an amusing wobble. Model footage is used repeatedly and receives extensive play.

Killer Kane (flatly portrayed by mustached Anthony Warde) is described as a genetically superior racketeer. Warde's two-dimensional performance is unstimulating compared to the full-tilt ham surrounding it. Being the bad guys, Kane and his men wear black uniforms.

Rogers and Wade are aided in their pursuit of justice by Dr. Huer, the scientist-general of Hidden City, and Lt. Wilma Deering (Constance Moore). Deering is unusual in that she is completely self-sufficient. The serial avoids the cliché of providing a skirt so she can get in trouble and be saved; Wilma holds her own. When she gets captured, the tomboyish heroine frees herself with quick thinking and helps to rescue Buck. In a time when subservience was the rule for actresses, Moore's performance provides a refreshing touch of women's lib. She is, however, the only woman in the cast, making audiences wonder what happened to all of the females during the years our heroes were asleep.

Among the disappointing aspects are the botched fight scenes. The directors either had little idea how to make a fist appear to hit a jaw or found the technique too time-consuming. Using fast motion, the filmed pugilism is championship wrestling at best.

Rogers attempts to gain an alliance with the people of Saturn. In the ringed planet's underground city, people get around in the "bullet railroad," a glass car that travels at jetlike speeds through the subterranean myriad of caves. The effects here are re-used clips of Queen Azura's "rocket subway" in *Flash Gordon's Trip to Mars*.

Some of the science fiction elements will seem familiar to modern fans. The jet-packs worn on the backs of the heroes enabling them to fly are similar to the one worn by James Bond, and the transporter elevator used in The Hidden City is a prototype for the "beam-up" device used on TV's *Star Trek*.

Despite Buck's outdating of Flash in the comics, the serial was viewed as a rehash of space-epics already seen. The similarity between the chapter-plays cannot be denied. The same actor portrayed both heroes—only the color of his hair had changed. The music, stolen from Universal features, and many of the sets were the same.

The film differs from the comic strip in several ways. In the strip Buck was the only one thrust in time, being a surveyor trapped in a mine cave-in, while Buddy and Wilma were brother and sister.

The serial was re-released in feature form (91 minutes) as *Destination Saturn*.

Buck Rogers in the 25th Century was an ABC-TV 30-minute live weekly series airing from 1950–51, starring Ken Dibbs as Buck, Lou Prentis as Wilma, and Harry Sothern as Dr. Huer.

Buck submerged for nearly 30 years before appearing again, this time in a telefilm and a series. The film—a series pilot—was bumped off TV network schedules when made in 1978 and received a short release in theaters before airing the following year. *Buck Rogers*, both the series and the film, starred Gil Gerard as Buck, Erin Gray as Wilma, and Henry Silva as Killer Kane. Both were highlighted by oddly appealing theme music.

Dick Tracy (Ralph Byrd again) returned to the screen in Republic's *Dick Tracy's G-Men* (1939), directed by William Witney and John English. Over the following few years this directorial team worked like yeomen, cranking out Republic science fiction weeklies.

As an example of the silly arbitrary changes Republic made when adapting heroes from other media, Dick Tracy was the only Chester Gould character in the movie. His adopted son Junior and the others were nowhere to be seen, and Tracy switched from a police detective to an FBI agent.

Irving Pichel, an actor who later became a director, portrayed Tracy's

Bela Lugosi's metallic chum in *The Phantom Creeps* **(Universal, 1939) is hardly designed to win friends. Will Lugosi become the ro-butt of the joke?**

arch-enemy, the bearded and mustached spy Zarnoff. Convicted of a long list of crimes including murder, Zarnoff has been sentenced to the gas chamber. Audiences were surprised when he is executed in the first episode. Serials returned characters from the dead every week, but seldom this literally. Fortunately for the remaining fourteen chapters, the spy's allies inject him with a reanimation formula so his anti-American espionage can resume.

In the final chapter, "The Last Stand," Tracy is bound to a tree in the desert. Zarnoff taunts and quaffs from a water hole only a few feet away, not knowing the water is poison. Zarnoff dies in the blazing sun as Tracy is rescued by fellow G-Men.

Lugosi made his final serial appearance in Universal's *The Phantom Creeps* (1939), directed by Ford Beebe and Saul A. Goodkin. That same year Lugosi was classic as Ygor in *Son of Frankenstein* for the same company.

Lugosi plays Dr. Alex Zorka, a power-hungry scientist whose genius has produced an invisibility belt, an eight-foot robot, and a meteorite element that spreads suspended animation across great areas. When his wife is killed accidentally, he goes mad and wages an all-out war against society. Confronting him are Captain Bob West (Robert Kent) of the Military Intelligence Department and reporter Jean Drew (Dorothy Arnold). After army planes bomb Zorka's lab to smithereens, he attempts simultaneous suicide and world annihilation, but manages only to destroy himself in the resulting earthquake. West is a hero and Jean gets her scoop.

Though Lugosi is rousing as he wails week after week about his mechanical man's menace, the robot does not come into play until the final episode. The scowling metallic warrior moves clumsily, arms waving, and we can't help but be disappointed when a single Army bullet puts it out of commission.

In 1940 Emperor Ming was back on Mongo without a scratch, hardly looking like he'd been tossed into a disintegration machine the year before. Charles Middleton again was Ming, as predictably nasty as ever, and the film was Universal's *Flash Gordon Conquers the Universe*, directed by Ford Beebe and Ray Taylor, the third and last serial featuring the golden-haired hero.

Buster Crabbe returned as Flash, and Frank Shannon once again played Zarkov. The two major changes in the cast were Carol Hughes as Dale Arden and Roland Drew as the bow-slinging Prince Barin, replacing Jean Rogers and Richard Alexander in those roles. The formerly brunette and evil Princess Aura was now good and played by blonde actress Shirley Deane.

In recent years this has been the most popular entry in the series. Universal has re-edited the chapterplay footage into three features, *Peril from the Planet Mongo*, *Space Soldiers Conquer the Universe*, and *The Purple Death from Outer Space*.

It is the prettiest serial ever made. Greater attention was given to costuming and set design than ever before. Even extras were lavishly costumed. But it has been faulted for its patient pacing. Crabbe is lethargic compared to previous Flash portrayals, and timing acceptable in a feature is particularly tiresome in cliffhanger format.

Much action occurs in Mongo's Arctic, known appropriately as Frigia. As Universal had no icebound back lot, they heavily padded the picture with stock footage from their tundra release, *White Hell of Pitz Palu* (1930). Careless cross-cutting between borrowed footage of tiny figures walking across ice to close-ups of the principles frequently and hilariously changes the numbers in Flash's party.

Among the interesting characters introduced here are the Rock Men, Mongo's version of Clay People, who speak the language of lost tribes from Earth's Gobi Desert backwards. Absurdly, Zarkov realizes this and is able to translate for the rest of crew.

Earth is being devastated by an epidemic called "The Plague of the Purple Death." When Flash, Dale, and Zarkov rocket into the stratosphere to investigate, they discover Ming's warships sprinkling deadly dust. On

Mongo, Flash and company join forces with Barin and Aura and invade Ming's palace, partially wrecking it. They then journey to Frigia in search of Polante, the Purple Death's antidote being found only there.

Ming, with Sonja (Anne Gwynne), Thong (Victor Zimmerman) and Torch (Don Rowan), attacks the Arctic expedition with a space ship. Dale and Zarkov are captured. Flash deflects a death ray attack to save them, sets the controls of a solarite ship on automatic, and aims it at Ming's headquarters. Bailing out at the last second, Flash crashes the ship into the stronghold. A terrific explosion ensues, bringing Ming to his third and final demise.

There was a short-lived *Flash Gordon* television series in 1953 filmed in Germany and starring Steve Holland in the lead, but has been termed "vastly inferior" to the serials. It starred Irene Champlin as Dale and Joseph Nash as Zarkov.

A soft-porn parody, *Flesh Gordon* (1974), produced by Bill Osco, was amateurish with the exception of its stop-motion animation.

In 1979 NBC-TV presented a color animated *Flash Gordon* series for children, produced by Don Christiensen.

Dino De Laurentiis produced the lavish and appropriately campy *Flash Gordon* (1980), with naive Sam Jones in the lead. Directed by Mike Hodges, the British release features Max von Sydow's hissable Ming and a rock-and-roll soundtrack by Queen.

Universal converted a favorite radio hero to film in *The Green Hornet* (1940), directed by Ford Beebe and Ray Taylor — the same team that had just completed *Flash Gordon Conquers the Universe*. George W. Trendle created the characters for a long-running radio show written by Fran Striker, originating from Detroit's WXYZ. The show starred Al Hodge, later to be film's *Captain Video*, as the Green Hornet's voice.

For the serial, the role of Britt Reid (alias TGH) went to Gordon Jones, later to gain girth and supply comedy relief in Roy Rogers westerns. Reid, a crusading publisher, dons his green mask at night to fight crime. At his side is houseboy and martial arts expert Kato (Keye Luke). They sleuth nocturnally in the Black Beauty — a sleek supercar outfitted with Kato's "energizer" — that exceeds 200 mph.

Their other tricks include a gun that shoots knockout gas and the ability to imitate any voice, an effect achieved through dubbing.

A twist. The cops think the Green Hornet is a crook. Subjected to frame-ups, he apportions his time between crook-chasing and cop-evading.

There was more plot in one episode than in many complete serials. Reid and his employees at *The Daily Sentinel* bare a crooked junkyard, thwart an organized busriders' attempt to cheat the bus company, foil a trucking company swindle scheme, halt a rigged election, and end a protection racket against dry cleaners.

As the Green Hornet investigates a syndicate-operated flying school, young pilot Gilpin is flying solo after only four hours of instruction. The apprentice aviator, who struggles but manages to land safely, was played by

Alan Ladd before his fame in films such as *This Gun for Hire* and *Shane*. The supporting cast was Anne Nagel as Reid's beautiful secretary Lenore Case and Wade Boteler as his dim Irish assistant Mike Oxford.

Realizing all of these crimes to be masterminded from a single source, the Green Hornet tracks the crook down despite police interference. The chapterplay was popular enough to warrant an immediate sequel. Though less than a year passed between *The Green Hornet* and *The Green Hornet Strikes Back* (also 1940), Universal made a major cast change. This time it was Warren Hull as Reid. Perhaps Gordon Jones was already starting to show signs of the spare tire that would eventually limit him to comedy. The other main characters remained the same—Keye Luke, Anne Nagel and Wade Boteler as Kato, Lenore and Mike.

Directed by Ford Beebe and John Rawlins, the film tells of the Green Hornet and Kato's pursuit of mastercrook Grogan (Pierre Watkins), who threatens society with gas guns and a superbomb.

The Green Hornet didn't appear on the screen again until 1966 on ABC-TV. The slick but unpopular series (it ran less than a year) starred Van Williams in the lead and martial arts legend Bruce Lee as Kato.

Although *The Shadow* was a popular radio mystery drama heard by millions each week, it was upon the hero's pulp magazine version that Columbia's 1940 serial was based. On radio, Lamont Cranston's alter-ego became completely invisible, while in the book magazines, written by Walter B. Gibson under the pen name Maxwell Grant, he dressed in black with mask, cape, and broad-brimmed hat. He clung to darkness to "shadow" enemies. This sleuth appeared in *The Shadow*, directed by James W. Horne. After Columbia's success with *The Spider's Web* (1938)—a rip-off of Gibson's character—they made the real McCoy after some difficulty obtaining the film rights.

The title role was played by Victor Jory, a menacing Canadian character actor best cast as cynical heavies. Cranston, a scientist and criminologist, pursues The Black Tiger, a masked arch-fiend sabotaging railroads, airplanes and factories with a death ray and nitrogen bulb explosives. In need of rescue is Cranston's friend and secretary, Margot Lane (Veda Ann Borg).

After The Black Dragon is zapped by his own electrical control board, we learn he is Stanford Marshall (J. Paul Jones), a solid citizen appointed by Police Commissioner Weston (Frank LaRue) to apprehend himself.

Boy heroes were abound in Universal's *Junior G-Men* (1940), starring the Dead End Kids. Belief in the premise here is absolutely essential. Lower East Side juvenile delinquents become Feds. There are other elements of science fiction as well.

Colonel Barton (Russell Hicks), inventor of a new explosive, has disappeared with other military and scientific VIP's. G-Man Jim Bradford (Phillip Terry) is assigned to investigate. The inventor's son Billy (Billy

Halop) is the runaway leader of a street gang including Gyp (Huntz Hall) and Terry (Gabriel Dell), who both later became Bowery Boys. Bradford approaches Billy and (get this) invites him to help the G-Men find his dad. Billy tells the coppa to take a powda. Punks and Feds team only after the agent saves Billy's life. The teenagers discover "The Order of the Flaming Torch," an anarchist band responsible for the kidnappings, plotting the snatching of a new aerial torpedo's inventor. After foiling the scheme the boys are inducted into the force as official Junior G-Men. There was a sequel, *Junior G-Men of the Air* (1942), to be discussed later.

Another bizarre use of superscience appeared in Republic's *King of the Royal Mounted* (1940), directed by William Witney and John English and based on the Zane Grey comic strip of the same name. The plot centers around "Compound X," an odd substance that both cures polio and sinks ships from afar with magnetic powers. Its inventor is Canadian mine-owner Merritt (Stanley Andrews), who is murdered by enemy agent Kettler (Robert Strange). Along with henchman Garson (Harry Cording), Kettler seeks Compound X for an unnamed enemy country.

Chasing Kettler by airplane, car, and boat is Sergeant King of the Mounties (Allan Lane), accompanied by Corporal Tom Merritt and his sister Linda (Robert Kellard and Lita Conway), the son and daughter of the late inventor. Tom sacrifices his life to save the world, leaving his best friend King to marry his sister. While captured on Kettler's Compound X-laden submarine, Tom slugs King and shoots him out the torpedo tube before blowing the sub, Kettler, and himself into oblivion. Allan Lane returned as Sergeant King in *King of the Mounties* (1942), once again battling the forces of ultrascientific evil.

Republic Studios repeatedly used this same play on words. In *King of the Texas Rangers* (1941) the hero was Tom King. Steve King was *King of the Forest Rangers* (1946), while Bert King was *King of the Carnival* (1955). In a serial discussed later, Jeff King became *King of the Rocket Men* (1949).

Witney and English made Republic's *Mysterious Dr. Satan* (1940) (also known in re-release as *Dr. Satan's Robot*). This robot did not look as menacing as Lugosi's in *The Phanton Creeps*, but he was more active. Dr. Satan's mechanical man resembles a walking hot water heater. This was one of Republic's fastest-paced serials, rich in nostalgic camp when viewed today. A rousing score by Cy Feuer, superior lighting, and good stunt work enhance the feverish tempo.

Dr. Satan, an extremely Italian master criminal (Eduardo Cianelli), needs a remote-control device invented by brilliant scientist Thomas Scott (C. Montague Shaw) to launch his robot on a terror campaign. He repeatedly threatens the life of the inventor's daughter Lois (Ella Neal).

Hero Bob Wayne (Robert Wilcox), when battling evil, dons the copper mask of his father, a fugitive from crooked justice in the old west. In action Wayne is known as "Copperhead." (Masked heroes like the Green Hornet and Copperhead became increasingly popular during the Forties, sometimes in script premises that never explained the mask's necessity.) Copperhead saves Lois each week, only to find his own neck in the balance.

Early, Dr. Satan proves his robot a legitimate menace by ordering it to crush a henchman gone awry. Later, Copperhead finds himself in those same clutches but manages to shut off the robot's operating controls before squashed. Copperhead survives an underwater trap, a spray of raw electricity, a wall of flame, and a blazing furnace sealed inside a coffinlike box. In the predictable ending, Dr. Satan squirms in his own creation's death grip as villain and robot tumble from a window to the street far below.

Captain Marvel, the first caped and costumed film hero, debuted in *Whiz Comics'* February 1940 issue, published by Fawcett to take advantage of *Superman's* comic success. A year later Marvel converted from page to screen in *The Adventures of Captain Marvel*, directed by Witney and English. Republic originally intended to film Superman, but substituted Marvel after difficulties in obtaining the former's film rights. A live Superman did not appear in the movies until seven years later in a Columbia serial.

The illustrated *Captain Marvel* was a satire of other comic books. The art work of C.C. Beck and writing of Otto Binder was starkly fundamental, rich with elements of wit. The red-suited character has most of the powers of Superman, with the exception of X-ray vision. Though he could fly and bullets bounced off of his chest, he was in reality nonpowered youngster Billy Batson. To transform into "The World's Mightiest Mortal" he called out "*Shazam!*" and the change occurred amid the crackle of enchanted lightning. He grew from a boy into a man wearing red tights trimmed in gold, a white cape, and gold boots. Across his chest was a gold lightning bolt.

The picture removed the satirical wit that made the comic do-gooder so popular, replacing it with serious professionalism. With Tom Tyler as Marvel, this was one of the best serials ever made.

Tyler (1903–1954) was the holder of a world weightlifting championship, yet had a slender frame and an angularly handsome face. He was primarily associated with westerns throughout his career, but his most recent work had been the title role in Universal's *The Mummy's Hand* (1940).

The special effects were superior. In a medium where film magic was budget-inhibited and uniformly sloppy, this appears quite real, thanks to the effects team Theodore and Howard Lydecker and stuntman Dave Sharpe who doubled for Tyler. For the flying scene, the Lydecker brothers propelled a full-sized dummy along hundreds of feet of wire at tremendous speeds, so the caped hero would appear to glide up the sides of skyscrapers and zoom along highways in pursuit of fleeing getaway cars.

Billy Batson (Frank Coghlan, Jr.), an archaeological expedition assistant radio operator in the Far Eastern "Valley of the Tombs," is the only member of this troupe not to cross a forbidden chamber threshold. After a volcanic eruption collapses the underground chamber, trapping the expedition, Billy encounters Shazam (gray-haired and bearded Nigel de Brulier), guardian of the tomb. His name comes from initials of six legendary heroes,

Rare unedited print of Tom Tyler displaying superstrength — here obviously a publicity shot — from *The Adventures of Captain Marvel* **(Republic, 1941).**

each famous for a different power. Shazam bestows all of these virtues on Billy as a reward for respecting the forbidden area, and orders him to protect The Scorpion, a powerful golden weapon whose full potency is not unleashed unless its ray is focused through five highly polished lenses. Shazam tells Billy his powers will last only as long as the weapon is in jeopardy. Meanwhile, the trapped scientists divide the five lenses among them so no one can have all the power. After Billy rescues the expedition as Captain Marvel, they return to America where one of the archaeologists becomes The Scorpion, a masked malefactor handled after the weapon he seeks. One by one he gathers the lenses from the other four to complete the ray.

Getting into trouble is pretty Betty Wallace (Louise Curry), the expedition's secretary, Marvel always arrives in time for rescue, once in mid-air as she tumbles toward certain death at a river gorge's bottom.

Once the Scorpion gathers all five of the lenses, only Captain Marvel stands between him and his dream of conquering the world. Using Betty as bait, the Scorpion captures Billy, knowing the sixteen-year-old is somehow Marvel but ignorant of the magical transformation. The Scorpion threatens to use the death ray on Betty unless Billy reveals the secret of his powers. Bound and gagged, the boy nods his agreement. The Scorpion yanks the gag away, Billy screams the magic word, transforms, and breaks loose. Marvel removes the Scorpion's hood, baring him as Professor Bently (Harry Worth), a typically arbitrary solution.

While trying to escape, Bently falls in front of a blast from his own ray gun and instantly disintegrates. Marvel throws the device in a molten lava pit so it can never again be used for evil. His mission for Shazam through, he loses his powers and becomes Billy Batson forever. Considering the popularity and quality here, it's odd that a sequel was never made.

Witney and English directed the final serial based on Chester Gould's super-sleuth (again Ralph Byrd) in *Dick Tracy vs. Crime, Inc.* (1941). Despite heavy reliance on footage from previous Tracy movies, an intelligent script by Ronald Davidson, Norman S. Hall, William Lively, Joseph O'Donnell, and Joseph Poland, and an original score by Cy Feuer, made this by far the series' best entry.

Tracy is summoned from Washington to New York to investigate the murders of members of the Council of Eight, a body of influential citizens organized to rid the city of arch-fiend The Ghost. Unbeknownst to all, The Ghost is council member Morton (Ralph Morgan). A humming device invented by fanatic Lucifer (John Davidson) endows The Ghost with invisibility while committing nefarious crimes. When visible, he hides behind a black head-shaped mask.

In a spectacular cliffhanger, The Ghost and Lucifer bomb New York Harbor's volcanic fault, causing an earthquake and tidal wave. Large buildings crumbling and washing away were spliced from RKO's feature *Deluge.*

Tracy invents a ray that neutralizes The Ghost's invisibility. Their punchface battle is filmed in negative to show the effects of Tracy's ray. The Ghost manages to smash Tracy's invention and flee but is electrocuted while attempting to cross high-tension wires.

Byrd later played Dick Tracy in RKO features *Dick Tracy's Dilemma* and *Dick Tracy Meets Gruesome* (both 1947, the latter with Karloff), and then again in the original *Dick Tracy* TV-series (1950-51).

In a sequel to *The Spider's Web* (1938), Warren Hull repeated as playboy Richard Wentworth (alias The Spider) in Columbia's *The Spider Returns* (1941), directed by James W. Horne. Writers were veteran George H. Plympton with new collaborator Jesse A. Duffy. Kenne Duncan repeated his role as The Spider's servant Ram Singh, while Mary Ainslee replaced Iris Meredith as Wentworth's girlfriend and co-sleuth Nina Van Sloan.

The cloaked and masked hero, still more than coincidentally similar to The Shadow, pursues the Gargoyle, whose X-ray belt has thrown the U.S. defense system into chaos. The ray controls machinery from afar while his X-ray eye serves as a superior surveillance system.

As in the first serial, Wentworth poses as underworld habitué Blinky McQuade to obtain information. But it is The Spider who infiltrates the Gargoyle's headquarters and unmasks him as McLeod, one of the nation's most respected businessmen.

The Dead End Kids returned to aid Feds battle Axis forces in their second science fiction serial *Junior G-Men of the Air* (1942), again straining logic with its premise. The juvenile delinquents were inducted as official *Junior G-Men* at the first serial's end, but here the boys are back on the streets, mistrustful of cops and looking for trouble. To show what brilliant minds lie behind those smart-mouthed facades, Ace Holden (Billy Halop), Bolts Larson (Huntz Hall), Stick Munsey (Gabriel Dell), and Greaseball Plunkett (Bernard Punsley) are assembling an airplane out of scrounged parts from an auto and airplane junkyard owned by Ace's father Eddie (Gene Reynolds). After G-Man Don Ames (Richard Lane) returns Eddie Holden's stolen pick-up truck, Junior G-Man Jerry Markham (Frank Albertson) persuades Ace and company to fight against a pair of enemy agents, who are scheming ultrascientific terrorism. They are the Baron (Lionel Atwill), and Araha (Turhan Bey).

After this it was determined that the Dead End Kids' talents best suited comedy, and they went on, with some personnel changes, to become the Bowery Boys.

In a sequel to *King of the Royal Mounted*, Allan Lane returned as Sergeant King in Republic's *King of the Mounties* (1942), here in conflict with the Oriental Axis Fifth Column in Canada. The bad guys, Admiral Yamata (Abner Biberman), Count Baroni (Nestor Paiva) and Marshall von Horst (William Vaugn) are softening Western Canada for a Jap attack, mercilessly bombing from a radar-immune mystery plane called the Falcon. When American Professor Brent (George Irving) invents a device that can detect the Falcon, he is murdered by Japs before King can save him. After Brent's lovely daughter Carol (Peggy Drake) continues her father's work, she too is abducted to Axis headquarters in a dormant volcano where the crater is a heliport for the Falcon. There is a King versus Japs fist-jaw session inside the volcano and explosives are accidentally knocked into boiling lava. King rescues Carol and expertly maneuvers the Falcon to safety before both volcano and enemy explode.

The script, by Taylor Caven, Ronald Davidson, William Lively, Joseph O'Donnell, and Joseph Poland, was inspired by the writings of Zane Grey.

As King battled Japs in Canada, Alan Armstrong fought Nazis under the caped and costumed guise of *Spy Smasher* (1942), another Republic serial. Also directed by William Witney, this was a superior chapterplay. Foremost among its qualities is the abnormally competent acting skills of Kane Richmond as both Alan and twin brother Jack (Jack Armstrong?). The miniatures of Theodore Lydecker—in particular the enemy agents' "bat plane"—were especially real. The camp-free script, written by a team led by Ronald Davidson, and Reggie Lanning's atmospheric cinematography lend to its appeal. Aging well, it was re-edited and released to TV in 1966 as the misleading *Spy Smasher Returns.*

Based on the *Whiz Comics* character, Spy Smasher wore a Superman-like costume when fighting Nazis. His garb was complete with gloves, diamondshaped chest emblem, and "V" (for victory) belt buckle.

Other characters converted from comics to film were kindly American Admiral Corby (white-haired Sam Flint), his daughter and Jack's fiancee Eve (former New York model and Howard Hughes protege Marguerite Chapman), and German villain The Mask (Hans Schumm).

Aided by spearhead evildoer Drake (the mustached Tristram Coffin), The Mask envisions U.S. economic ruin through counterfeit currency. He also endangers the hero with ray guns and a television spy system.

In a stunning cliffhanger, Spy Smasher is shot off a rooftop, falling to his death on pavement. Audiences wondered how scriptwriters would scribe their way out of that one and were surprised the next week to find the character really dead—with Jack, posing as his brother, taking the fatal tumble. Spy Smasher avenges Jack's death in the conclusion, leaping from his motorboat seconds before it crashes into the Nazi's submarine, burying The Mask and his crew at sea.

Next to Superman, the most popular comics costumed hero has been Batman, who used cunning and detective skills rather than superhuman powers to capture criminals. Like Spy Smasher, Batman was a vulnerable mortal and perfect for the cliffhanger format.

The creation of teen artist Bob Kane, "The Batman" debuted in *Detective Comics* in 1939. When he was not living his life as millionaire Bruce Wayne, he dressed in blue-gray tights, midnight blue boots, mask and gloves, and flowing black cape cut like bat wings. His mask had pointy ears.

There was a bat-shaped emblem on the center of his muscular chest. From his gold utility belt, he pulled an endless assortment of gadgets. No matter what Batman needed to escape from a life-threatening jam, one could rest assured that it was in that belt.

In 1940 Kane introduced the Dynamic Duo's other half, Robin the Boy Wonder. Robin, actually Dick Grayson, the youngest of family trapeze act "The Flying Graysons," pledges to battle crime for eternity after his parents are murdered for refusing to cooperate with a mobster protection racket. His destiny is found as Bruce Wayne's adopted ward. The pair base operations in the ultra-modern "Bat Cave" below Wayne Manor and sleuth the night streets in the sleek "Batmobile." Sole knowledge of their identities belongs to Wayne's butler, Alfred. Robin's circus training pars him with Batman as they swing on Bat-ropes or scale skyscrapers.

Unfortunately, Batman and Robin's adaptation to the screen, Columbia's *Batman* (1943), directed by Lambert Hillyer, was one of the hokiest and cheapest serials ever made, chock full of unintentional laughs. Cast in the lead were two uncharming, unathletic and unknown actors — 4-F by necessity. Lewis Wilson as Batman was pudgy around the middle, a portion of his anatomy obvious in tights. (Oddly, the flab reappeared in the Sixties *Batman* TV-series with actor Adam West flaunting his spare tire.) Robin was Douglas Croft, who was much too old for the part. In one of many continuity difficulties encountered, a hairy-legged stuntman doubles for the bare-legged "boy."

As was true of all wartime serials, domestic crime was pushed aside for international intrigue. Japanese Dr. Daka (gamely portrayed by J. Carroll Naish) is a superspy trying to internally seize U.S. control. The villain's ethnicity offered scriptwriters Victor McLeod, Leslie Swabacker, and Harry Fraser an opportunity to use all conceivable racial slurs. "You're as yellow as your skin!" Robin exclaims when face-to-face with Daka. One chapter was called "The Nipponese Trap."

Daka controls an army of zombie slaves, lobotomized by silly helmets not unlike that which Killer Kane forced upon Buck Rogers.

Avoiding expensive retakes, botched scenes became prints. During one fight scene Batman's cape falls off. After a brief cut to Alfred the butler (British William Austin), we return to the fight to find the cape magically returned to place. Audiences are never too young to miss such deviations.

Even when scenes were filmed correctly they were often ridiculous. When Batman swings on a rope to a painter's scaffolding beside a skyscraper, he accidentally knocks the workman off, leaving him dangling by his fingertips far above the street. Cliffhanger solutions were equally absurd. Batman is a passenger on a plane that crashes into the ground with a terrific explosion. Instead of acceptably opening the next segment with Batman leaping to safety at the last second, he stumbles dazed but unhurt from the smouldering wreckage.

Heroes and Daka first meet in the final segment, before the villain

Badly in need of a tailor, Robert Lowery and John Duncan pose as *Batman and Robin* **(Columbia, 1949).**

falls into his own alligator-stocked pit, a wasted opportunity. Audiences were already familiar with the principles. A passable product would have called for an immediate sequel. But moviegoers were disgruntled at the baffling inadequacies—even for a serial.

The second and last chapterplay featuring the Caped Crusader and the Boy Wonder wasn't made for six years. It was no surprise that *Batman and Robin* (1949), a Sam Katzman production, found both Lewis Wilson and Douglas Croft replaced with new actors.

All serial mysteries but one were based on the identity of the masked villain. If the hero wore a mask we knew who he was, even if the other characters didn't. A switcheroo was pulled in Republic's *The Masked Marvel* (1943), featuring an unknown masked hero. Directed by Spencer Gordon Bennett (b. 1893) and exceptionally photographed by Reggie Lanning, it was re-released in 1966 edited into feature form as *Sakima and the Masked Marvel*. The hero confronts Japanese terrorist Sakima (Caucasian

Johnny Arthur) who with main henchman Mace (Anthony Warde) contaminates American fuel with a secret formula that explodes craft in mid-air.

The Marvel — in form-fitting mask over eyes and nose — is one of four identically dressed insurance company special agents. Though he is revealed as Bob Barton (David Bacon), the youngest of the agents, actor Bacon did not play the Masked Marvel. He was portrayed throughout by stuntman/actor Tom Steele, also the robot in *The Mysterious Dr. Satan*. Necessitated by frugality, Steele also played several bit parts. At one point, through crosscutting, he chases himself up a flight of stairs. As Steele's voice was inappropriately high-pitched, his lines were dubbed by baritone radio actor Gayne Whitman, radio's Chandu the Magician.

The Marvel joins the case after the World Wide Insurance Company's chief executive is murdered by Sakima, raising the dander of daughter Alice Hamilton (demure Louise Curry), Marvel's sole confidant. The hero gains victory when he leaps from Sakima's hideout window moments before the Jap succumbs to his own time bomb.

Republic originally intended to keep Marvel's identity a secret, deciding to unmask the hero only after it was determined there would be no sequel. The character was one of few masked heroes originating on film rather than adapted from comic books or pulp fiction.

The first comic book costumed hero, predating Batman and Superman, was The Phantom. He was created by cartoonist Lee Falk, originator of *Mandrake the Magician*. Both strips debuted in 1936. With his wolf-dog Devil at his side, The Phantom — the African jungle's white protector — wore royal purple tights and a "skull ring" that left its imprint on the cheek of many a foe. The Phantom possessed superhuman strength but was not invulnerable. Africans thought him immortal because he had been around for four hundred years, not knowing his genetic powers were passed from generation to generation.

The Phantom was adapted to the screen by Columbia, the firm responsible for *Batman* earlier in the year. Though not a major production, *The Phantom* (1943) was vastly superior to *Batman*, primarily because of the direction of B. Reeves "Breezy" Eason, and a less absurd script by a team headed by Morgan B. Cox. Cast in the lead as "The Ghost Who Walks" was Tom Tyler, who previously played Captain Marvel and the Mummy.

Godfrey Prescott (Tyler) grieves beside his fatally wounded father. The torch passed, he becomes The Phantom. Prescott's fiancée Diana (Jeanne Bates) and her father, Professor Davidson (Frank Shannon), are searching for The Lost City of Zoloz where they expect to find a hidden treasure. Their quest is impeded by local thug Singapore Smith (Joe Devlin) and master criminal Dr. Bremmer (Kenneth MacDonald). The latter wants to instigate war among African tribes so Zoloz can be used as a secret air base site. Before it's over the Phantom survives an avalanche, poison gas, walls of flame, and massive explosions.

Director William Witney continued his busy schedule by making

Republic's *G-Men vs. the Black Dragon* (1943), about three allied secret agents battling Japs. American Special Investigator Rex Bennett (young Rod Cameron), British secret agent Vivian Marsh (bespectacled Constance Worth), and Chinese secret service agent Chang (Ronald Got) confront The Black Dragon Society, led by insidious Haruchi (mustached Nino Pipitone). Members of the society, played by Caucasians altered by make-up, dress like cheap American gangsters.

Haruchi and henchmen sink American ships at will, secretly mixing incendiary ingredients with the ships' paint. Chang infiltrates the society to steal an enemy submarine locater, more powerful than radar or sonar, and delivers it to Professor Nicholson (veteran C. Montague Shaw), who uses it to sink Jap U-boats. When the enemy comes for their device, Nicholson is tortured and killed.

In the conclusion, Rex awaits decapitation by the villain when Vivian and Chang arrive, forcing Haruchi to flee in a TNT-packed speedboat. Rex pursues, makes a death-defying leap into the villain's moving bomb, and grapples with Haruchi. Rex dives into seawater seconds before the boat crashes into a surfacing Jap submarine.

Much footage from this serial was reused in Republic's *Flying Disc Men from Mars* (1951).

G-Man Rex Bennett (again Rod Cameron) returned in Republic's *Secret Service in Darkest Africa* (also 1943) to battle Nazis under the direction of Spencer G. Bennett.

Baron von Rommler (Lionel Royce) is a Nazi trying to coax North African Arabs toward Axis control posing as great Arab leader Sultan Abou Ben Ali. The villain plans to vanquish allies with a death ray and secret suspended animation formula. Rex is aided by Janet Blake (Joan Marsh), an American foreign correspondent working undercover as a United Nations secret agent (unrelated to today's U.N.), and French officer Pierre LaSalle (Duncan Renaldo). Despite the displayed ultrascientific weaponry, when Bennett discovers Sultan Ali to be the Gestapo agent, they choose to swashbuckle through their final confrontation with swords. The hero impales Von Rommler ending the Nazi's North African spy complex.

As was the case with *G-Men vs. the Black Dragon*, Republic reused yards of footage from this serial for *Flying Disc Men from Mars*. *Secret Service in Darkest Africa* was later edited to feature length and re-released as *The Baron's African War*.

Republic Studios, notorious for arbitrary changes in characters adapted from other media, did a particularly horrendous butcher job on *Captain America* (1944), directed by John English and Elmer Clifton.

Captain America (alias Steve Rogers of the U.S. Army) was created by Joe Simon and Jack "King" Kirby in 1941 for Timely (later to become Marvel) Comics. Rogers was a handsome blonde given an injection of super-strength serum. With teenage chum Bucky Barnes, "Cap" battled Nazis with his fists, his red, white, and blue shield providing his sole protection.

When the movie version came out three years later Timely Comics was incensed at Republic's alterations. The film hero did not have chemically-induced strength, had no sidekick, carried no shield, was a civilian, and wasn't even Steve Rogers. He is actually Grant Gardner, District Attorney, who under the guise of Captain America combats domestic crime with a .38 police special. No explanation is given for the character's origin or why he bothers to wear a mask. Dick Purcell portrayed the star-spangled hero, whose costume *was* patterned after Simon and Kirby's creation.

The villain is museum curator Dr. Maldor, also known as the Scarab (the masterful Lionel Atwill), who murders those members of a fruitful archaeological expedition he believes to be cheating him of his fair share of the accrued wealth and fame. Inventions used to kill are "The Purple Death," a poison unrelated to Ming's plague, and a dynamic vibrator (not a marital aid) which transformed light and sound rays into forces of mass destruction.

Captain America is helped by pretty assistant Gail Richards (Lorna Gray). In the final episode, when Captain America and the Scarab meet face to face, the hero does not kill the villain with his .38 but rather brings him in to the police so, as Grant Gardner, he can send the doctor to the chair.

A screen adaptation of the real "Cap" was not made until CBS-TV produced the telefilm *Captain America* (1979), with blonde Reb Brown playing the Star-Spangled Avenger.

Possession of the Peratron, a matter transmission device, furnishes the conflict in Universal's *The Great Alaskan Mystery* (1944), directed by Ray Taylor and Lewis D. Collins. A similar invention would become the premise for *The Fly* (1958).

The Peratron, invented by kindly American scientist Dr. Miller (Ralph Morgan) can only be perfected with a rare element exclusive to the Alaskan tundra. Together with daughter Ruth (the delicious Marjorie Weaver), and hero Jim Hudson (Milburn Stone), Dr. Miller begins a long trek into the arctic, heading for an old ore mine owned by Jim's father (Joseph Crehan). The group is unaware that Miller's assistant Dr. Hauss (Martin Kosleck) is a fascist spy in cahoots with a pair of Nazis (Harry Cording and Samuel S. Hinds). The evildoers often try to sabotage the frigid expedition, but are killed themselves in the end by Dr. Miller's death ray.

Republic's tiresome *The Manhunt of Mystery Island* (1945) is most famous for Captain Mephisto (mustached Roy Barcroft, 1902–1969), a super-scientific mastermind seeking an American radio-atomic power transmitter. Mephisto was the cruel 18th-Century buccaneer ruler of Mystery Island, a tiny speck in the Pacific. In current time Mephisto returns to his crimes via a "Transformation Chair," in which a modern-day criminal (we don't know who until the final reel) changes his blood's molecular structure to become the pirate. It is unclear why becoming Mephisto is desirable, but it let special effects men Howard and Theodore Lydecker use the same transformation scene in all fifteen episodes, a lethargy-inducing repetition since it had to be filmed without revealing the modern-day criminal's face.

Dr. Forrest (Forrest Taylor), inventor of the atomic energy transmitter, is kidnapped by Mephisto's henchmen. Forrest's daughter Claire (Linda Sterling, previously the dominatrix heroine of *Zorro's Black Whip*) enlists the aid of famous criminologist Lance Reardon (Richard Baily) and together sleuth their way to Mystery Island. There they learn Mephisto is one of four men, each a part owner of the island and blood relative of the original pirate. They are Professor Hargreaves (Forbes Murray), Edward Armstrong (Jack Ingram), Frederick Braley (Harry Strang), and Paul Melton (Edward Cassidy).

When Forrest is saved, Mephisto flees; so the doctor employs his television scanner, small enough to be concealed in his pocket, to locate the corsair's hide-out. Lance finally notifies authorities in the final episode but invades Mephisto's headquarters before they arrive. The buccaneer knocks Lance cold and straps him to the transformation machine, planning to return to his true self while changing Lance into Mephisto so the hero will be arrested by police. The scheme is foiled when Claire bursts in, talks with his pistol, and offs the pirate on the spot. Mephisto in death is revealed to be Braley. No one gasped with surprise. As usual, the suspects were indistinguishable, scriptwriters not wanting the mystery to get in action's way.

In one of Universal's last wartime chapterplays, *The Master Key*, Milburn Stone fights Nazis as Federal Investigator Tom Brant who, joined by private detective Jack Ryan (Dennis Moore) and reporter Janet Lowe (Jan Wiley), searches for American inventor Professor Elwood Henderson (Byron Foulger). The professor is a mineralogical scientist, and inventor of the Orotron, a machine that extracts massive quantities of gold from the ocean.

The Nazis, led by identified scapegrace the Master Key, want the machine to create U.S. financial panic. The Master Key is female Dorothy Newton (Maris Wrixon), secretary to Police Chief O'Brien (Russell Hicks), speaking with an electronically-altered voice. For once audiences were genuinely pleased with the surprise ending. When Dorothy attempts to flee by air, FBI agents blow her plane out of the sky.

Robots made their overdue return to serials in Columbia's *The Monster and the Ape* (1945), directed by Howard Bretherton. The picture had the pleasant notoriety of being the last science fiction serial with a Nazi villain and was later re-edited into a 100-minute feature.

Professor Arnold (Ralph Morgan) is demonstrating his new invention, the Metalogen Man, at the Bainbridge Research Foundation. The robot, constructed to aid hero Ken Morgan (Robert Lowery) and the corporation he represents, is being admired by Professor Ernst (George MacReady), secretly a Nazi agent. His plot to steal the robot is thwarted by a trained gorilla Thor, your basic man in a monkey suit. The ape is eventually shot dead, sacrificing his life for freedom, and Ernst splatters after falling from a high embankment.

With peace in Europe, Republic returned to outer space once again to find their villain in *The Purple Monster Strikes* (1945), directed by Spencer G. Bennett and Fred C. Brannon. The Purple Monster was actually a Martian Caucasian in gold-scaled purple tights. He behaved like an American gangster.

Dr. Cyrus Layton (James Craven), American inventor of an interplanetary jet in his Griffith Park observatory, monitors the approach of a glowing purple meteor through his powerful telescope. He drives to a rocky area in California where the coffin-shaped object crashes to Earth in a ball of flame. Rather than using animation for this image, the Lydecker brothers actually plunged the object into the rocks and caused the explosion upon impact. Tightwad producers must have winced when the scene had to be reshot after the first take ruptured an underground water line.

Out of the wreckage steps the Purple Monster (Roy Barcroft, Captain Mephisto in *Manhunt of Mystery Island* now clean-shaven), who says, "I am from the planet you call Mars," and explains his perfect English by the monitoring of his planet's "distance eliminator." He reveals the ability to become raw energy and infiltrate any human body. As Martian space travel is obviously imperfect, he seeks Dr. Layton's spaceship to wage all-out war on Earth. After killing the scientist with a capsule of Martian atmosphere (without explaining how he can breathe our air and remain healthy), he assumes Layton's form and is pursued throughout the film's remainder by lawyer Craig Foster (Dennis Moore), close friend of Layton's pretty daughter Sheila (Linda Sterling). The hero never considers informing the authorities of Earth's peril but is determined to take on the extraterrestrial single-handed with his bosomy girlfriend at his side.

The Martian enlists the aid of dim Earthling hoodlums who seem to like the idea of a Martian takeover. Also helping him is the Emperor of Mars (John Davidson), who sends a pretty Martian named Marcia (Mary Moore) to Earth, where she meets an ugly doom at the bottom of an abyss.

Craig and Sheila evade the usual cliffhanger scrapes, most notably the "electro-annihilator," a Martian disintegrator ray which always misses by inches. When Sheila and Craig realize her father is the Purple Monster, the villain returns to normal and attempts flight in Dr. Layton's rocketship, only to be blasted by his own annihilator gun, aimed more carefully by the hero.

The costumed man from Mars returned in a 1951 Republic sequel *Flying Disc Men from Mars*, which consisted predominantly of spliced footage from *The Purple Monster Strikes*, *G-Men vs. the Black Dragon*, and *Secret Service in Darkest Africa*.

Barcroft, effective as the villain, did not like the idea of wearing tights. To play the Purple Monster, he had to lose thirty pounds in as many days before filming could begin.

The most frightening villain in chapterplay history was the title character in Republic's *The Crimson Ghost* (1946), directed by William Witney and Fred C. Brannon. The villain wore the skull mask of the Grim Reaper, his eyes peering from black sockets. He seemed reminiscent of Lon Chaney's make-up in *The Phantom of the Opera*. His lipless mouth was stretched back into a sardonic grin baring rotted teeth. He wore a red cloak and gloves decorated with his hands' skeletal construction—much like the ads for "X-Ray Specs" found on the inside covers of comic books. The villain was played by uncredited stuntman Bud Geary, and his voice was supplied by I. Stanford Jolley, who also had a bit part as henchman Blackton.

Professor Chambers (Kenne Duncan), an internationally famous physicist, is demonstrating his invention, the Cyclotron, for four colleagues, one of whom is secretly The Ghost. The Cyclotron is a coiled counter-atomic ray gun able to short-circuit all electrical current within miles. After the exhibition, two Ghost henchmen arrive to abduct both scientist and invention. They wear metallic collars, removal of which means instant death. Professor Chambers smashes the Cyclotron so it can't be stolen, and the kidnapping is halted by the intervention of hero Duncan Richards (Charles Quigley), a renowned criminologist and Chambers' friend. During the ensuing scuffle one thug escapes while the other is knocked cold. When Chambers thoughtlessly removes the collar, an electric light flashes brightly, and the bad guy is zapped instantly dead.

The heroine is Duncan's secretary Diana Fransworth (the busy Linda Sterling). In the end The Ghost is unmasked as Professor Parker (Joe Forte), a seemingly kind old man who had been "helping" the good guys.

With the war just over, Universal was already setting its sights on World War III in *Lost City of the Jungle* (1946), directed by Ray Taylor and Lewis D. Collins. Sir Eric Hazarius (Lionel Atwill in his final screen role), a villainous warmonger who seeks Meteorium 245, the only known defense against the atom bomb and found exclusively in the jungle city Pendrang. Hazarius plans to throw the world into a new conflict and emerge from the rubble as its leader. Confronting him at every turn are United Peace Foundation investigator Rod Stanton (Russell Hayden), Pendrang local Tal Shan (Keye Luke, Kato in *The Green Hornet* serials), and Marjorie Elmore (Jane Adams), daughter of brilliant American scientist Dr. Elmore (John Eldredge).

Hazarius eventually unearths a chest full of Meteorium 245 from the "Tomb of the Glowing Goddess" far below the lost city, but as he and henchman Grebb (John Gallaudet) are fleeing by plane they fight over the element. The chest topples and spills, and the released power blows them apart.

Sadly, Atwill died of pneumonia due to lung cancer in the middle of production, forcing Universal to use a double for the back of Hazarius' head. The firm also enlarged the role of Grebb and repeatedly used the same grainy shot of Atwill nodding approval.

The Pacific war left a worse taste in American mouths during the later Forties than did the war in Europe. It was common for screen villains to be Oriental years after the Japanese were once again our allies. Such was the case in Republic's *The Black Widow* (1947), directed by Spencer G. Bennett and Fred C. Brannon. Interestingly the villain was female—Sombra

(Caucasian Carol Forman made up to look Oriental), the daughter of "Asian" King Hitomu, who seeks world domination after stealing a new American atomic rocket engine. Armed with science fiction gadgets including an invention that can change her car's color while it is in motion, she hides behind the front of a fortune-telling establishment aided by gangster Ward (Anthony Warde), and scientist-turned-traitor Jaffa (I. Stanford Jolley). One by one, associates of Henry Weston (Sam Flint), inventor of the engine, are poisoned by spider venom—thus giving the villainess her title monicker.

When local newspaper *The Daily Clarion* learns of the murders, they hire amateur criminologist Steve Volt (Bruce Edwards) to investigate, assisted by reporter Joyce Winters (Virginia Lindley). Sombra is bitten by one of her own spiders in the climax. Colt shoots all of the other gangsters dead and saves Joyce so she can eagerly phone her paper.

Serials were well past their prime when Columbia made the space adventure *Brick Bradford* (1947), a feeble attempt to imitate *Flash Gordon* and *Buck Rogers*. The script, written by George H. Plympton and others, was so uninspired that it was difficult to believe Plympton the same man who helped pen the original *Flash Gordon* serial eleven years before. The shoddy production was set by "quickie" producer Sam Katzman. Though there are many scenes that are *supposed* to be funny, all of the humor is unintentional. What can be said about a film that costumes its evil moon-men in tee-shirts, Bermuda shorts, and sneakers? The bad guys seem more like suburban beer-drinkers than aliens. Though based on the King Features Syndicate comic strip, it bears little resemblance to its creator's intention.

Director Spencer G. Bennett, who had led many above-average serials dating back to the silent era, realized he had a dog on his hands and did little to punch up this mishmash of misguided pulp.

The U.N. assigns hero Brick (gamely portrayed by Kane Richmond) to protect the Interceptor Ray—an anti-missile device perfected by Dr. Tymak (John Merton)—from villain Laydron (Charles Quigley), who wants the ray for his terror campaign. Brick is accompanied on his adventures by Professor Salisbury (Pierre Watkin), Salisbury's daughter June (Linda Johnson), and young sidekick Sandy Sanderson (Rick Vallin).

To perfect the Interceptor Ray, Dr. Tymak needs the element Lunarium, found only on the moon. He invents a "crystal door" with a threshold which magically leads to the lunar surface. Once there Tymak is captured by moon meanies and has to be rescued by Brick.

The moon scenes boggle the most accepting mind. Earthlings can breathe normally and are unaffected by the change in gravity. Above the lunar surface is a bright sunshiny sky, replete with puffs of cottony clouds.

Back on Earth, Brick and Sandy fearlessly enter the "Time Top," a spinning time-travel machine, to secure an 18th Century English formula that Tymak needs. After battling pirates, they return to the present time to rescue Tymak from Laydron and his henchmen.

Columbia later made space serials *Captain Video* (1951) and *The Lost Planet* (1953), which were just as bad.

Jack Armstrong, the All-American Boy was one of radio's most popular programs through the Thirties and early Forties. When the program began in 1933, Jack was a high school student who had adventures in faraway places with friends Billy and Betty Fairfield and their explorer Uncle Jim Fairfield. By the late Forties the program had changed considerably, and its popularity had waned. Jack had grown up and was an agent for the Scientific Bureau of Investigation. Uncle Jim had been replaced by Vic Hardy, head of the S.B.I. It took 14 years for Jack to make his first, and only, screen appearance. Owners of the property, cereal-makers General Mills, wanted an inflated price for film rights while the program was in its heyday. That price had decreased considerably when Columbia made *Jack Armstrong* (1947), directed by Wallace Fox.

Producer Sam Katzman was smart enough to revert back to the old format. Jack was again in high school and popular Uncle Jim was reinstated. Vic Hardy remained, but as a famous scientist rather than a chief investigator.

Youthful John Hart plays Jack and Joe Brown and Rosemary La Planche portray Billy and Betty. Pierre Watkin plays Uncle Jim and Hugh Prosser is Vic Hardy. Uncle Jim now heads an aviation company developing atomic engines.

The villain is Jason Grood (Charles Middleton, Ming in the *Flash Gordon* serials), who is plotting worldwide takeover with his cosmic annihilator ray, poisonous gas, Tanilic Light, and the aeroglobe, an artificial satellite in orbit around the Earth. Hoping to add Fairfield's engine to his arsenal, Grood recruits the aid of badnik Professor Zorn (Wheeler Oakman). Hardy is kidnapped and taken to Grood's base of operation on an enchanted island. Jack, Billy, and Betty aren't far behind, never once thinking that it might be wiser to call police. In the conclusion, Jack, in All-American fashion, blows Grood and his cronies up with a hurled hand grenade.

In Republic's *G-Men Never Forget* (1947), the last and least effective of the Fed series, government agent Ted O'Hara (Clayton Moore) battles notorious Vic Murkland (Roy Barcroft), whose face has been scientifically altered to make him a precise double for local Police Commissioner Cameron (Barcroft also). Directed by Fred C. Brannon and Yakima Cannutt, the film also starred Stanley Price as evil scientist Dr. Benson and stylish Ramsay Ames as a pretty police sergeant. The heroes escape devilish gases, floodwaters, falling bombs, and exploding fuel before the villain's identity is revealed and his protective insurance racket is squelched.

Appropriately, the world's most popular superhero became the biggest serial moneymaker of all time in 1948 when Columbia made *Superman*, a Sam Katzman production, directed by Spencer G. Bennett and Thomas Carr. With anticipation piqued by the time of its release, it was

Lois Lane (Noel Neill) and the Man of Steel (Kirk Alyn) discuss the value of platoni-cism in *Superman* (Columbia, 1948).

immediately booked into first-run theaters nationwide, many of which had never shown a serial before.

The "Man of Steel" was created by writer Jerry Siegal and artist Joe Shuster, while both were still in their teens. The pair, after many rejections, sold the concept to National Comics (later to become DC) for $200. With the sale the pair lost all rights to their work and never received another dime.

Superman made his premiere in the first issue of *Action Comics* in 1938 and was a smash. The original character could only leap an eighth of a mile and had skin so thick that an exploding shell was needed to pierce it. His Kryptonese parents were originally named Jor-L and Lora, but were later changed to Jor-El and Lara. Superman's adopted Earth parents went through several name changes. Originally named John and Mary Kent, by the time the movie was made they were Eben and Sarah, but soon after changed to Jonathan and Martha, their current names.

It took ten years to bring Superman to Hollywood in a live-action film because of National Comics' insistence on complete scripting control. Twice, in 1940 and '41, Republic announced the making of a Superman serial, but neither panned out. Instead they made *The Mysterious Dr. Satan* and *The Adventures of Captain Marvel*, using plot and special effects originally planned for the Man of Steel. The first project was scrubbed because of conflicts with the publisher, and the second was abandoned after the 1941 release of 17 Superman cartoons with Bud Collyer, radio's Superman, providing the heroic voice.

Columbia purchased the film rights after Sam Katzman convinced them it was a moneymaking proposition. No Katzman film had ever finished in the red, no matter how bad it was. Even *Brick Bradford* made money.

The studio considered many actors, including Buster Crabbe, for the title role. Crabbe turned them down, thinking himself already stringently typecast.

Although he was a bit slight for the part, Columbia picked handsome Kirk Alyn (b. 1915), correctly feeling his face perfectly suited. Alyn demonstrated an ability to be both heroic as Superman and wimpish as alter-ego Clark Kent. Columbia's silly publicity department announced that the *real* Superman would play himself in the film. Theater posters listed Superman among actor credits, and during the film Alyn is credited with playing Clark Kent, but not the hero.

Though most of the serial works, the special effects are disappointing, hardly up to the standards set by *The Adventures of Captain Marvel*. Katzman originally intended to dangle Alyn by invisible strings in front of moving rear-projected clouds, the simulation technique used in the *Superman* TV-series and the 1951 feature *Superman and the Mole Men*, both starring George Reeves. After much blundering and physical pain to Alyn, Katzman fired his special effects crew and used animation for Superman's flight. We see a cartoon hero flying and Alyn landing, a technique considered cheating even at the time. To compensate, the writing crew, headed by

George H. Plympton, kept excellently to the flavor of the comic book as the arbitrary changes that flawed some screen adaptations were prohibited.

Stuntman Paul Stader was intended to double for Alyn's action scenes, but the star was forced into his own stunts when Stader hurt his leg early in production leaping from a speeding truck.

The first episode appropriately began with the character's origin, opening on doomed Krypton where Jor-El (Nelson Leight) tries to convince leaders that everyone must flee by rocket or die. Scoffed at, he wraps his baby child in a blanket (later to provide material for Superman's invulnerable uniform), places him in a cigar-shaped missile, and launches him toward Earth where atmosphere and inhabitants are compatible. Krypton explodes seconds after the baby blasts off.

The rocket lands on the plains of Ohio and is discovered by Ma and Pa Kent (Edward Cassidy and Virginia Carroll), who take the baby home and adopt him. When the boy grows up and realizes his super powers, Pa Kent explains his origin. Clark promises to use his superiority for truth, justice, and the American way.

As an adult, Clark moves to Metropolis (a thinly-veiled New York City), where he becomes a reporter for *The Daily Planet*, thinking the job will keep the underworld accessible. There he meets grouchy editor Perry White (Pierre Watkin), Lois Lane (snotty Noel Neill, who repeated the role in *Superman and the Mole Men* and on TV), and cub reporter Jimmy Olsen (Tommy Boyd).

Metropolis is ravaged by crime, led by the Spider Lady (Carol Forman, the first blonde villainness) and her deadly reducer ray. She also has Kryptonite, a meteor fragment that robs Superman of all powers. Superman neutralizes the Kryptonite by lining his uniform with lead and finally sees that justice is met. (It was decided that Superman's famous uniform was to be gray and brown—since these colors filmed better in black and white.) The Spider Lady and her henchmen are destroyed by their own powerful ray.

After this serial's sequels *Atom Man vs. Superman* (1950) with Alyn, *Superman and the Mole Men* (1951), a Lippert feature, and *The Adventures of Superman* (1953–7), a syndicated weekly TV-series, the Man of Steel left the screen until Christopher Reeve played the role in *Superman—the Movie* (1978) and *Superman II* (1981), opposite Margot Kidder as a *much* sexier Lois Lane.

It had been six years since *Batman* (presumably enough time for everyone to forget how bad it was) when Columbia made the sequel *Batman and Robin* (also known as *The New Adventures of Batman and Robin*, and *The Return of Batman*) in 1949. It was no better. The same producer and director (Sam Katzman and Spencer G. Bennett) who successfully made *Superman* the previous year flopped, with so many cut budget corners and misguided decisions that this chapterplay, along with its predecessor, is easily among history's worst films.

Robin with a tattoo?

At least they put tights on the Boy Wonder's legs this time so his body hair would not change drastically when doubled by an ape-like stuntman. The Batmobile, a limo in the original, was reduced to a '49 Merc. The Caped Crusader's uniform, in particular his mask, did not fit. It was clear that Batman could not see a thing; his eyes didn't line up with the holes.

Batman and Robin (now played by Robert Lowery and sourpussed John Duncan) are called into Gotham City's police headquarters where Commissioner Gordon (Lyle Talbot, later Lex Luthor in *Atom Man vs. Superman*) assigns them to retrieve a remote-control device stolen by the cloaked and masked Wizard. The device, enabling its possessor to operate machinery from afar, is the invention of eccentric and wheelchair-bound Professor Hammil (William Fawcett). The Wizard plans to use the remote for a diamond heist. The Dynamic Duo, along with magazine photographer Vicki Vale (Jane Adams), pursue him until he is captured and unmasked as Professor Hammil himself. Who would have thought?

In the cutesy denouement, Vicki is starting to suspect that Batman is really millionaire Bruce Wayne (and that would make Robin his ward Dick Grayson, right, Vic?) but her suspicions are waylaid when Batman uses a tape recorder to have a phone conversation with Bruce.

Batman took a screen vacation until 1966 when the Batman TV series began. The show ran through 1968 and spawned one feature, also called *Batman* (1966). Both starred campy Adam West and Burt Ward as the principles and a delicious flock of celebrity villains.

Instead of adapting a superhero from another medium an original was created for Republic's *King of the Rocket Men* (1949), directed by Fred C. Brannon and highlighted by the Lydecker brothers' special effects.

Rocket Man (there was only one) is actually Jeff King (mustached Tristram Coffin), a young scientist who wears a bullet-shaped helmet over his face, a black leather jacket, and a rocket-powered backpack enabling his flight. He also carries a ray gun resembling a German Luger.

Two members of Science Associates, a private research project developing futuristic weapons, are attacked by evil Dr. Vulcan, a mystery villain always shown as a shadow. One is killed and the other, Dr. Milland, is left for dead. Dr. Vulcan steals a powerful "decimator ray" and flees.

Jeff, a fellow member of the project, hides Milland in a remote cave where the professor outfits him in the neat flying suit to avenge the attack. On the chest of Jeff's jacket is a charmingly simple control panel consisting of three dials: "*On-Off, Up-Down, Fast-Slow.*" Jeff quickly learns how to operate it and flies like a bird. The Lydecker brothers used a life-sized dummy propelled across wires to simulate flight, similar to their effects for *The Adventures of Captain Marvel* (1941), and a solution to the flying problem that obviously never occurred to Sam Katzman when he was making

Opposite: With both futuristic weapon and thug smoking, Tristram Coffin goes for the .38 in *King of the Rocket Men* (Republic, 1949).

Superman. Aiding Jeff is Glenda Thomas (Mae Clarke, who played Elizabeth in Universal's *Frankenstein* 18 years before and, at 39, was getting a bit mature to play serial heroines), a photographer for *Miracle Science* magazine.

After failed attempts to retrieve the decimator, Jeff watches in horror as Dr. Vulcan uses it in the final segment, unleashing a devastating earthquake and tidal wave on New York. As in *Dick Tracy vs. Crime, Inc.* (1941), footage from RKO's *Deluge* showed the Big Apple crumbling. Moments later, in the most impressive effect in the film, Rocket Man smashes helmet-first through the Vulcan's window and destroys the decimator with his ray gun. Rocket Man leaves, allowing Air Force bombers to blow the villain and his cronies up.

Republic falsely assumed a sequel, so never revealed the mystery villain's identity. We'll never know. Much Lydecker effects footage from this chapterplay was reused in Republic's *Radar Men from the Moon* and *Zombies of the Stratosphere* (both 1952).

The vast radar system along the U.S. border is attacked by the sinister leader of the most dangerous ring of saboteurs in the annals of military intelligence in Republic's *Radio Patrol vs. Spy King* (1949), directed by Fred C. Brannon, with special effects by the Lydeckers. Chris Calvert (Kirk Alyn, fresh from his new fame as Superman), an operator for the Radar Defense Bureau, and brilliant radar scientist Joan Hughes (Jean Dean), battle Baroda, the title spy in cahoots with a potential enemy nation. At Baroda's side is henchwoman Nitra (Eve Whitney).

The villain attacks with a radar-beam neutralizer, captures Joan and Chris, bombards them with gamma rays, and attempts to inject them with a subservience serum. Surviving unscratched, the heroes waste Baroda and turn Nitra over to police.

The serial was on its last legs at the turn of the decade. Though studios produced serials into the Fifties, they would soon be a dead form, replaced in the habits of America's youth by television.

Filmography

Abbott and Costello Meet Frankenstein (1948). Black and white, 92 minutes, Universal.
Director: Charles T. Barton. *Producer*: Robert Arthur. *Screenplay*: John Grant, Frederick I. Rinaldo, Robert Lees. Based on characters created by Mary Shelley and Bram Stoker. *Cinematography*: Charles Van Enger. *Special Effects*: David S. Horsely, Jerome H. Ash. *Art Directors*: Bernard Herzbrun, Hillyard Brown. *Editor*: Frank Gross. *Make-up*: Bud Westmore. *Music*: Frank Skinner.
Cast: Bud Abbott, Lou Costello; Bela Lugosi as Dracula, Lon Chaney, Jr., as Lawrence Talbot/The Wolf Man, Glenn Strange as the Frankenstein Monster, Lenore Aubert, Frank Ferguson, Jane Randolph, Joe Kirk, Vincent Price (voice only).

The Absent-Minded Lecturer (*Le Conférencier Distrait*) (1899-French). Black and white, silent, 65 feet, Star Films.
Director and Producer: Georges Méliès

Ace Drummond (1936). Black and white, serial, 13 episodes, 26 reels, Universal.
Directors: Ford Beebe, Cliff Smith. *Associate Producers*: Barney Sarecky, Ben Koenig. *Screenplay*: Wyndham Gittens, Norman S. Hall, Ray Trampe. Based on a newspaper feature created by Eddie Rickenbacker. *Cinematography*: Richard Fryer.
Cast: John King, Jean Rogers, Noah Beery, Jr., Guy Bates, William Hall, Diana Gibson, Russell Wade, Lon Chaney, Jr., House Peters, Jr.

An Adventure at the Bottom of the Sea (1906 French). Black and white, silent, 349 feet, Pathé.

Adventure Unlimited see *White Pongo*

The Adventures of Captain Marvel (1941). Black and white, 12 episodes, 25 reels, Republic.
Directors: William Witney, John English. *Producer*: Hiram S. Brown. *Screenplay*: Ronald Davidson, Norman S. Hall, Arch B. Heath, Joseph Poland, Sol Shor. Based on characters appearing in Fawcett Publications' *Captain Marvel* comics. *Cinematography*: William Nobels. *Special Effects*: Howard Lydecker, Theodore Lydecker. *Editors*: Edward Todd, William Thompson. *Music*: Cy Feuer.
Cast: Tom Tyler as Captain Marvel, Frank Coghlan, Jr., as Billy Batson, William Benedict as Murphy, Louise Currie as Betty Wallace, "?" as The Scorpion, Robert Strange as John Malcolm, Harry Worth as Professor Bentley, Bryant Washburn as Henry Carlyle, John Davidson as Tal Chotali, George Pembroke as Dr.

Stephen Lang, Peter George Lynn as Dwight Fisher, Reed Hadley as Rahman Bar, Jack Mulhall as Howell, Kenneth (Kenne) Duncan as Barnett, Nigel de Brulier as Shazam, John Bagni as Cowan, Carelton Young as Martin, Leland Hodgson as Major Rawley, Stanley Price as Owens, Ernest Sarracino as Akbar, Tetsu Komai as Chan Lai.

Aelita: The Revolt of the Robots (1924 Soviet). Black and white, silent, 6050 feet (approx. 45 minutes), Mezharabpom/Amkino.
   Director: Yakov A. Protazanov. *Scenario*: Fyodor Otzep, Alexei Faiko. *Based on* Alexei Tolstoy's play. *Cinematography*: Yuri A. Zhelyabuzhsky, Emil Schonemann. *Art Directors*: Isaac Rabinovitch, Alexandra Exter, Victor Simov, Sergei Kozlovski.
   Cast: Nikolai Tseretelli as Los, Igor Ilinski as Gusev, Yulia Solntseva as Aelita, Konstantin Eggert, Nikolai Batalov, Yuri Zavadsky, Valentina Kuinzhi, V. Orlova.

The Aerial Anarchists (1911 British). Black and white, silent, 700 feet, Kineto.
   Director: Walter Booth.

The Aerial Submarine (1910 British). Black and white, silent, 600 feet, Kineto.
   Director: Walter Booth.

Aerial Torpedo see *The Airship Destroyer*

Aerial Warfare see *The Airship Destroyer*

The Aerocab and Vacuum Provider see *Professor Puddenhead's Patents*

After Death (*Dopo la Morte*) (1913 Italian). Black and white, silent, 2150 feet, Cines/Kleine.
   Cast: Hispernia.

Air Fury see *Air Hawks*

Air Hawks (1935). Black and white, 66 minutes, Columbia. Also known as *Air Fury*.
   Director: Albert Rogell. *Screenplay*: Griffin Jay, Grace Neville. Based on a story by Ben Pivar. *Cinematography*: Henry Freulich. *Editor*: Richard Cahoon.
   Cast: Ralph Bellamy, Wiley Post, Edward Van Sloan, Tala Birell, Douglas Dumbrille.

The Air Torpedo (1913 German). Black and white, three reels, Deutsche Kinematographen/Warner Brothers.
   Producer: Louis Gero.

The Airship (1908). Black and white, silent, Vitagraph. Also known as *100 Years Hence*.
   Director and Producer: J. Stuart Blackton.

The Airship Destroyer (1909 British). Black and white, silent, 1,350 feet. Also known as *Aerial Warfare, Aerial Torpedo, The Battle in the Clouds, The Possibilities of War in the Air, Death in the Air, Romance of the Inventor of the First Aerial Torpedo*.

Algol (1920 German). Black and white, silent.
Director: Hans Werkmeister. *Screenplay*: Hans Brenert. *Sets*: Paul Scheerbart.
Cast: Emil Jennings as Mephisto, John Gottowt, Kathe Haack, Ernst
Hoffman.

Algy Tries Physical Culture (1910 British). Black and white, silent, Gaumont.

Alraune (1918 German). Black and white, silent, Luna-Film.
Based on Hans Heinz Ewers' novel.

Alraune (1918 Hungarian). Black and white, silent, Phoenix.
Directors: Michael Curtiz, Odor Fritz. *Screenplay*: Richard Falk. Based on
Hans Heinz Ewers' novel.

Alraune (1928 German). Black and white, silent, Amafilm/UFA. Also known
as *Daughter of Destiny, Unholy Love*.
Director and screenplay: Henrik Galeen. Based on Hans Heinz Ewers' novel.
Cinematography: Franz Planer. *Art Directors*: Walter Reimann, Max Heilbronner.
Cast: Brigitte Helm as Alraune, Paul Wegener, Ivan Petrovich, Alexander
Sascha.

Alraune (1930 German). Black and white, 87 minutes, UFA/Carlton. Also
known as *Daughter of Evil*.
Director: Richard Oswald. *Screenplay*: Charlie Roellinghoff, R. Welsbach.
Based on Hans Heinz Ewers' novel. *Cinematography*: Gunther Kramph. *Art Directors*: Otto Erdmann, Hans Sohnle. *Music*: Bronislaw Kaper.
Cast: Brigitte Helm as Alraune, Albert Basserman, Agnes Straub, Kathe
Haack.

Alraune and the Golem (1919 German). Black and white, silent, Riesenbio-
skopfilm.
Cinematography: Guido Seeber. *Art Director*: Nils Chrisander.

Der Anderer (*The Other*) (1913 German). Black and white, silent, Vitaskop.
Director: Max Mack. Based on Paul Lindau's play.
Cast: Albert Basserman, Emmerich Hanus, Relly Ridon, Hanni Weisse, Leon
Rosemann, Otto Collot, C. Lengling, Paul Passarge.

Der Anderer (1930 German). Black and white, 92 minutes, Terra/Tobis Foren-
films. Also known as *The Man Within, Dr. Hallers*.
Directors: Max Glass, Robert Wiene. *Screenplay*: Johannes Brandt. Based on
Paul Lindau's play. *Cinematography*: Nikolaus Farkas.
Cast: Fritz Kortner, Kathe von Nagy, Heinrich George, Hermine Sterler,
Ursula von Dieman, Eduard von Winterstein.

Angel on the Amazon (1948). Black and white, 86 minutes, Republic.
Director and associate producer: John H. Auer. *Screenplay*: Lawrence Kim-
ble. Based on a story by Earl Fenton. *Cinematography*: Reggie Lanning. *Special
Effects*: Howard Lydecker, Theodore Lydecker. *Editor*: Richard L. Van Enger.
Music: Nathan Scott.
Cast: Vera Ralston, George Brent, Brian Aherne, Constance Bennett, Richard
Crane, Walter Reed.

Another Wild Idea (1934). Black and white, two reels, M-G-M. *Directors*: Charley Chase, Edward Dunn. *Producer*: Hal Roach. *Editor*: William Terhune.
Cast: Charley Chase, Betty Mack, Harry Bowen, Tiny Sanford, Frank Austin, Harry Bernard, Carlton Griffin.

The Ape (1940). Black and white, 62 minutes, Monogram. *Director*: William Nigh. *Producer*: Scott R. Dunlap. *Associate Producer*: William T. Lackey. *Screenplay*: Curt Siodmak, Richard Carroll. Based on Adam Hull Shirk's play. *Cinematography*: Harry Neumann. *Art Director*: E.R. Hickson. *Editor*: Russell Schoengarth. *Music*: Edward Kay.
Cast: Boris Karloff as Dr. Adrian, Gertrude W. Hoffman, Henry Hall, Maris Wrixon, Gene O'Donnell.

The Ape Man (1943). Black and white, 64 minutes, Monograms. Also known as *Lock Your Doors*.
Director: William Beaudine. *Producers*: Sam Katzman, Jack Dietz. *Screenplay and associate producer*: Barney Sarecky. Based on Karl Brown's story "They Creep in the Dark". *Cinematography*: Mack Stengler. *Art Director*: David Milton. *Editor*: Carl Pierson.
Cast: Bela Lugosi, Louise Currie, Wallace Ford, Henry Hall, Minerva Urecal, Jack Mulhall, Wheeler Oakman, Ralph Littlefield, J. Farrell MacDonald.

An Apish Trick (1909 French). Black and white, silent, short, Pathé.

The Arc (1919 German). Black and white, silent, short. *Director*: Richard Oswald. Based on Werner Scheff's novel. *Cinematography*: Karl Freund.
Cast: Eugen Klöpfer.

Arrest Bulldog Drummond (1938). Black and white, 60 minutes, Paramount. *Director*: James Hogan. *Executive Producer*: William LeBaron. *Associate Producer*: Stuart Walker. *Screenplay*: Stuart Palmer. Based on H.C. "Sapper" McNeile's novel *The Final Count*. *Cinematography*: Ted Tedzlaff. *Art Directors*: Hans Dreier, Franz Bachelin. *Editor*: Stuart Gilmore.
Cast: John Howard, Heather Angel, H.B. Warner, Reginald Denny, E.E. Clive, George Zucco.

The Astronomer's Dream (1898 French). Hand-colored, silent, short, Pathécolor. Also known as *The Man in the Moon*.
Director: Georges Méliès.

At the Edge of the World (1927 German). Black and white, silent, 90 minutes, UFA.
Director: Karl Grune. *Cinematography*: F.A. Wegner. *Art Directors*: A.D. Neppach, Albert Steinruck.
Cast: Brigitte Helm, Max Schreck, Wilhelm Dieterle, Imre Raday, Viktor Janson, Camilla von Hellay, Erwin Faber, Jean Bradin.

L'Atlantide (1921 French). Black and white, silent, French version: 8,223 feet. American version: 6,601 feet. Thalman/Metro. Also known as *Lost Atlantis, Missing Husbands*.
Director and Screenplay: Jacques Feyder. Based on Pierre Benoit's novel.

Cinematography: Georges Specht, Victor Morin. *Art Director*: Manuel Orazi. *Cast*: Stacia Napierkovska, Jean Angelo, Georges Melchior, André Roanne, Maria-Louise Iribe, Abel-Kader-Beh-Ali.

L'Atlantide (1932 German). Black and white, 80 minutes, Nero/International Road Shows. Also known as *The Mistress of Atlantis*. *Director*: G.W. Pabst. *Producer*: Seymour Nebenzel. Based on Pierre Benoit's novel. *Cinematography*: Eugene Shuftan. *Music*: Wolfgang Zeller. *Cast*: Brigitte Helm as Antinea, Gustav Diessl, Heinz Klingenberg, Tela Tschai, Vladimir Sokolov, John Stuart, Odette Florelle, Jean Angelo, Pierre Blanchar.

The Atomic Monster see *Man-Made Monster*

Atomic Rocketship see *Flash Gordon*

The Automatic House (1915). Black and white, silent, one reel, United Film Service.

The Automatic Laundry (1908). Black and white, silent, 361 feet, Lubin.

The Automatic Monkey (1909 French). Black and white, silent, 324 feet, Gaumont.

The Automatic Motorist (1911 British). Black and white, silent, 610 feet, Kineto. *Director*: Walter Booth.

The Automatic Servant (1908). Black and white, silent, 367 feet, Urban-Eclipse.

Balaoo the Demon Baboon (1913 French). Black and white, silent, three reels, Éclaire. *Director*: Victorin Jasset. Based on Gaston Leroux's novel. *Cast*: Bataille as Balaoo; Henri Gouget as Dr. Coriolisi; Camille Bardou.

The Baron's African War see *The Secret Service in Darkest Africa*

Batman (1943). Black and white, serial, 15 episodes, 30 reels, Columbia. *Director*: Lambert Hillyer. *Producer*: Rudolph C. Flothow. *Screenplay*: Victor McLeod, Leslie Swabacker, Harry Fraser. Based on comic book characters created by Bob Kane. *Cinematography*: James Brown, Jr. *Cast*: Lewis Wilson as Batman/Bruce Wayne, Douglas Croft as Robin/Dick Grayson, J. Carrol Naish as Dr. Daka, William Austin as Alfred, Shirley Patterson as Linda, Charles C. Wilson as Captain Arnold, Charles Middleton as Ken Colton, Robert Fiske as Foster, Michael Vallon as Preston, Gus Glassmire as Martin Warren.

Batman and Robin (1949). Black and white, serial, 15 episodes, 31 reels, Columbia. Also known as *The Return of Batman, New Adventures of Batman and Robin*. *Director*: Spencer G. Bennett. *Producer*: Sam Katzman. *Screenplay*: George H. Plympton, Joseph Poland, Royal K. Cole. Based on comic book characters created by Bob Kane. *Cinematography*: Ira H. Morgan. *Music*: Mischa Bakaleinikoff.

Cast: Robert Lowery as Batman/Bruce Wayne, John Duncan as Robin/Dick Grayson, Jane Adams as Vicki, Lyle Talbot as Commissioner Gordon, Ralph Graves as Harrison, Don Harvey as Nolan, William Fawcett as Hammil, Leonard Penn as Carter, Rick Vallin as Brown, Michael Whalen as Dunne, Greg McClure as Evans, House Peters, Jr., as Earl, Jim Diehl as Jason, Rusty Wescoatt as Ives.

Battle in the Clouds see ***The Airship Destroyer***

Before I Hang (1940). Black and white, 71 minutes, Columbia.
Director: Nick Grindé. *Producer*: Wallace MacDonald. *Screenplay*: R.D. Andrews. Based on a story by R.D. Andrews, Karl Brown. *Cinematography*: Benjamin Kline. *Art Director*: Lionel Banks. *Editor*: Charles Nelson.
Cast: Boris Karloff as Dr. John Garth, Evelyn Keyes, Bruce Bennett, Pedro de Cordoba, Edward Van Sloan, Don Beddoe, Robert Fiske.

Behind the Door see ***The Man with Nine Lives***

Beyond the Veil see ***The Secret Kingdom***

The Birth of a Robot (1934 British). Color, seven minutes.
Directors: Humphrey Jennings, Len Lye. *Producer*: Charles H. Dand.

Black Dragons (1942). Black and white, 64 minutes, Monogram.
Director: William Nigh. *Producers*: Sam Katzman, Jack Dietz. *Associate Producer*: Barney Sarecky. *Screenplay*: Harvey H. Gates. *Cinematography*: Art Reed. *Art Director*: Dave Milton. *Editor*: Carl Pierson. *Music*: Lange and Porter.
Cast: Bela Lugosi, Joan Barclay, Clayton Moore, George Pembroke, Bob Frazer, Bob Fiske, Kenneth Harlan.

Black Dragons of Manzanar see ***G-Men versus the Black Dragon***

Black Friday (1940). Black and white, 70 minutes, Universal.
Director: Arthur Lubin. *Associate Producer*: Burt Kelly. *Screenplay*: Curt Siodmak, Eric Taylor. *Cinematography*: Elwood Bredell. *Art Director*: Jack Otterson. *Editor*: Philip Cahn.
Cast: Boris Karloff as Dr. Ernest Sovac, Stanley Ridges as Professor George Kingsley, Anne Nagel as Sonny Rogers, Bela Lugosi as Eric Marney, Anne Gwynne as Jean Savoc, Virginia Brissac as Margaret, Paul Fix, Jack Mulhall, James Craig.

The Black Widow (1947). Black and white, serial, 13 episodes, Republic. Also known as *Sombra, the Spider Woman*.
Directors: Spencer G. Bennett, Fred C. Brannon.
Cast: Bruce Edwards as Steve Colt, Virginia Lindley as Joyce Winters, Carol Forman as Sombra, Anthony Warde as Ward, Virginia Carroll as Ruth Dayton, I. Stanford Jolley as Jaffa, Theodore Gottlieb as King Hitomu, Ramsay Ames as Dr. Curry, Gene Stutenroth as Walker, Sam Flint as Harry Weston, Tom Steele as Bard, Dale Van Sickel as Bill, LeRoy Mason as Dr. Godfrey, Forrest Taylor as Bradley, Ernie Adams as Blinky, Keith Richards as Burns.

Blake of Scotland Yard (1927). Black and white, silent, serial, 12 episodes, Universal.
Director: Robert F. Hill. *Scenario*: William Lord Wright. Based on a story by Robert F. Hill.

Cast: Hayden Stevenson as Angus Blake, Gloria Gray as Lady Diana Blanton, Grace Cunard as the Woman in White.

Blake of Scotland Yard (1936 British). Black and white, serial, 15 episodes, Victory.
Director: Bob Hill. *Producer*: Sam Katzman.
Cast: Ralph Byrd as Jerry Sheehan, Joan Barclay as Hope Mason, Dickie Jones as Bobby, Herbert Rawlinson as Sir James Blake, Lloyd Hughes, Nick Stuart.

A Blind Bargain (1922). Black and white, silent, Goldwyn.
Director: Wallace Worsley. *Producer*: Samuel Goldwyn. *Scenario*: J.G. Hawks. Based on Barry Pain's novel *The Octave of Claudius*. *Cinematography*: Norbert Brodine.
Cast: Lon Chaney, Raymond McKee, Jacqueline Logan, Virginia True Boardman, Fontaine LaRue.

Blonde Gorilla see *White Pongo*

The Blue Light (1932 German/Italian). Black and white, 90 minutes, Sokal/DuWorld.
Director: Leni Riefenstahl. *Screenplay*: Leni Riefenstahl, Bela Balazs, Hans Schneeberger. *Cinematography*: Hans Schneeberger.
Cast: Leni Reifenstahl, Mathias Wieman.

The Brain Snatcher see *The Man Who Lived Again*

Brick Bradford (1947). Black and white, serial, 15 episodes, Columbia.
Directors: Spencer G. Bennett, Thomas Carr. *Producer*: Sam Katzman. *Screenplay*: George H. Plympton, Arthur Hoerl, Lewis Clay.
Cast: Kane Richmond as Brick Bradford, Pierre Watkin as Professor Salisbury, Rick Valin as Sandy Sanderson, Linda Johnson as June Saunders, John Merton as Dr. Tymak, Charles Quigley as Laydron, Jack Ingram as Albers, Fred Graham as Black, Leonard Penn as Byrus, Wheeler Oakman as Walther, Carol Forman as Queen Khana, Charles King as Creed, John Hart as Dent, Helene Stanley as Carol Preston, Nelson Leigh as Prescott, Robert Barron as Zuntar, George de Normand as Meaker.

The Bride of Frankenstein (1935). Black and white, 75 minutes, Universal.
Director: James Whale. *Producer*: Carl Laemmle, Jr. *Screenplay*: John L. Balderston. Based on characters created by Mary Shelley. *Cinematography*: John Mescall. *Special Effects*: John Fulton. *Music*: Franz Waxman.
Cast: Boris Karloff as the Monster, Colin Clive as Dr. Henry Frankenstein, Ernest Thesiger as Dr. Praetorius, Valerie Hobson as Elizabeth, Elsa Lanchester as Mary Shelley/The Bride, Una O'Connor as Minnie, O.P. Heggie as the Blind Hermit, Dwight Frye as Karl, Lucien Prival as the butler, John Carradine as the lost hunter, Anne Darling as the shepherdess, E.E. Clive, Walter Brennan, Douglas Walton, Gavin Gordon, Neil Fitzgerald, Reginald Barlow, Mary Gordon, Tempe Piggott, Ted Billings, Grace Cunard, Rollo Lloyd, Harry Northrup, Joseph North, D'Arcy Corrigan, Jack Curtis, Helen Gibson, Frank Terry.

Buck Rogers (1939). Black and white, serial, 12 episodes, 384 minutes, Crystal (Universal). Also known in feature form as *Planet Outlaws* (1953) and *Destination Saturn* (1965).
Directors: Ford Beebe, Saul A. Goodkind. *Associate Producer*: Barney

Sarecky. *Screenplay*: Norman S. Hall, Ray Trampe. Based on characters created by Philip Nowlan, Dick Calkins. *Cinematography*: Jerome Ash. *Editors*: Alvin Todd, Louis Sackin.

Cast: Larry "Buster" Crabbe as Colonel Anthony "Buck" Rogers, Jackie Moran as George "Buddy" Wade, C. Montague Shaw as Dr. Huer, Constance Moore as Lieutenant Wilma Deering, Anthony Warde as Killer Kane, Henry Brandon as Lasca, Jack Mulhall as Captain Rankin, Guy Usher as Aldar, William Gould as Marshall Kragg, Philson Ahn as Prince Tallen, Wheeler Oakman as Pattin, Kenneth Duncan as Lieutenant Lacy, Carleton Young as Scott, Reed Howes as Roberts.

By Radium Rays (1914). Black and white, silent, two reels, Gold Seal.

The Cabinet of Dr. Caligari (1919 German). Black and white. 69 minutes, UFA.

Director: Robert Wiene. *Producer*: Erich Pommer. *Scenario*: Karl Mayer, Hans Janowitz. Based on a story on Hans Janowitz. *Cinematography*: Willy Hameister. *Art Directors*: Walter Riemann, Walter Röhrig, Herman Warm.

Cast: Werner Krauss as Dr. Caligari, Conrad Veidt as Césare, Lil Dagover, Rudolf Lettinger, Friedrich Feher, Rudolf Klein-Rogge, Hans Heinz von Twardowsky.

Captain America (1943). Black and white, serial, 15 episodes, 31 reels, Republic. Also known as *Return of Captain America*.

Directors: John English, Elmer Clifton. *Screenplay*: Royal Cole, Ronald Davidson, Basil Dickey, Jesse Duffy, Harry Fraser, Grant Nelson, Joseph Poland. *Cinematography*: John MacBurnie. *Special Effects*: Howard Lydecker, Theodore Lydecker.

Cast: Dick Purcell as Grant Gardner/Captain America, Lorna Gray as Gail Richards, Lionel Atwill as Dr. Maldor/the Scarab, Charles Trowbridge as Commissioner Dryden, Russell Hicks as Major Randolph, George J. Lewis as Matson, John Davidson as Gruber, Norman Nesbitt as newscaster, Frank Reicher as Professor Lyman, Hugh Sothern as Professor Dodge, Tom Chatterton as Henley, Robert Frazer as Dr. Clinton Lyman, John Hamilton as Hillman, Crane Whitley as Dirk, Edward Keane as Dr. Baracs, John Bagni as Monk, Jay Novello as Simms.

Captain Mephisto and the Transformation Machine see *Manhunt of Mystery Island*

Captive Wild Woman (1943). Black and white, 61 minutes, Universal.

Director: Edward Dmytryk. *Associate Producer*: Ben Pivar. *Screenplay*: Henry Sucher, Griffin Jay. Based on a story by Ted Fithian, Neil P. Varnick, Maurice Pivar. *Cinematography*: George Robinson. *Art Director*: John B. Goodman. *Editor*: Milton Carruth. *Make-up*: Jack Pierce. *Music*: Hans J. Salter.

Cast: Acquanetta as Paula Dupree, John Carradine as Dr. Sigmund Walters, Evelyn Ankers, Milburn Stone, Martha MacVicar (Vickers), Lloyd Corrigan, Paul Fix.

The Case of the Missing Brides see *The Corpse Vanishes*

Chandu the Magician (1932). Black and white, 70 minutes, 20th Century–Fox.

Directors: William Cameron Menzies, Marcel Varnel. *Screenplay*: Barry Conners, Philip Klein. Based on radio series by Harry A. Earnshaw, Vera M. Oldham, R.R. Morgan. *Cinematography*: James Wong Howe. *Editor*: Harold Schuster.

Cast: Edmund Lowe as Chandu; Bela Lugosi, Irene Ware, Henry B. Walthall, Herbert Mundin.

The Challenge of King Kong see *White Pongo*

The Chemist (1936). Black and white, 21 minutes, 20th Century-Fox. *Producer*: Al Christie. Based on a story by David Freedman. *Cinematography*: George Webber.
Cast: Buster Keaton, Marilyn Stuart, Earl Gilbert.

The City of Lost Men see *The Lost City*

Code of the Air (1928). Black and white, silent, 5,700 feet, Bischoff. *Director*: James P. Hogan. *Screenplay*: Barry Barenger. *Cinematography*: William Miller.
Cast: William V. Mong, Arthur Rankin, Mae Cooper, Ken Harlan, June Marlow.

The Comet's Comeback (1916). Black and white, silent, short, Mutual.
Cast: John Steppling, Carol Halloway, Dick Rosson, John Sheehan.

Congo Pongo see *White Pongo*

Conquest of the Air (1901 French). Black and white, silent, short, Pathé. *Director*: Ferdinand Zecca.

Conquest of the Air (1906 French). Black and white, silent, short, Pathé. *Director*: Gaston Vellé.

The Conquest of the Pole (1912 French). Black and white, silent, 650 feet, Star.
Director: Georges Méliès.
Cast: Georges Méliès as Mabuloff.

The Corpse Vanished see *Revenge of the Zombies*

The Corpse Vanishes (1942). Black and white, 64 minutes, Monogram. Also known as *The Case of the Missing Brides*.
Director: Wallace Fox. *Producers*: Sam Katzman, Jack Dietz. *Associate Producer*: Barney Sarecky. *Screenplay*: Harvey Gates. Based on a story by Sam Robins, Gerald Schnitzer. *Cinematography*: Art Reed. *Art Director*: David Milton. *Editor*: Robert Golden. *Music*: Lange and Porter.
Cast: Bela Lugosi, Luana Walters, Tristram Coffin, Minerva Urecal, Vince Barnett, Elizabeth Russell, George Eldredge, Angelo Rositto.

Counterblast (1948 British). Black and white, 100 minutes, British National. *Director*: Paul L. Stein. *Screenplay*: Jack Whittingham. Based on a story by Guy Morgan. *Cinematography*: James Wilson. *Music*: Hans May.
Cast: Mervyn Johns as Dr. Karl Brucker; Nova Pilbeam, Robert Beatty, Karel Stepanek, Margaretta Scott.

The Crazy Ray (1923 French). Black and white, silent, 61 minutes. Also known as *Paris Qui Dort, Paris Asleep*.

Director, Screenplay, and Editor: René Clair. *Cinematography*: Maurice Defassjaux, Paul Guichard.
Cast: Henri Rollan, Albert Préjéan, Charles Martinelli.

The Creeper (1948). Black and white, 64 minutes, Reliance/20th Century–Fox.
Director: Jean Yarbrough. *Producers*: Bernard Small, Ben Pivar. *Screenplay*: Maurice Tombragel. Based on a story by Don Martin. *Cinematography*: George Robinson. *Editor*: Saul A. Goodkind. *Make-up*: Ted Larson. *Music*: Milton Rosen.
Cast: Onslow Stevens, Eduardo Ciannelli, June Vincent, Ralph Morgan, Janis Wilson.

The Crimson Ghost (1946). Black and white, serial, 12 episodes, Republic. Also known in feature form as *Cyclotrode X*.
Directors: William Witney, Fred C. Brannon.
Cast: Charles Quigley as Duncan Richards, Linda Stirling as Diana Farnsworth, Clayton Moore as Ashe, I. Stanford Jolley as Blackton/the voice of the Crimson Ghost, Kenne Duncan as Professor Chambers, Forrest Taylor as Van Wyck, Emmet Vogan as Anderson, Sam Flint as Maxwell, Joe Forte as Professor Parker, Stanley Price as Fator, Wheaton Chambers as Wilson, Tom Steele as Stricker, Dale Van Sickel as Harte, Rex Lease as Bain, Fred Graham as Zane, Bud Wolfe as Gross, Bud Geary as the Crimson Ghost (no screen credit).

Cyclotrode X see *The Crimson Ghost*

Daughter of Destiny see *Alraune* (1928)

The Daughter of Evil see *Alraune* (1930)

D-Day on Mars see *The Purple Monster Strikes*

The Deadly Ray from Mars see *Flash Gordon's Trip to Mars*

Death in the Air see *The Airship Destroyer*

The Death Ray (1924). Black and white, silent, two reels, Pathé.
Supervisor: H. Grindell Matthews.

The Debilatory Powder (1908 French). Black and white, silent, 434 feet, Pathé.

Destination Saturn see *Buck Rogers*

The Devil Commands (1941). Black and white, 65 minutes, Columbia.
Director: Edward Dmytryk. *Producer*: Wallace MacDonald. *Screenplay*: Robert D. Andrews, Milton Gunzberg. *Cinematography*: Allen G. Sigler. *Special Effects*: Phil Faulkner. *Music*: M.W. Stoloff.
Cast: Boris Karloff as Dr. Julian Blair; Walter Baldwin, Shirley Warde, Amanda Duff, Richard Fiske, Anne Revere, Ralph Penny, Dorothy Adams, Kenneth MacDonald.

The Devil Doll (1936). Black and white, 79 minutes, M-G-M.
Director: Tod Browning. *Producer*: E.J. Mannix. *Screenplay*: Garret Fort, Guy Endore, Erich von Stroheim. Adapted by Tod Browning from Abraham Merritt's novel *Burn, Witch, Burn*. *Cinematography*: Leonard Smith. *Art* Director:

Cedric Gibbons. *Music*: Franz Waxman.
Cast: Lionel Barrymore, Maureen O'Sullivan, Frank Lawton, Robert Grieg, Lucy Beaumont, Henry B. Walthall, Grace Ford, Rafaela Ottiano.

The Devil Monster (1946). Black and white, Weiss.
Cast: Barry Norton, Blanche Mahaffy.

The Devil's Brood see *House of Frankenstein*

The Devil's Castle (1896 French). Black and white, silent, short, Robert-Houdin.
Director: Georges Méliès.

The Diamond Maker (1909). Black and white, silent, 490 feet, Blackton.
Director and Producer: J. Stuart Blackton.

The Diamond Maker (1913). Black and white, silent, two reels, Rex.
Cast: Robert Z. Leonard, Marguerita Fischer.

The Diamond Maker (1914 Italian). Black and white, silent, two reels, Cines.

The Diamond Master (1929). Black and white, silent, serial, ten episodes, 20 reels, Universal.
Director: Jack Nelson. *Screenplay*: George H. Plympton, Carl Krusada. Based on Jacques Futrelle's novel.
Cast: Louise Lorraine, Hayden Stevenson, Louis Stern.

The Diamond Queen (1921). Black and white, silent, serial, 18 episodes, 36 reels, Universal.
Director: Edward Kull. *Screenplay*: George W. Pyper, Robert F. Roden. Based on Jacque Futrelle's novel *The Diamond Master*.
Cast: Eileen Sedgewick, Al Smith, Lon Short, Frank Clarke.

Dick Barton — Special Agent (1948 British). Black and white, 70 minutes, Hammer.
Director: Alfred Goulding. *Screenplay*: Alan Stranks, Alfred Goudling. Based on a BBC radio serial. *Cinematography*: Stanley Clinton.
Cast: Don Stannard as Dick Barton, George Ford as Dr. Casper, Jack Shaw, Gillian Maude.

Dick Barton Strikes Back (1949 British). Black and white, 73 minutes, Exclusive.
Director: Godfrey Grayson. *Screenplay*: Ambrose Grayson. Based on a BBC radio serial. *Cinematography*: Cedric Williams.
Cast: Don Stannard as Dick Barton, James Raglan, Sebastian Cabot.

Dick Tracy (1937). Black and white, serial, 15 episodes, 31 reels, Republic.
Directors: Ray Taylor, Alan James. Based on a story by Morgan Cox and George Morgan from comic strip characters created by Chester Gould. *Cinematography*: William Nobles, Edgar Lyons.
Cast: Ralph Byrd as Dick Tracy, John Piccori as Dr. Moloch, Richard Beach as Gordon Tracy (before), Carleton Young as Gordon Tracy (after), Kay Hughes as Gwen, Smiley Burnette as Mike McGurk, Lee Van Atta as Junior, Francis X.

Bushman as Anderson, Fred Hamilton as Steve, John Dilson as Brewster, Wedge-wood Nowell as Clayton, Theodore Lorch as Paterno, Edwin Stanley as Odette, Harrison Greene as Claggerstein, Herbert Webber as Martino, Buddy Roosevelt as Burke, George de Normand as Flynn, Bryon K. Foulger as Korvitch.

Dick Tracy Meets Gruesome (1948). Black and white, 65 minutes, RKO. *Director*: John Rawlins. *Producer*: Herman Scholm. *Screenplay*: Robinson White, Eric Taylor. Based on comic strip characters created by Chester Gould. *Cinematography*: Frank Redman. *Special Effects*: Russel Cully. *Music*: Paul Sawtell.
     Cast: Ralph Byrd as Dick Tracy, Boris Karloff as Gruesome, Anne Gwynne, June Clayworth.

Dick Tracy versus Crime, Inc. (1941). Black and white, serial, 15 episodes, 31 reels, Republic. Also known as *Dick Tracy versus the Phantom Empire*. *Directors*: William Witney, John English. *Screenplay*: Ronald Davidson, Norman S. Hall, William Lively, Joseph O'Donnell, Joseph Poland. Based on comic strip characters created by Chester Gould. *Cinematography*: Reggie Lanning. *Music*: Cy Feuer.
     Cast: Ralph Byrd as Dick Tracy, John Davidson as Lucifer, Ralph Morgan as Morton, Michael Owen as Billy Carr, Jan Wiley as June Chandler.

Dick Tracy versus the Phantom Empire see *Dick Tracy versus Crime, Inc.*

Dick Tracy's G-Men (1939). Black and white, serial, 15 episodes, 31 reels, Republic.
     Directors: William Witney, John English. *Screenplay*: Barry Shipman, Franklin Adreon, Rex Taylor, Ronald Davidson, Sol Shor. Based on comic strip characters created by Chester Gould. *Cinematography*: William Nobles.
     Cast: Ralph Byrd as Dick Tracy, Irving Pichel as Zarnoff, Ted Pearson as Steve, Phyllis Isley (Jennifer Jones) as Owen, Walter Miller as Robal, George Douglas as Sandoval, Kenneth Harlan as Anderson, Robert Carson as Scott, Julian Madison as Foster, Ted Mapes as first G-man, William Stahl as second G-man, Robert Wayne as third G-man, Joe McGuinn as Tommy, Kenneth Terrell as Ed, Harry Humphrey as Warden Stover, Harrison Greene as Baron.

The Dinosaur and the Missing Link (1917). Black and white, silent, five minutes, Manikin (Edison). *Director*: Willis H. O'Brien.

Dr. Brompton-Watt's Adjuster (1912), Black and white, silent, 325 feet, Edison.

Dr. Cyclops (1939). Color, 75 minutes, Paramount. *Director*: Ernest B. Schoedsack. *Producer*: Dale Van Every. *Screenplay*: Tom Kilpatrick. *Cinematography*: Henry Sharp, Winton Hock. *Special Effects*: Farciot Edouart. *Mechanical Special Effects*: Wallace Kelly. *Art Directors*: Hans Dreyer, Earl Hedrick.
     Cast: Albert Dekker as Dr. Thorkel, Charles Halton as Dr. Bulfinch, Janice Logan as Dr. Mary Mitchell, Thomas Coley as Bill Stockton, Frank Yaconelli as Pedro, Victor Kilian as Steve Baker.

Dr. Hallers see *Der Anderer* (1930).

Dr. Jekyll and Mr. Hyde (1908). Black and white, silent, 1035 feet, Selig Poly-scope. Also known as *The Modern Dr. Jekyll*.
Based on Luella Forepaugh's play and Robert Louis Stevenson's novel.

Dr. Jekyll and Mr. Hyde (Den Skaebnesvangre Opfindelse) (1910 Danish). Black and white, short, Nordisk (Great Northern).
Director and Screenplay: August Blom. Based on Robert Louis Stevenson's novel (as are all following versions). *Producer*: Ole Olsen.

Dr. Jekyll and Mr. Hyde (1912). Black and white, silent, one reel, Thanhouser. *Director*: Lucius Henderson.
Cast: James Cruze as Dr. Jekyll/Mr. Hyde, Marguerite Snow, Harry Benham.

Dr. Jekyll and Mr. Hyde (1913 British). Two-color, silent, two reels, Kineto-Kinemacolor.

Dr. Jekyll and Mr. Hyde (1913). Black and white, silent, two reels, Universal. *Director*: King Baggott. *Producer*: Carl Laemmle.
Cast: King Baggot as Dr. Jekyll/Mr. Hyde, Jane Gail, Matt Snyder, Howard Crampton, William Sarell.

Dr. Jekyll and Mr. Hyde (1914). Black and white, silent, short, Starlight.

Dr. Jekyll and Mr. Hyde (1920). Black and white, silent, 63 minutes, Para-mount.
Director: John S. Robertson. *Producer*: Adolph Zukor. *Screenplay*: Clara S. Berenger. *Cinematography*: Roy Overbough.
Cast: John Barrymore as Dr. Jekyll/Mr. Hyde, Martha Mansfield as Millicent, Brandon Hurst as Sir George Carewe, Nita Naldi as the dancer, Charles Lane, Louis Wolheim.

Dr. Jekyll and Mr. Hyde (1920). Black and white, silent, Arrow Film Corp.
Cast: Hank Mann as Dr. Jekyll/Mr. Hyde.

Dr. Jekyll and Mr. Hyde (1920). Black and white, silent, Pioneer.
Producer: Louis B. Meyer.
Cast: Shelton Lewis as Dr. Jekyll/Mr. Hyde; Gladys Field, Alexander Shan-non, Dora Mills Adams, Leslie Austin.

Dr. Jekyll and Mr. Hyde (1932). Black and white, 98 minutes, Paramount.
Director and Producer: Rouben Mamoulian. *Screenplay*: Samuel Hoffenstein, Percy Heath. *Cinematography*: Karl Struss. *Make-up*: Wally Westmore.
Cast: Fredric March as Dr. Jekyll/Mr. Hyde, Holmes Herbert as Dr. Lanyon, Rose Hobart as Muriel Carew, Miriam Hopkins as Ivy Pierson, Halliwell Hobbes as General Carewe; Arnold Lucy, Tempe Piggott, Edgar Norton.

Dr. Jekyll and Mr. Hyde (1941). Black and white, 127 minutes, M-G-M.
Director and Producer: Victor Fleming. *Screenplay*: John Lee Mahin. *Cin-ematography*: Joseph Ruttenberg. *Special Effects*: Warren Newcombe. *Make-up*: Jack Dawn. *Music*: Franz Waxman.
Cast: Spencer Tracy as Dr. Jekyll/Mr. Hyde, Ingrid Bergman as Ivy, Lana Turner as Millicent, Donald Crisp, Barton MacLane, C. Aubrey Smith, Sara Allgood, Ian Hunter, Billy Bevan.

Dr. Mabuse (1922 German). Black and white, silent, two parts, 20 reels, Decla-Bioscop/UFA.
Director: Fritz Lang. *Scenario*: Thea von Harbou. Based on a story by Norbert Jacques. *Cinematography*: Carl Hoffman. *Art Directors*: Otto Hunt, Stahl-Urach.
Cast: Rudolph Klein-Rogge as Dr. Mabuse, Paul Richter as Hull, Bernard Goetzhe, Aud Egede Nissen, Alfred Abel, Gertrude Welcker.

Dr. Maniac see *The Man Who Lived Again*

Dr. Renault's Secret (1942). Black and white, 58 minutes, 20th Century-Fox.
Director: Harry Lachman. *Producer*: Sol M. Wurtzel. *Screenplay*: William Bruckner, Robert F. Metzler. Based on Gaston LeRoux's novel *Balaoo*. *Cinematography*: Virgil Miller. *Music*: David Raskin, Emil Newman.
Cast: J. Carrol Naish as Balaoo, George Zucco as Dr. Renault, Mike Mazurki, Lynne Roberts, Jack Norton, John Shepperd (Shepherd Strudwick), Bert Roach, Eugene Borden.

Doctor Satan's Robot see *Mysterious Dr. Satan*

Doctor X (1932). Black and white, 80 minutes, First National/Warner Brothers.
Director: Michael Curtiz. *Screenplay*: Earl Baldwin, Robert Tasker. Based on a play by Howard Comstock, Allen C. Miller. *Cinematography*: Ray Rennahan, Richard Tower. *Art Director*: Anton Grot. *Editor*: George Amy.
Cast: Lionel Atwil as Dr. Xavier, Fay Wray, Lee Tracy, Preston Foster, Robert Warwick, Mae Busch, George Rosener, Leila Bennett, Arthur Edmund Carewe, John Wray, Tom Dugan, Harry Beresford, Willard Robertson, Thomas Jackson, Harry Holman, Selmer Jackson.

The Doctor's Experiment; or, Reversing Darwin's Theory (1908 British). Black and white, silent, short, Gaumont.

The Duality of Man (1910 British). Black and white, silent, short, Wrench.
Based on Robert Louis Stevenson's novel *The Strange Case of Dr. Jekyll and Mr. Hyde*.

The Eagle of the Night (1928). Black and white, silent, serial, 10 episodes, 20 reels, Pathé.
Director: Jimmie Fulton.
Cast: Franke Clarke, Shirley Palmer, Earle Metcalf, Rag Wilson, Joseph Swickard, Max Hawley, Jack Richardson, Maurice Costello.

The Effects of a Rocket (1911). Black and white, silent, short, 420 feet.

The Electric Girl (1914). Black and white, silent, one reel, Éclair.

The Electric Man see *Man-Made Monster*

The Electric Policeman (1909 French). Black and white, silent, 352 feet, Gaumont.

The Electric Villa (1911 French). Black and white, silent 420 feet, Pathé.

End of Adventure see *The Girl from Scotland Yard*

The End of the World (1916 Danish). Black and white, silent, six reels, Nordisk. *Director*: August Blom. *Screenplay*: Otto Rung. *Cinematography*: John Ankerstjerne.

The End of the World (1930 French). Black and white, French version: 105 minutes. U.S. version: 54 minutes. L'Écran d'Art/Auten. *Director and Screenplay* (French version): Abel Gance. *Director* (U.S. version): V. Ivanoff. *Screenplay* (U.S. version): H.S. Kraft. Based on Camille Flammarion's novel. *Cinematography*: Jules Kruger, Nicolas Rudakov, Roger Hubert. *Art Directors*: Lazare Meerson, Jean Perrier. *Music* (French version): Ondes Martenot, Michel Michelet. *Music* (U.S. Version): M. Levine, R. Siohan, W. Zederbaum.

Cast: Abel Gance, Colette Darfeuil, Sylvia Grenade, Samson Fainsilber, Georges Colin.

The Exploits of Elaine (1915). Black and white, silent, serial, 14 episodes, 28 reels, Star/Pathé. *Directors*: L.J. Gasnier, George B. Seitz. *Producers*: Theodore W. Wharton, Leopold V. Wharton. *Scenario*: Arthur B. Reeve, Charles W. Goddard. Based on a story by Arthur B. Reeve and Basil Dickey.

Cast: Pearl White as Elaine, Shelton Lewis as the Clutching Hand, Arnold Daly, Creighton Hale, William Riley Hatch.

Face of Marble (1946). Black and white, 70 minutes, Monogram. *Director*: William Beaudine. *Producer*: Jeffrey Bernard. *Screenplay*: Michael Jacoby. Based on a story by William Thiele, Edmund Hartmann. *Cinematography*: Harry Neumann. *Special Effects*: Robert Clarke. *Art Director*: David Milton. *Editor*: William Austin. *Music*: Edward Kay.

Cast: John Carradine, Claudia Drake, Robert Shayne, Maris Wrixon, Thomas E. Jackson, Willie Best.

The Feathered Serpent (1948). Black and white, 61 minutes, Monogram. *Director*: William Beaudine.

Cast: Roland Winters as Charlie Chan, Keye Luke as Number One Son, Victor Sen Yung as Number Two Son, Mantan Moreland, Carol Forman, Robert Livingston, Nils Asther, Beverly Jons, Leslie Denison, George Lewis, Martin Garralaga, Erville Alderson, Charles Stevens, Milton Ross, Fred Cordova, Jay Silverheels.

The Fifth Man (1914). Black and white, silent, three reels, Selig. *Director*: F.J. Grandon. *Screenplay*: James Oliver Curwood. *Cast*: Charles Clary, Bessie Eyton, Roy Watson.

The Fighting Marines (1935). Black and white, serial, 12 episodes, 25 reels, Mascot. *Directors*: B. Reeves "Breezy" Eason, Joseph Kane. *Producer*: Barney Sarecky. *Screenplay*: Barney Sarecky, Sherman L. Lowe.

Cast: Grant Withers as Corporal Lawrence, Adrian Morris as Sergeant McGowan, Ann Rutherford as Frances Schiller, Robert Warwick as Colonel Bennet.

Fire of Life (1912 Danish). Black and white, silent, two reels, Nordisk (Great Northern).

Director: Schedler Sorenson. *Scenario*: Xenius Rostock.
Cast: Valdemar Psitander, Julie Henriksen, Else Fröhlich, Frederick Skondrup, Elith Pio, Alfred Boeson.

First Men in the Moon (1919 British). Black and white, silent, feature, Gaumont.
Director: J.V. Leigh.
Cast: Bruce Gordon, Hector Abbas, Heather Thatcher, Lionel D'Arragan, Cecil Morton York.

The Flaming Disk (1920). Black and white, silent, serial, 18 episodes, 36 reels, Universal.
Director: Robert F. Hill. Based on a story by Arthur Henry Gooden, Jerry Ash.
Cast: Elmo Lincoln, Monty Montague, Louise Lorraine, Lee Kohlmar, Roy Watson, George Williams, Jenks Harris.

Flash Gordon (1936). Black and white, serial, 13 episodes, 416 minutes, Universal. Also known as *Space Soldiers, Atomic Rocketship, Spaceship to the Unknown*.
Director: Frederick Stephani. *Screenplay*: Frederick Stephani, George H. Plympton, Basil Dickey, Lee O'Neill. Based on comic strip characters created by Alex Raymond. *Special Effects*: John P. Fulton.
Cast: Larry "Buster" Crabbe as Flash Gordon, Jean Rogers as Dale Arden, Charles Middleton as Emperor Ming, Priscilla Lawson as Princess Aura, John Lipson as King Vultan, Richard Alexander as Prince Barin, Frank Shannon as Dr. Hans Zarkov, Duke York, Jr., as King Kala, Earl Askam as Officer Torch, Theodore Lorch as High Priest, James Pierce as King Thun, Muriel Goodspeed as Zona, Richard Tucker as Gordon, Sr.

Flash Gordon Conquers the Universe (1940). Black and white, serial, 12 episodes, 384 minutes, Universal. Also known as *Peril from the Planet Mongo, Space Soldiers Conquer the Universe, The Purple Death from Outer Space*.
Directors: Ford Beebe, Ray Taylor. *Screenplay*: George H. Plympton, Basil Dickey, Barry Shipman. Based on comic strip characters created by Alex Raymond.
Cast: Larry "Buster" Crabbe as Flash Gordon, Charles Middleton as Emperor Ming, Frank Shannon as Dr. Hans Zarkov, Carol Hughes as Dale Arden, Anne Gwynne as Sonja, Roland Drew as Prince Barin, Shirley Deane as Princess Aura, Victor Zimmerman as Thong, Don Rowan as Torch, Michael Mark as Karm, Sigmund Nilssen as Korro, Lee Powell as Roka, Edgar Edwards as Turan, Ben Taggart as Lupi, Harry C. Bradley as Keedish.

Flash Gordon's Trip to Mars (1939). Black and white, serial, 15 episodes, 480 minutes, Universal. Also known as *Space Soldiers' Trip to Mars*.
Directors: Ford Beebe, Robert F. Hill. *Screenplay*: Ray Trampe, Norman S. Hall, Wyndham Gittens, Herbert Dolmas. Based on comic strip characters created by Alex Raymond.
Cast: Larry "Buster" Crabbe as Flash Gordon, Jean Rogers as Dale Arden, Charles Middleton as Emperor Ming, Frank Shannon as Dr. Hans Zarkov, Beatrice Roberts as Queen Azura, Richard Alexander as Prince Barin, C. Montague Shaw as Clayface, Donald Kerr as Happy Hapgood, Wheeler Oakman as Tarnak.

The Flying Serpent (1946). Black and white, 59 minutes, Producer's Releasing Corporation.
Director: Sherman Scott (Sam Newfield). *Producer*: Sigmund Neufeld. *Screenplay*: John T. Neville. *Cinematography*: Jack Greenhalgh. *Art Director*: Edward C. Jewell. *Editor*: Holbrook N. Todd. *Make-up*: Bud Westmore. *Music*: Leo Erdody.
Cast: George Zucco, Ralph Lewis, Hope Kramer (Crane), Eddie Acuff, Milton Kibbee, Wheaton Chambers, James Metcalf, Henry Hall.

Fourteen Million Leagues from the Earth see *Sky Ship*

F.P. 1 Does Not Answer (1932 German). Black and white, 90 minutes, UFA/Fox/Gaumont.
Director: Earl Hartl. *Producer*: Erich Pommer. *Screenplay*: Walter Reisch, Curt Siodmak. *English Dialogue*: Robert Stevenson, Peter MacFarland. *Cinematography*: Günther Rittau, Konstantin Tschet.
Cast (English version): Leslie Fenton as Captain Droste, Conrad Veidt as Major Ellissen, Jill Esmond as Claire Lennartz, George Merritt as Lubin, Donald Calthrop as photographer, Nicholas Hannen, Warwick Ward, William Freshman, Dr. Philip Manning.
Cast (German version): Hans Albers, Sybille Schmitz, Paul Hartmann, Peter Lorre, Rudolph Platte, Hermann Speelmans.
Cast (French version): Charles Boyer, Jean Murat, Pierre Brasseur, Danielle Parola, Marcel Vallée, Ernest Ferny.

Frankenstein (1910). Black and white, silent, 975 feet, Edison.
Director: J. Searle Dawley. Based on Mary Shelley's novel.
Cast: Charles Ogle as the monster.

Frankenstein (1931). Black and white, 71 minutes, Universal.
Director: James Whale. *Producer*: Carl Laemmle, Jr. *Screenplay*: Robert Florey, Garret Fort, Francis Edwards Faragoh. *Adaptation*: Robert Florey, John L. Balderston (from Peggy Webling's play). Based on Mary Shelley's novel. *Cinematography*: Arthur Edeson. *Special Effects*: John P. Fulton. *Special Electrical Effects*: Ken Strickfaden. *Art Director*: Charles D. Hall. *Sets*: Herman Rosse. *Make-up*: Jack Pierce.
Cast: Colin Clive as Dr. Henry Frenkenstein, Mae Clarke as Elizabeth, John Boles as Victor Morris, Boris Karloff as the monster, Edward Van Sloan as Dr. Waldman, Dwight Frye as Fritz, Frederick Kerr as Baron Frankenstein, Lionel Belmore as Vogel the Burgomaster, Forrester Harvey as Hans Kramer, Marilyn Harris as Maria Kramer.

Frankenstein Meets the Wolf Man. Black and white, 72 minutes, Universal.
Director: Roy William Neill. *Producer*: George Waggner. *Screenplay*: Curt Siodmak. *Cinematography*: George Robinson. *Special Effects*: John P. Fulton. *Editor*: Edward Curtis. *Make-up*: Jack Pierce. *Music*: Hans Salter.
Cast: Lon Chaney, Jr., as Lawrence Talbot/the wolf man; Bela Lugosi as the Frankenstein monster, Patric Knowles as Dr. Frank Mannering; Maria Ouspenskaya as Maleva; Ilona Massey as Baroness Frankenstein, Lionel Atwill as the Major, Dwight Frye as Rudd, Dennis Hoey, Eddie Parker.

Die Frau im Mond see *Woman in the Moon*

From Death to Life (1911). Black and white, silent, short, Rex.

From Mars to Munich (1925). Black and white, silent, one reel, 20th Century–Fox.

The Gap (1937 British). Black and white, 38 minutes, Instructional Films. *Director*: Donald Carter. *Cast*: Patric Curwen, Carleton Hobbs, G.H. Mulcaster, Jack Vyvyan, Charles Danville, Norman Wooland, Foster Carlin.

The Germ of Mystery (1916). Black and white silent, three reels, Selig. *Director*: William Robert Daly. *Scenario*: L.V. Jefferson. *Cast*: Guy Oliver, Fritzi Burnette, Lillian Hayward.

Germanic Love (1916). Black and white, silent, one reel, Vogue/Mutual. *Director*: Rube Miller. *Scenario*: Thomas Delmar. *Cast*: Arthur Tavares, Henry Kernan, Madge Kirby, Alice Neice.

The Ghost of Frankenstein (1942). Black and white, 68 minutes, Universal. *Director*: Erle C. Kenton. *Producer*: George Waggner. *Screenplay*: Scott Darling. Based on a story by Eric Taylor from characters created by Mary Shelley. *Cinematography*: Milton Krasner, Woody Bredell. *Art Director*: Jack Otterson. *Make-up*: Jack Pierce. *Music*: Charles Previn.
    Cast: Sir Cedric Hardwicke as Dr. Ludwig Frankenstein, Lon Chaney, Jr., as the monster; Bela Lugosi as Ygor; Evelyn Ankers, Ralph Bellamy, Lionel Atwill, Doris Lloyd, Olaf Hytten, Leyland Hodgson, Janet Ann Gallow, Otto Hoffman, Dwight Frye, Barton Yarborough, Holmes Herbert, Lawrence Grant, Brandon Hurst, Julius Tannen, Harry Cording, Dick Alexander, Ernie Stanton, George Eldredge, Jimmy Phillips, Teddy Infuhr, Michael Mark, Lionel Belmore.

Ghost Patrol (1936). Black and white, 58 minutes, Puritan. *Director*: Sam Newfield. *Producers*: Sig Neufeld, Leslie Simmonds. *Screenplay*: Wyndham Gitten. Based on a story by Joe O'Donnell. *Cinematography*: John Greenhalgh. *Editor*: Jack English.
    Cast: Tim McCoy, Claudia Dell, Slim Whitaker, Walter Miller, Wheeler Oakman, Jim Burtis, Lloyd Ingraham.

The Ghost of Slumber Mountain (1919). Black and white, silent, 1000 feet, World.
    Director, Producer and Scenario: Herbert M. Dawley. *Special Effects*: Willis H. O'Brien, Herbert M. Dawley.
    Cast: Willis H. O'Brien, Herbert M. Dawley.

The Girl from Scotland Yard (1937). Black and white, 62 minutes, Paramount. Also known as *End of Adventure*.
    Director: Robert Vignola. *Producer*: Emanuel Cohen. *Screenplay*: Doris Anderson, Dore Schary. Based on a story by Coningsby Dawson from characters created by Edgar Wallace. *Cinematography*: Robert Pittack. *Editor*: George McGuire.
    Cast: Karen Morley, Eduardo Ciannelli, Robert Baldwin, Katherine Alexander, Milli Monti, Lloyd Crane, Bud Flanagan.

Girl in the Moon see *Woman in the Moon*

G-Men Never Forget (1947). Black and white, serial, 12 episodes, 24 reels, Republic.

Directors: Fred C. Brannon, Yakima Canutt. *Producer*: Mike Frankovich. *Screenplay*: Franklin Adreon, Basil Dickey, Jesse Duffy, Sol Shor. *Cinematography*: John McBurnie. *Editors*: Cliff Bell, Sam Starr. *Music*: Mort Glickman.

Cast: Clayton Moore as Ted O'Hara, Roy Barcroft as Vic Murkland/Commissioner Cameron, Ramsay Ames as Sergeant Frances Blake, Tom Steele as Parker, Dale Van Sickel as Cook, Edmund Cobb as Brent, Stanley Price as Dr. Benson, Jack O'Shea as Slater, Barry Brooks as George, Doug Aylesworth as Hayden, Frank O'Connor as district attorney, Dian Fauntelle as Miss Stewart, Eddie Acuff as Fiddler, George Magrill as Staley, Ken Terrell as Kelsey.

G-Men versus the Black Dragon (1943). Black and white, serial, 15 episodes, 31 reels, Republic.
Director: William Witney. *Associate Producer*: W.J. O'Sullivan. *Screenplay*: Ronald Davidson, Joseph Poland, William Lively, Joseph O'Dennel. *Cinematography*: Bud Thackery. *Special Effects*: Howard Lydecker. *Art Director*: Russell Kimball. *Editors*: Edward Todd, Tony Martinelli. *Music*: Mort Glickman.

Cast: Constance Worth as Vivian Marsh, Rod Cameron as Rex Bennett, Roland Got as Chang, Nino Pepitone as Haruchi, C. Montague Shaw as Professor Nicholson, Noel Cravat as Ranga, George J. Lewis as Lugo, Maxine Doyle as Marie, Allen Jung as Fugi, Donald Kirk as Muller, Ivan Miller as inspector, Walter Fenner as Williams, Harry Burns as Tony, Forbes Murray as Kennedy, Hooper Atchley as Caldwell, Robert Homans as Captain Gorman.

Go and Get It (1920). Black and white, silent, 6,300 feet, Marshall Neilan Productions.
Directors: Marshall Neilan, Henry R. Symonds. *Producer*: Marshall Neilan. *Scenario*: Marion Fairfax. *Cinematography*: David Kesson. *Art Director*: Ben Carré.

Cast: Pat O'Malley, Noah Beery, Wesley Barry, Agnes Ayres, Bull Montana, J. Barney Skerry, Charles Hill Mailes, Walter Long.

Gold (1934 German). Black and white, 80 minutes, UFA.
Director (German version): Karl Hartl. *Director* (French version): Serge de Poligny. *Screenplay*: Rolf E. Vanloo. *Cinematography*: Guenther Rittau, Otto Baecker, Werner Bohne. *Art Director*: Otto Hunte. *Music*: Hans-Otto Borgmann.

Cast (German version): Hans Albers, Brigitte Helm, Lien Deyers, Friederich Kayssler, Ernst Karchow.

Cast (French version): Pierre Blanchar, Brigitte Helm, Line Noro, Jacques Dumesnil, Roger Karl.

The Golem (1914 German). Black and white, silent, Bioscop/Hawk. Also known as *The Monster of Fate*.
Directors: Paul Wegener, Henrik Galeen. *Scenario*: Henrik Galeen. Based on Gustav Meyrink's novel. *Cinematography*: Guido Seeber. *Art Director*: Robert A. Dietrich. *Costumes*: R. Gliese.

Cast: Paul Wegener, Lyda Salmonova, Henrik Galeen, Carl Ebert.

The Golem (1916 Danish). Black and white, silent.
Director: Urban God. Based on Gustav Meyrink's novel.

The Golem (1936 Czech). Black and white, 88 minutes AB/Metropolis. Also known as *The Legend of Prague*.
Director: Julien Duvivier. *Producer*: Charles Philipp. *Screenplay*: Julien Duvivier, André-Paul Antoine. Based on Gustav Meyrink's novel. *Cinematography*:

Vaclav Vich, Jan Stallich. *Art Directors*: A. Andrejeff, S. Kopecky. *Editor*: Martin J. Lewis. *Music*: Joseph Kumok.

Cast: Harry Baur as Emperor Rudolph II, Charles Dorat as Rabbi Jacob, Ferdinand Hart as the Golem; Germain Aussey, George Voskovec, Roger Karl, Gaston Jacquet, Roger Duchesne, Aimos, Jany Holt.

The Golem (How He Came Into the World) (1920 German). Black and white, silent, six reels, Union-UFA.

Directors: Paul Wegener, Carl Boese. *Scenario*: Paul Wegener, Henrik Galeen. *Cinematography*: Karl Freund, Guido Seeber. *Art Director*: Hans Pölzig. *Costumes*: Rochus Gliese.

Cast: Paul Wegener as the Golem, Lyda Salmonova, Albert Steinruck, Ernst Deutsch, Hanns Sturm, Grete Schröder, Ferdinand von Atlen, Henrik Galeen, Lothar Müthel, Otto Gebühr, Max Kronert, Dora Paetzold.

Der Golem und die Tanzerin (*The Golem and the Dancing Girl*) (1917 German). Black and white, silent, Bioscop/Union.

Director: Paul Wegener.

Cast: Paul Wegener as himself, Lyda Salmonova as the dancing girl, Rochus Gliese.

The Great Alaskan Mystery (1944). Black and white, serial, 13 episodes, 26 reels, Universal. Also known as *The Great Northern Mystery*.

Directors: Ray Taylor, Lewis D. Collins. *Associate Producer*: Henry MacRae. *Screenplay*: Maurice Tombragel, George H. Plympton. Based on a story by Jack Foley. *Cinematography*: William Sickner.

Cast: Ralph Morgan as Dr. Miller; Marjorie Weaver as Ruth; Milburn Stone as Jim Hudson, Joseph Crehan as Bill, Martin Kosleck as Dr. Hauss, Fuzzy Knight, Anthony Warde, Jay Novello.

The Great Northern Mystery see *The Great Alaskan Mystery*

The Great Radium Mystery (1919). Black and white, silent, serial, 18 episdoes, 36 reels, Universal. Also known as *The Radium Mystery*.

Directors: Robert F. Hill, Robert Broadwell. *Scenario*: Frederick Bennett.

Cast: Cleo Madison, Robert Reeves, Eileen Sedgwick, Edwin Brady, Robert Kortman, Jeff Osborne, Gordon McGregor, Robert Grey.

The Greatest Power (1917). Black and white, silent, five reels, Metro/Rolfe.

Director: Edwin Carewe. *Screenplay*: Albert Shelby Le Vino. Based on a story by Louis B. Wolheim.

Cast: William B. Davidson, Ethel Barrymore, Harry S. Northrup, William Black, Frank Currier, Cecil Owen.

The Green Hornet (1940). Black and white, serial, 13 episodes, 26 reels, Universal.

Directors: Ford Beebe, Ray Taylor. *Associate Producer*: Henry MacRae. *Screenplay*: George H. Plympton, Basil Dickey, Morrison C. Wood, Lyonel Margolies. Based on a radio serial created by Fran Striker. *Cinematography*: William Sickner, Jerome Ash.

Cast: Gordon Jones as the Green Hornet/Brett Reid, Keye Luke as Kato; Wade Boteler as Michael Oxford, Anne Nagel as Lenore Case, Philip Trent as Jasper Jenks, Edward Earle as Felix Grant, Alan Ladd as Gilpin, Walter McGrail as Dean,

John Kelly as Hawks, Gene Rizzi as Carney, Douglas Evans as Motinson, Ralph Dunn as Andy, Arthur Loft as Joe Ogden, Cy Kendall as Monroe.

The Green Hornet Strikes Again (1940). Black and white, serial, 15 episodes, 30 reels, Universal.
Directors: Ford Beebe, John Rawlins. *Screenplay*: George H. Plympton, Basil Dickey, Sherman L. Lowe. Based on a radio serial created by Fran Striker. *Cinematoraphy*: Jerome Ash.
Cast: Warren Hull as the Green Hornet/Brett Reid, Keye Luke as Kato, Pierre Watkins as Grogan, Wade Boteler as Michael Oxford, Anne Nagel as Lenore Case, Eddie Acuff as Lowry, C. Montague Shaw as Weaver, Joe A. Devlin as Dolan, William Hall as Don DeLuca, Dorothy Lovett as Frances Grayson, Jay Michael as Foranti.

The Green Terror (1919 British). Black and white, silent, 6,524 feet, Gaumont.
Director: Will Kellino. *Scenario*: G.W. Clifford. Based on Edgar Wallace's story.
Cast: Aurele Sydney, Maud Yates, Heather Thatcher, W.T. Ellwanger, Cecil duGue, Arthur Poole.

The Hand of Peril (1916). Black and white, silent, five reels, World/Paragon.
Director, Producer, and Scenario: Maurice Tourneur. Based on a story by Arthur Stringer.
Cast: House Peters, Doris Sawyer, June Elvidge, Ralph Delmore.

The Hands of Orlac (*Orlacs Haende*) (1925 Austrian). Black and white, silent, Pan-film. Also known as *The Sinister Hands of Dr. Orlak*.
Director: Robert Wiene. *Scenario*: Ludwig Kerzt. Based on Maurice Rernard's novel. *Cinematography*: G. Krampf, Hans Androschin. *Art Director*: S. Wessely.
Cast: Conrad Veidt, Carmen Cartellieri, Fritz Kortner, Alexandra Sorina, Paul Askonas, Fritz Strassny.

Heaven Ship see *Sky Ship*

Hellevision (1939). Black and white, Roadshow Attractions.

The Hidden Hand (1942). Black and white, 68 minutes, Warner Brothers.
Director: Ben Stoloff. *Producer*: William Jacobs. *Screenplay*: Anthony Coldwey, Raymond Schrock. *Cinematography*: Henry Sharp. *Art Director*: Stanley Fleischer. *Editor*: Harold McLeron.
Cast: Craig Stevens, Elizabeth Fraser, Frank Wilcox, Julie Bishop, Cecil Cunningham, Ruth Ford, Roland Drew, Milton Parsons, Willie Best, Wade Boteler, Creighton Hale, Monte Blue.

Hidden Power (1939). Black and white, 60 minutes, Columbia.
Director: Lewis D. Collins. *Producer*: Larry Darmour. *Screenplay*: Gordon Rigby. *Cinematography*: James S. Brown, Jr., *Editor*: Dwight Caldwell.
Cast: Jack Holt, Dickie Moore, Gertrude Michael, Regis Toomey, Holmes Herbert, Helen Brown.

High Treason (1929 British). Black and white, British version: 95 minutes. U.S. version: 69 minutes, Gaumont/Tiffany.
Director: Maurice Elvey. *Screenplay*: L'Estrange Fawcett. Based on Pemberton

Billing's play. *Art Director*: Andrew Mazzei. *Music*: Patrick K. Heale, Walter Collins. *Cast*: Benita Hume, Basil Gill, Raymond Massey, Jameson Thomas, Humberston Wright, Milton Rosmer, Henry Vibart, Rene Ray.

Homunculus (1916 German). Black and white, silent, six parts, 360 minutes, Bioscop. Also known as *The Revenge of Homunculus, Homunculus the Leader*. *Director*: Otto Rippert. *Scenario*: Otto Rippert, Robert Neuss. Based on Robert Reinart's novel. *Cinematography*: Carl Hoffman. *Art Director*: Robert A. Dietrich.
  Cast: Frederick Kühne, Olaf Fonss, Maria Carmik Mechtild Their, Aud Egede Nissen, Lupu Pick.

Homunculus the Leader see **Homunculus**

The Horror (1933?). Black and white, F.P./Stanley.
Directed and Produced by Bud Pollard.

House of Dracula (1945). Black and white, 67 minutes, Universal.
Director: Erle C. Kenton. *Producer*: Paul Malvern. *Executive Producer*: Joe Gershenson. *Screenplay*: Edward T. Lowe. Based on a story by George Bricker, Dwight V. Babcock from characters created by Mary Shelley, Bram Stoker. *Cinematography*: George Robinson. *Art Directors*: John B. Goodman, Martin Obzina. *Editor*: Russell Schoengarth. *Make-Up*: Jack Pierce. *Music*: Hans J. Salter.
  Cast: Lon Chaney, Jr., as Lawrence Talbot/the Wolf Man, John Carradine as Dracula, Glenn Strange as the Frankenstein Monster, Martha O'Driscoll, Lionel Atwill, Jane Adams, Onslow Stevens, Beatrice Gray, Ludwig Stossel, Skelton Knaggs.

House of Frankenstein (1945). Black and white, 71 minutes, Universal. Also known as *The Devil's Brood*.
Director: Erle C. Kenton. *Producer*: Paul Malvern. *Screenplay*: Edward T. Lowe. Based on a story by Curt Siodmak from characters created by Mary Shelley, Bram Stoker. *Cinematography*: George Robinson. *Special Effects*: John P. Fulton. *Art Directors*: John B. Goodman, Martin Obzina. *Editor*: Philip Cahn. *Sound*: Bernard B. Brown. *Make-Up*: Jack Pierce. *Music*: H.J. Salter.
  Cast: Boris Karloff as Dr. Neimann, Lon Chaney, Jr., as Lawrence Talbot/the Wolf Man, J. Carrol Naish as Daniel, John Carradine as Dracula, Anne Gwynne as Rita, Glenn Strange as the Frankenstein Monster, George Zucco as Professor Lampini, Elena Verdugo as Alonka, Peter Coe, Lionel Atwill.

House of Mystery see **Night Monster**

The House that Went Crazy (1914). Black and white, silent, one reel, Selig.

The Hypnotic Spray (1909 British). Black and white, silent, 360 feet, Gaumont.

If (1916 British). Black and white, silent, 4,800 feet, London.
Director: Stuart Kinder.
Cast: Iris Delaney, Judd Green, Ernest Leicester.

I'm an Explosive (1933 British). Black and white, 50 minutes, George Smith Productions.
Director and Screenplay: Adrian Brunel. *Producer*: Harry Cohen.

Cast: Bill Hartnell, Gladys Jennings, Sybil Grove, Harry Terry, Eliot Makeham, D.A. Clarke-Smith, George Dillon, Blanche Adele.

The Impossible Voyage (1904 French). Black and white, silent, 1414 feet, Star.
Director: Georges Méliès.
Cast: Georges Méliès.

The Inventor (1910). Black and white, silent, 900 feet, Pathé.

The Inventors (1934 British). Black and white, two reels, Educational Films.
Producer: Al Christie. Based on a story by William Watson, Sig Herzig.
Editor: Barney Rogan.
Cast: Chase Taylor, Budd Hulick.

The Inventor's Galvanic Fluid see *Liquid Electricity*

The Inventor's Secret (1911 Italian). Black and white, silent, 2,100 feet, Cines.

The Inventor's Son (1911 British). Color, silent, short, Kinemacolor.
Director: David Miles.

Invisibility (1909 British). Black and white, silent, 650 feet, Hepworth.
Directors: Cecil Hepworth, Lewin Fitzhamon.
Cast: Lewin Fitzhamon.

The Invisible Agent (1942). Black and white, 81 minutes, Universal.
Director: Edwin L. Marin. *Producer*: Frank Lloyd. *Screenplay*: Curt Siodmak. *Cinematography*: Lester White. *Special Effects*: John P. Fulton, Bernard B. Brown. *Art Director*: Jack Otterson. *Editor*: Edward Curtiss. *Music*: Charles Previn.
Cast: Jon Hall as Frank Raymond, Peter Lorre as Ikito, Ilona Massey, Sir Cedric Hardwicke, J. Edward Bromberg, John Litel, Albert Basserman, Holmes Herbert, Keye Luke.

The Invisible Fluid (1908). Black and white, silent, 662 feet, Biograph.

The Invisible Killer (1940). Black and white, 61 minutes, Producer's Releasing Corporation.
Director: Sherman Stout. *Associate Producer*: Sigmund Neufeld. *Screenplay*: Joseph O'Donnell. Based on a story by Carter Wayne. *Cinematography*: Jack Greenhalgh. *Editor*: H.N. Todd.
Cast: Grace Bradley, Roland Drew, William Newill, Ernie Adams.

The Invisible Man (1933). Black and white, 71 minutes, Universal.
Director: James Whale. *Producer*: Carl Laemmle, Jr. *Screenplay*: R.C. Sherriff. Based on H.G. Wells' novel. *Cinematography*: Art Edeson. *Miniature Cinematography*: John Mescall. *Special Effects*: John P. Fulton. *Art Director*: Charles D. Hall. *Editors*: Maurice Pivar, Ted Kent.
Cast: Claude Rains as Jack Griffin, Gloria Stuart as Flora Cranley, William Harrigan as Dr. Kemp, Henry Travers as Dr. Cranley, Una O'Connor as Jenny Hall, Forrester Harvey as Herbert Hall, Holmes Herbert as Chief of Police, E.E. Clive as Jaffers, Dudley Digges as Chief of Detectives, Harry Stubbs as Inspector Bird, Donald Stuart as Inspector Lane, Merle Tottenham as Milly, Jameson Thomas as

Doctor, Dwight Frye as reporter, Walter Brennan as bicycle owner, John Carradine as informer.

The Invisible Man Returns (1940). Black and white, 81 minutes, Universal. *Director*: Joe May. *Associate Producer*: Kenneth Goldsmith. *Screenplay*: Curt Siodmak, Lester Cole. Based on a story by Joe May, Curt Siodmak, a "sequel" to H.G. Wells' novel *The Invisible Man*. *Cinematography*: Milton Krasner. *Special Effects*: John P. Fulton. *Editor*: Frank Gross. *Music*: H.J. Salter.

Cast: Vincent Price as Sir Geoffrey Radcliffe, Nan Grey as Helen Manson, Sir Cedric Hardwicke as Richard Cobb, John Sutton as Dr. Frank Griffin, Cecil Kellaway as inspector, Alan Napier, Forrester Harvey, Frances Robinson, Ivan Simpson, Edward Fielding, Harry Stubbs.

The Invisible Man's Revenge (1944). Black and white, 77 minutes, Universal. *Director and Producer*: Ford Beebe. *Screenplay*: Bertram Millhauser. "Suggested" by H.G. Wells' novel *The Invisible Man*. *Cinematography*: Milton Krasner. *Special Effects*: John P. Fulton. *Art Director*: John B. Goodman. *Editor*: Saul A. Goodkind. *Music*: H.J. Salter.

Cast: Jon Hall as Robert Griffin, Evelyn Ankers as Julie, John Carradine as Dr. Dupree; Gale Sondergaard as Irene, Alan Curtis as Jasper; Leon Errol, Ian Wolfe, Billy Bevan, Lester Matthews.

The Invisible Ray (1920). Black and white, silent, serial, 15 episodes, 31 reels, Forham Amusement Corporation. *Director*: Harry A. Pollard. *Producer*: Jesse J. Goldberg. *Scenario*: Guy McConnell.

Cast: Ruth Clifford, Jack Sherrill, Edward Davis, Sidney Bracey, Corinne Uzzell.

The Invisible Ray (1936). Black and white, 81 minutes, Universal. *Director*: Lambert Hillyer. *Producer*: Edmund Granger. *Screenplay*: John Colton. Based on a story by Howard Higgin, Douglas Hodges. *Cinematography*: George Robinson. *Special Effects*: John P. Fulton. *Art Director*: Albert D'Agostion. *Editor*: Bernard Burton. *Music*: Franz Waxman.

Cast: Bela Lugosi as Dr. Benet, Boris Karloff as Janos Rukh, Violet Kemble Cooper as Mrs. Rukh, Frances Drake, Frank Lawton, Walter Kingsford, Beulah Bondi.

The Invisible Thief (1905 French). Black and white, silent, 377 feet, Pathé. *Directors*: Gaston Velle, Gabriel Moreau. *Cast*: Charles Lepire.

The Invisible Woman (1941). Black and white, 72 minutes, Universal. *Director*: A. Edward Sutherland. *Associate Producer*: Burt Kelly. *Screenplay*: Robert Lees, Fred Rinaldo, Gertrude Purcell. Based on a story by Joe May, Curt Siodmak. *Cinematography*: Elwood Bredell. *Special Effects*: John P. Fulton. *Art Director*: Jack Otterson. *Editor*: Frank Gross. *Music*: Charles Previn.

Cast: John Barrymore as Professor Gibbs; John Howard as Dick Russell, Virginia Bruce as Kitty Carroll, Charles Ruggles as George; Charles Lane as Growley; Oscar Homolka as Blackie Cole, Shemp Howard, Maria Montez, Margaret Hamilton, Edward Brophy.

The Iron Claw (1916). Black and white, serial, 20 episodes, 40 reels, Pathé.
Director: Edward José. *Scenario*: George Brackett Seitz.
Cast: Pearl White, Creighton Hale, Sheldon Lewis, Harry Fraser, J.E. Dunn.

Island of Lost Souls (1933). Black and white, 70 minutes, Paramount.
Director: Erle C. Kenton. *Screenplay*: Philip Wylie, Waldemar Young. Based
on H.G. Wells' novel *The Island of Dr. Moreau*. *Cinematography*: Karl Struss.
Special Effects: Gordon Jennings. *Art Director*: Hans Dreier. *Make-Up*: Wally West-
more.
Cast: Charles Laughton as Dr. Moreau, Richard Arlen as Edward Parker,
Leila Hyams as Ruth Thomas, Kathleen Burke as Lota, Bela Lugosi as the Sayer of
the Law, Stanley Fields as Captain Davies; Joe Bonomo, George Irving, Tetsu
Komai, Alan Ladd, Randolph Scott.

The Island of Terror (*Ile d'Epouvante*) (1913 French). Black and white, silent,
3000 feet, Eclipse.

It's Good to Be Alive (1933). Black and white, 69 minutes, 20th Century–Fox.
Director: Alfred Werker. *Screenplay*: Paul Perez, Arthur Kober. *Cinematog-
raphy*: Robert Planck. *Editor*: Barney Wolf.
Cast: Paul Roulien, Gloria Stuart, Edna May Oliver, Edward Van Sloan,
Herbert Mundin, Robert Grieg, Emma Dunn.

Jack Armstrong (1947). Black and white, serial, 15 episdoes, 31 reels,
Columbia.
Director: Wallace Fox. *Producer*: Sam Katzman. *Screenplay*: Arthur Hoerl,
Lewis Clay, Royal K. Cole, Leslie Swabacker. Based on the radio program *Jack
Armstrong, the All-American Boy*. *Cinematography*: Ira H. Morgan. *Editor*: Earl
Turner. *Music*: Lee Zahler.
Cast: John Hart as Jack Armstrong, Charles Middleton as Jason Grood,
Pierre Watkin as Jim Fairfield, Hugh Prosser as Vic Hardy, Joe Brown as Billy Fair-
field, Rosemary LaPlanche as Betty Fairfield, Clair James as Alura, Wheeler Oakman
as Professor Zorn, Jack Ingram as Blair, Eddie Parker as Slade, John Merton as
Gregory Pierce, Gene Stutenroth as Dr. Albour, Russ Vincent as Umala.

Janus-Faced see *Der Januskopf*

Der Januskopf (1920 German). Black and white, silent, Lippow/Decla-
Bioscop. Also known as *Janus-Faced*, *Love's Mockery*.
Director: Friedrich Wilhelm Murnau. *Scenario*: Hans Janowitz. *Cine-
matography*: Carl Hoffman, Karl Freund, Carl Weiss. *Art Director*: Heinrich
Richter.
Cast: Conrad Veidt, Bela Lugosi, Margarete Schlegel, Willy Keyser-Heyl,
Margarete Kupfer, Gustav Botz, Jaro Furth, Magnus Stifter, Marga Reuter, Lansa
Rudolph, Danny Gurtler.

Jungle Captive (1945). Black and white, 63 minutes, Universal. Also known as
Wild Jungle Captive.
Director: Harold Young. *Executive Producer*: Ben Pivar. *Associate Producer*:
Morgan B. Cox. *Screenplay*: M. Coates Webster, Dwight V. Babcock. Based on a
story by Dwight V. Babcock. *Cinematography*: Maury Gertsman. *Art Directors*:
John B. Goodman, Robert Clatworthy. *Editor*: Fred R. Feitshans, Jr., *Music*: Paul
Sawtell.

Cast: Otto Kruger, Amelita Ward, Phil Brown, Vicky Lane, Jerome Cowan, Rondo Hatton, Robert Shayne.

Jungle Woman (1944). Black and white, 54 minutes, Universal.
Director: Reginald LeBorg. *Producer*: Will Cowan. *Executive Producer*: Ben Pivar. Based on a story by Henry Sucher. *Cinematography*: Jack McKenzie. *Art Directors*: John B. Goodman, Abraham Grossman. *Editor*: Ray Snyder. *Music*: Paul Sawtell.
Cast: Acquanetta as Paula Dupree, Evelyn Ankers, J. Carrol Naish, Samuel S. Hinds, Lois Collier, Milburn Stone, Pierre Watkin, Heinie Conklin, Alec Craig, Douglas Dumbrille.

Junior G-Men (1940). Black and white, serial, 12 episodes, 24 reels, Universal.
Directors: Ford Beebe, John Rawlins. *Screenplay*: George H. Plympton, Basil Dickey.
Cast: Russell Hicks as Colonel Barton, Billy Halop as Billy, Philip Terry as Jim Bradford, Cy Kendall as Brand, Huntz Hall as Gyp, Gabriel Dell as Terry, Bernard Punsley as Lug, Roger Daniels as Midge, Kenneth Lundy as Buck, Kenneth Howell as Harry Trent.

Junior G-Men of the Air (1942). Black and white, serial, 12 episodes, 25 reels, Universal.
Directors: Ray Taylor, Lewis D. Collins. *Associate Producer*: Henry MacRae. *Screenplay*: Paul Huston, George H. Plympton, Griffin Jay. *Cinematography*: William S. Sickner.
Cast: Billy Halop as Ace Holden, Huntz Hall as Bolts Larson, Gabriel Dell as Stick Munsey, Bernard Punsley as Greaseball Plunkett, Gene Reynolds as Eddie Holden, Richard Lane as Don Ames, Lionel Atwill as the Baron, Turhan Bey as Araka, Noel Cravat as Monk, John Bleifer as Beal, Edward Foster as Comora, Frank Albertson as Jerry Markham.

Just Imagine (1930). Black and white, 113 minutes, 20th Century–Fox.
Director: David Butler. *Screenplay*: David Butler, Ray Henderson, G.G. DeSylva, Lew Brown. *Art Directors*: Stephen Gooson, Ralph Hammeras. *Songs*: G.G. DeSylva, Ray Henderson, Lew Brown.
Cast: El Brendel as Single O, Maureen O'Sullivan as LN-18, John Garrick as J-21, Marjorie White as D-6, Frank Albertson, Hobart Bosworth, Kenneth Thomson, Misha Auer, Joseph Girard, Sidney DeGray, Joyzelle.

The Kaiser's Shadow (1918). Black and white, silent, five reels, Ince. Also known as *The Triple Cross*.
Director: R. William Neill. *Producer*: Thomas H. Ince. *Scenario*: Octavus Roy Cohen, J.H. Giesy.
Cast: Dorothy Dalton, Thurston Hall, Edward Cecil.

King Kong (1933). Black and white, 110 minutes, RKO Radio.
Directors and Producers: Merian C. Cooper, Ernest B. Schoedsack. *Executive Producer*: David O. Selznick. *Screenplay*: James Creelman, Ruth Rose. Based on a story by Merian C. Cooper, Edgar Wallace, from an idea conceived by Merian C. Cooper. *Cinematography*: Edward Linden, Vernon L. Walker, J.O. Taylor. *Technical Director and Special Effects*: Willis H. O'Brien, Marcel Delgado. *Art Directors*: Carroll Clark, Al Herman. *Art Technician*: Mario Larrinaga. *Sets*: Mario Larrinaga, Byron Crabbe. *Editor*: Ted Cheesman. *Music*: Max Steiner.

Cast: Robert Armstrong as Carl Denham, Fay Wray as Ann Darrow, Bruce Cabot as Jack Driscoll, Frank Reicher as Captain Englehorn, Victor Wong as Charley, Noble Johnson as native chief, Steve Clemento as witch king, James Flavin as second mate, Sam Hardy as Weston, Roscoe Ates as photographer, Dick Curtis as crewman, Paul Porcasi as fruit vendor, LeRoy Mason as theater patron, Sandra Shaw as woman dropped by Kong.

King of the Mounties (1942). Black and white, serial, 12 episodes, 25 reels, Republic.
Director: William Witney. *Associate Producer*: W.J. O'Sullivan. *Screenplay*: Taylor Caven, Ronald Davidson, William Lively, Joseph O'Donnell, Joseph Poland. *Cinematography*: Bud Thackery. *Special Effects*: Howard Lydecker. *Editors*: Edward Todd, Tony Martinelli.
Cast: George Irving as Professor Brent, Peggy Drake as Carol Brent, Abner Biberman as Admiral Yamata, Nestor Paiva as Count Baroni, William Vaughn as Marshal von Horst, Allan Lane as Sergeant King, Gilbert Emery as Commissioner, Russell Hicks as Marshal Carleton, Bradley Page as Blake, Douglas Dumbrille as Harper, William Blakewell as Ross, Duncan Renaldo as Pierre, Francis Ford as Collins, Jay Novello as Lewis, Anthony Warde as Stark, Norman Nesbitt as radio announcer, John Hiestand as Lane, Allen Jung as Sato, Paul Fung as Jap bomber, Awon Dale as Craig.

King of the Rocket Men (1949). Black and white, serial, 12 episodes, 25 reels, Republic. Also known in feature form as *Lost Planet Airmen*.
Director: Fred C. Brannon. *Associate Producer*: Franklin Adreon. *Screenplay*: Royal Cole, William Lively, Sol Shor. *Cinematography*: Ellis W. Carter. *Special Effects*: Howard Lydecker, Theodore Lydecker. *Editors*: Cliff Bell, Sam Starr. *Music*: Stanley Wilson.
Cast: Tristram Coffin as Jeff King, Mae Clarke as Glenda Thomas, Don Haggerty as Tony Dirken, House Peters, Jr., as Burt Winslow, James Craven as Professor Millard, I. Stanford Jolley as Professor Bryant, Douglas Evans as chairman, Ted Adams as Martin Conway, Stanley Price as Gunther Von Strum, Dale Van Sickel as Martin, Tom Steele as Knox, David Sharpe as Blears, Eddie Parker as Rowan, Michael Ferro as Turk, Frank O'Connor as guard, Buddy Roosevelt as Philips.

King of the Royal Mounted (1940). Black and white, serial, 12 episodes, 25 reels, Republic. Also known as *The Yukon Patrol*.
Directors: William Witney, John English. *Associate Producer*: Hiram S. Brown, Jr. *Screenplay*: Franklyn Adreon, Norman S. Hall, Joseph Poland, Barney A. Sarecky, Sol Shor. *Cinematography*: William Nobles. *Music*: Cy Feuer.
Cast: Allan Lane as Sergeant King, Robert Strange as Kettler, Robert Kellard as Corporal Tom Merritt, Jr., Lita Conway as Linda Merritt, Herbert Rawlinson as Inspector King, Harry Cording as Wade Garson, Bryant Washburn as Crandall, Budd Buster as Vinegar Smith, Stanley Andrews as Tom Merritt, Sr., John Davidson as Dr. Shelton, John Dilson as Dr. Wall, Paul McVey as Excellency Zarnoff, Lucien Prival as Admiral Johnson, Norman Willis as Captain Tarner, Tony Paton as LeCouteau.

King of the Zombies (1941). Black and white, 67 minutes, Monogram.
Director: Jean Yarbrough. *Producer*: Linsley Parsons. *Screenplay*: Edmund Kelso. *Cinematography*: Mack Stengler. *Art Director*: Charles Clague. *Editor*: Richard Currier. *Music*: Edward Kay.

Cast: Dick Purcell, Joan Woodbury, Mantan Moreland, Henry Victor, John Archer, George Zucco.

The Lady and the Doctor see **The Lady and the Monster**

The Lady and the Monster (1944). Black and white, 86 minutes, Republic. Also known as *The Lady and the Doctor*, *Tiger Man*. *Director and Producer*: George Sherman. *Screenplay*: Dane Lussier, Frederick Kohner. Based on Curt Siodmak's novel *Donovan's Brain*. *Cinematography*: John Alton. *Special Effects*: Theodore Lydecker. *Art Director*: Russell Kimball. *Editor*: Arthur Roberts. *Music*: Walter Scharf.

Cast: Vera Hruba Ralston, Erich von Stroheim, Richard Arlen, Sidney Blackmer, Helen Vinson, Mary Nash, Lola Montez.

The Last Hour (1930 British). Black and white, 75 minutes, Nettleford Films. *Director*: Walter Forde. *Producer*: Archibald Nettleford. *Screenplay*: H. Fowler Mear. Based on Charles Bennett's play.

Cast: Stewart Rome, Richard Cooper, Wilfred Shine, Billy Shine, Kathleen Vaughn, Alexander Field, James Raglan, George Bealby, Frank Arlton.

The Last Man on Earth (1924). Black and white (tinted), silent, seven reels, Fox.

Director and Producer: Jack G. Blystone. *Scenario*: Donald W. Lee. Based on a story by John D. Swain. *Cinematography*: Allan Davey.

Cast: Earle Foxe, Derelys Perdue, Grace Cunard, Gladys Tennyson, Buck Black, Maryon Aye, Clarissa Selwynne, Marie Astaire, Jean Johnson.

Latest Style Airship (1908 French). Black and white, short, Pathé. *Director*: Ferdinand Zecca.

Laughing at Danger (1924). Black and white, silent, six reels, FBO. *Director*: James W. Horne. Based on a story by Frank Howard Clark. *Cinematography*: William Marshall.

Cast: William Talmadge, Eva Novak, Joe Harrington, Joe Girard, Stanhope Wheatcroft.

Legally Dead (1923). Black and white, silent, 6,076 feet, Universal. *Director*: William Parke. *Screenplay*: Harvey Gates. Based on a story by Charles Furthman. *Cinematography*: Richard Fryer.

Cast: Milton Sills, Brandon Hurst, Claire Adams, Margaret Campbell, Edwin Sturgis, Faye O'Neill.

The Legend of Prague see **The Golem** (1936).

Let There Be Light (1915). Black and white, silent, two reels, American-Flying A. *Director*: William Bertram. *Cast*: Helen Rosson, Charles Newton, E. Forrest Taylor.

Lieutenant Rose, R.N., and His Patent Aeroplane (1912 British). Black and white, silent, 1032 feet, Clarendon.

Life in the Next Century (1909 French). Black and white, silent, 300 feet. Lux. *Director*: Gérard Bourgeois.

Life Without Soul (1915). Black and white, silent, Ocean.
Director: Joseph W. Smiley.
Cast: Percy Darrell Standing as the monster.

The Liquid Air (1909 French). Black and white, silent, 450 feet, Gaumont.

Liquid Electricity (1907). Black and white, silent, 450 feet, Blackton.
Director and Producer: J. Stuart Blackton.

The Living Ghost (1942). Black and white, 61 minutes, Monogram.
Director: William Beaudine. *Producer*: A.W. Hackel. *Screenplay*: Joseph
Hoffman. Based on a story by Howard Dimsdale. *Cinematography*: Mack Stengler.
Editor: Jack Ogilvie. *Music*: Frank Sanucci.
Cast: James Dunn, Joan Woodbury, Vera Gordon, Paul McVey, J. Farrell
MacDonald, Minerva Urecal, George Eldredge, Jan Wiley.

Lock Your Doors see *The Ape Man*

Lost Atlantis see *L'Atlantide*

The Lost City (1935). Black and white, serial, 12 episodes, 24 reels, Regal. Also
known as *The City of Lost Men*.
Director: Harry Revier. *Producer*: Sherman S. Krelberg. *Screenplay*: Pereley
Poore Sheehan, Eddie Graneman, Leon D'Usseau. Based on a story by Zelma
Carroll, George Merrick, Robert Dillon. *Cinematography*: Roland Price, Edward
Linden. *Art Director*: Ralph Berger. *Music*: Lee Zahler.
Cast: Kane Richmond as Bruce Gordon, William "Stage" Boyd as Zolok,
Claudia Dell as Natcha, Josef Swickard as Manyus, George F. "Gabby" Hayes as
Butterfield, Eddie Fetherstone as Jerry, William Bletcher as Gorzo, Milburn Moranti
as Andrews, Margot D'Use as Queen Rama, Jerry Frank as Appolyn, Ralph Lewis as
Reynolds, William Millman as Colton, Gino Corrado as Ben Ali, Sam Baker as
Hugo.

The Lost City of the Jungle (1946). Black and white, serial, 13 episodes, 26
reels, Universal.
Directors: Ray Taylor, Lewis D. Collins. *Executive Producer*: Morgan B. Cox.
Associate Producer: Joseph O'Donnell. *Screenplay*: Joseph F. Poland, Paul Houston,
Tom Gibson. *Cinematography*: Gus Peterson.
Cast: Russell Hayden as Rod Stanton, Jane Adams as Marjorie Elmore,
Lionel Atwill as Sir Eric Hazarias, Keye Luke as Tal Shan, Helen Bennett as Indra,
Ted Hecht as Doc Harris, John Eldredge as Dr. Elmore, John Miljan as Caffron,
John Gallaudet as Grebb, Ralph Lewis as Kurtz.

Lost Planet Airmen see *King of the Rocket Men*

The Lost World (1925). Black and white (with tinted sequences), 60 minutes,
First National.
Director: Harry O. Hoyt. *Producers*: Earl Hudson, Watterson R. Rothacker.
Screenplay: Marion Fairfax. Based on Sir Arthur Conan Doyle's novel. *Cinematographer*: Arthur Edeson. *Special Effects*: Willis H. O'Brien. *Models*: Marcel Delgado.
Cast: Wallace Beery as Professor Challenger; Bull Montana as the missing
link; Lewis Stone, Bessie Love, Arthur Hoyt, Lloyd Hughes.

Love's Mockery see *Der Januskopf*

The Mad Doctor of Market Street (1942). Black and white, 61 minutes, Universal.
Director: Joseph H. Lewis. *Associated Producer*: Paul Malvern. *Screenplay*: Al Martin. *Cinematography*: Jerome Ash. *Art Director*: Jack Otterson. *Editor*: Ralph Dixon. *Music*: Hans Salter.
   Cast: Una Merkel, Claire Dodd, Lionel Atwill, Nat Pendleton, Anne Nagel, Richard Davies, Noble Johnson.

The Mad Ghoul (1943). Black and white, 65 minutes, Universal.
Director: James Hogan. *Producer*: Ben Pivar. *Screenplay*: Brenda Weisberg, Paul Gangelin. Based on a story by Hans Kraly. *Cinematography*: Milton Krasner. *Make-Up*: Jack Pierce. *Music*: Hans Salter.
   Cast: David Bruce as Ted Allison, Evelyn Ankers as Isabel Lewis, George Zucco as Alfred Morris, Charles McGraw as Detective Garrity, Turhan Bey as Eric Iverson, Robert Armstrong as Ken "Scoop" McClure, Milburn Stone as Detective Simms.

Mad Love (1935). Black and white, 83 minutes, M-G-M.
Director: Karl Freund. *Producer*: John W. Considine. *Screenplay*: P.J. Wolfson, John L. Balderston. Adapted by Guy Endore, Karl Freund from Maurice Renard's novel, *Les Mains d'Orlac. Cinematography*: Chester Lyons, Greg Toland. *Music*: Dmitri Tiomkin.
   Cast: Peter Lorre as Dr. Gogol, Colin Clive as Stephen Orlac, Frances Drake as Madame Orlac, Edward Brophy as Rollo, Ted Healy, Sara Haden, Isabel Jewell, Cora Sue Collins, Keye Luke, Henry Kolker, Harold Huber, Charles Trowbridge, May Beatie, Ian Wolfe, Rollo Lloyd, Murray Kinnell, Clarence Wilson, Billy Gilbert, Frank Darien, Harvey Clark, Edward Norris, Philo McCullough.

The Mad Monster (1942). Black and white, 72 minutes, Prodcuer's Releasing Corporation.
Director: Sam Newfield. *Producer*: Sigmund Neufeld. *Screenplay*: Fred Myton. *Special Effects*: Gene Stone. *Make-Up*: Harry Ross. *Music*: David Chudnow.
   Cast: George Zucco as Dr. Lorenzo Cameron; Glenn Strange as Pedro; Johnny Downs, Anne Nagel, Sarah Padden, Gordon DeMain.

Madrid in the Year 2000 (1925 Spanish). Black and white, silent, feature, Madrid.
Director and Screenplay: Manuel Noriega. *Cinematography*: Antonio Macasoli.
   Cast: Roberto Ingesias, Roberto Rey, Juan Nada, Javier Rivera, Amelia Sanz Cruzado.

The Magician (1926). Black and white, silent, M-G-M.
Director and Producer: Rex Ingram. *Assistant to the Director*: Michael Powell. *Screenplay*: Rex Ingram. Based on Somerset Maugham's story. *Cinematography*: John F. Seitz. *Production Manager*: Harry Lachman. *Art Director*: Henri Menessier. *Editor*: Grant Whytock.
   Cast: Alice Terry, Paul Wegener, Ivan Petrovich, Firmin Gemier, Gladys Hamer, Henry Wilson, Stowitz, Michael Powell.

The Magnetic Fluid (1912 French). Black and white, silent, 510 feet, Pathé.

The Magnetic Kitchen (1908 French). Black and white, silent, short, Pathé. *Director*: Segundo de Chomon.

Magnetic Removal (1908 French). Black and white, silent, 672 feet, Pathé.

The Magnetic Squirt (1909 French). Black and white, silent, 480 feet, Le Lion.

the Magnetic Vapor (1908). Black and white, silent, 345 feet, Lubin.

The Man from Mars see *Radio Mania*

The Man in Half-Moon Street (1944). Black and white, 92 minutes, Paramount.
Director: Ralph Murphy. *Producer*: Walter MacEwen. *Screenplay*: Charles Kenyon. Adapted by Garret Fort from Barré Lyndon's play. *Cinematography*: Henry Sharp. *Editor*: Tom Neff. *Sound*: Philip Wisdom. *Make-Up*: Wally Westmore. *Music*: Miklos Rozsa.
Cast: Nils Asther as Julian Karell, Helen Walker as Eve Brandon. Reinhold Schunzel as Dr. Kurt Van Bruecken, Paul Cavanagh as Dr. Henry Latimer, Edmond Breon as Sir Humphrey Brandon, Morton Lowry as Allen Guthrie, Matthew Boulton as Inspector Garth, Brandon Hurst as Simpson the butler, Aminta Dyne as Lady Minerva Aldergate, Arthur Mulliner as Sir John Aldergate, Edward Fielding as Colonel Ashley, Reginald Scheffield as Mr. Taper the art critic, Eustace Wyatt as Inspector Lawson, Forrester Harvey as Harris the cabbie, Konstantin Shayne as Dr. Vishanoff, Leyland Hodgson as Dr. Albertson, Harry Cording, Clive Morgan, Arthur Blake, Ernie Adams, Norman Ainsley, Edward Cooper, John Sheehan, Frank Baker, T. Arthur Hughes, Frank Moran, John Power, Don Gallaher, Bob Stevenson, Bobby Hale, Cy Ring, Wilson Benge, George Broughton, Robert Cory, Frank Hagney, Al Ferguson.

The Man in the Moon (1898) see *The Astronomer's Dream*

Man in the Moon (1909 French). Black and white, silent, 317 feet, Gaumont.

The Man They Could Not Hang (1939). Black and white, 72 minutes, Columbia.
Director: Nick Grindé. *Producer*: Wallace MacDonald. *Screenplay*: Karl Brown. Based on a story by Leslie White, George Sayre. *Cinematography*: Benjamin Kline. *Editor*: William Lyon. *Music*: M.W. Stoloff.
Cast: Boris Karloff, Lorna Gray, Robert Wilcox, Roger Pryor, Ann Doran, Don Beddoe, Charles Trowbridge, James Craig, Byron Foulger.

The Man They Couldn't Arrest (1933 British). Black and whtie, 72 minutes, Gaumont.
Director: T. Hays Hunter. *Screenplay*: T. Hays Hunter, Angus MacPhail, Arthur Wimperis. *Cinematography*: Leslie Rowson. *Editor*: Ian Dalrymble.
Cast: Hugh Wakefield, Gordon Harker, Renée Clama, Nicholas Hannen, Garry Marsh, Dennis Wyndham.

The Man Who Changed His Mind see *The Man Who Lived Again*

The Man Who Lived Again (1936 British). Black and white, 61 minutes,

Gaumont. Also known as *The Man Who Changed His Mind, The Brain Snatcher, Dr. Maniac.*
Director: Robert Stevenson. *Screenplay*: L. du Garde Peach, Sidney Gillitat, John Balderston. *Cinematography*: Jack Cox. *Editor*: R.E. Dearing. *Make-Up*: Roy Ashton.
   Cast: Boris Karloff as Dr. Laurience, Anna Lee as Clare Wyatt, John Loder, Frank Cellier, Lyn Harding, Cecil Parker, Donald Calthrop.

The Man with Nine Lives (1940). Black and white, 73 minutes, Columbia. Also known as *Behind the Door.*
   Director: Nick Grindé. *Screenplay*: Karl Brown. Based on a story by Harold Shumate. *Art Director*: Lionel Banks. *Editor*: Al Clark.
   Cast: Boris Karloff as Dr. Leon Karvall, Roger Pryor, Jo Anne Sayers, Stanley Brown, John Dilson, Hal Faliaferro, Charles Trowbridge, Ernie Adams.

The Man with Two Lives (1942). Black and white, 65 minutes, Monogram.
   Director: Phil Rosen. *Producer*: A.W. Hacke. *Screenplay*: Joseph Hoffman. *Cinematography*: Harry Neumann. *Editor*: Martin G. Cohn. *Music*: Frank Sanucci.
   Cast: Edward Norris, Eleanor Lawson, Marlo Dwyer, Frederick Burton, Kenne Duncan, Anthony Warde, Hugh Sothern, Addison Richard.

The Man Within see *Der Anderer*

Manhunt in the African Jungle see *The Secret Service in Darkest Africa*

Manhunt of Mystery Island (1945). Black and white, serial, 15 episodes, 31 reels, Republic. Also known as *Captain Mephisto and the Transformation Machine.*
   Directors: Spencer G. Bennett, Wallace Grissell, Yakima Canutt. *Associate Producer*: Ronald Davidson. *Screenplay*: Albert DeMond, Basil Dickey, Jesse Duffy, Alan James, Grant Nelson, Joseph Poland. *Cinematography*: Bud Thackery. *Special Effects*: Howard Lydecker, Theodore Lydecker. *Music*: Richard Cherwin.
   Cast: Forrest Taylor as Dr. Forrest, Linda Sterling as Claire Forrest, Roy Barcroft as Captain Mephisto, Forbes Murray as Hargraves, Jack Ingram as Edward Armstrong, Harry Strang as Frederick Braley, Edward Cassidy as Paul Melton, Richard Baily as Lance Reardon, Kenne Duncan as Brand, Frank Alten as Raymond, Lane Chandler as Reed, Russ Vincent as Ruga, Dale Van Sickel as Barker, Tom Steele as Lyons, Duke Green as Harvey.

Maniac (1934). Black and white, 59 minutes, Roadshow Attractions.
   Director and Producer: Dwain Esper. *Screenplay*: Hildegarde Stadie.
   Cast: Horace Carpenter as Dr. Marasholtz; Bill Woods as Maxwell; Phyllis Diller.

Man-Made Monster (1941). Black and white, 59 minutes, Universal. Also known as *The Atomic Monster, The Electric Man.*
   Director: George Waggner. *Associate Producer*: Jack Bernard. *Screenplay*: Joseph West. *Cinematography*: Elwood Bredell. *Special Effects*: John P. Fulton. *Art Director*: Jack Otterson. *Editor*: Arthur Hilton. *Make-Up*: Jack Pierce. *Music*: Charles Previn.
   Cast: Lionel Atwill as Dr. Rigas; Lon Chaney, Jr., Anne Nagel, Frank Albertson, Samuel S. Hinds, William B. Davidson, Ben Taggert, Connie Bergen.

M.A.R.S. see *Radio Mania*

Mars Attacks the World see *Flash Gordon's Trip to Mars*

Mars Calling see *Radio Mania*

The Mask of Fu Manchu (1932). Black and white, 72 minutes, M-G-M. *Directors*: Charles Vidor, Charles Brabin. *Producer*: Irving Thalberg. *Screenplay*: Irene Kuhn, Edgar Allan Woolf, John Willard. Based on Sax Rohmer's novel. *Cinematography*: Tony Gaudio. *Art Director*: Cedric Gibbons. *Editor*: Ben Lewis. *Cast*: Boris Karloff as Dr. Fu Manchu, Lewis Stone as Sir Dennis Nayland Smith, Karen Morely as Sheila Barton, Charles Starrett as Terrence Granville, Myrna Loy as Fah Lo Suee, Jean Hersholt as Professor Von Berg, Lawrence Grant as Sir Lionel Barton, David Torrence as McLeod, E. Alyn Warren as Gay Lo Sung.

The Masked Marvel (1943). Black and white, serial, 12 episodes, 24 reels, Republic. Also known in feature form (1966) as *Sakima and the Masked Marvel*. *Director*: Spencer G. Bennett. *Associate Producer*: W.J. O'Sullivan. *Screenplay*: Royal K. Cole, Ronald Davidson, Basil Dickey, Jesse Duffy, Grant Nelson, George H. Plympton, Joseph Poland. *Cinematography*: Reggie Lanning. *Special Effects*: Howard Lydecker. *Editors*: Earl Turner, Wallace Grissell. *Music*: Mort Glickman.
Cast: David Bacon as Bob Bartion, Tom Steele as the Masked Marvel (no screen credit), Gayne Whitman as the voice of the Masked Marvel (no screen credit), Johnny Arthur as Sakima, William Forrest as Martin Crane, Howard Hickman as Warren Hamilton, Louise Currie as Alice.

The Master Key (1945). Black and white, serial, 13 episodes, 26 reels, Universal. *Directors*: Ray Taylor, Lewis D. Collins. *Producer*: Morgan Cox. *Screenplay*: Joseph O'Donnell, George H. Plympton, Ande Lamb. Based on a story by Jack Natteford, Dwight V. Babcock. *Cinematography*: William Sickner, Maury Gertsman. *Cast*: Milburn Stone as Tom Brant, Jan Wiley as Janet Lowe, Dennis Moore as Jack Ryan, Addison Richards as Garret Donahue, Bryon Foulger as Professor Elwood Henderson, Maris Wrixon as Dorothy Newton, Sarah Padden as Aggie, Russell Hicks as Chief O'Brien, Alfred LaRue as Migsy, George Lynn as Herman.

The Master of the World (1914). Black and white, silent, three reels, Film Releases of America. *Producer*: Karl Werner.

The Master of the World (*Der Herrn Der Welt* (1935 German). Black and whtie, 90 minutes, Ariel-Film. *Director*: Harry Piel. *Screenplay*: George Muehlen-Schulte. *Cast*: Walter Janssen, Sybille Schmitz.

The Mechanical Butchers (1898 French). Black and white, silent, short, Lumiére.

The Mechanical Husband (1910). Black and white, silent, short, LCC.

The Mechanical Legs (1908 French). Black and white, silent, short, Gaumont.

The Mechanical Man (1915). Black and white, silent, one reel, Universal. *Director*: Allen Curtis. *Scenario*: Clarence Badger. *Cast*: Max Asher.

Mechanical Mary Anne (1910 British). Black and white, silent, short, Hepworth. *Director*: Lewin Fitzhamon.

The Mechanical Statue and the Ingenious Servant (1907). Black and white, silent, 450 feet, Blackton. *Director and Producer*: J. Stuart Blackton.

Men with Steel Faces see *The Phantom Empire*

A Message from Mars (1913 British). Black and white, silent, 4000 feet, United Kingdom Films.
Director and Screenplay: J. Wellett Waller. Based on Richard Ganthony's play. *Producer*: Nicholson Ormsby-Scott.
Cast: E. Holman Clark as Ramiel, Charles Hawtrey, Crissie Bell, Hubert Willis, Frank Hector, Kate Tyndale, Evelyn Beaumont, Eileen Temple, R. Crompton, B. Stanmore, Tonie Reith.

A Message from Mars (1909 New Zealand). Black and white, silent, short.
Producer: Franklyn Barrett. Based on Richard Ganthony's play.

A Message from Mars (1921). Black and white, silent, 5,187 feet, Metro.
Director and Producer: Maxwell Karger. *Scenario*: Arthur Zellner, Arthur Maude. Based on Richard Ganthony's play. *Cinematography*: Arthur Martinelli.
Cast: Aphonz Ethier as the Martian; Bert Lytell, Raye Dean, Gordon Ash, Maude Milton, Leonard Mudie.

Metropolis (1927 German). Black and white, silent, 120 minutes, UFA/Paramount.
Director: Fritz Lang. *Producer*: Erich Pommer. *Scenario*: Fritz Lang, Thea von Harbou. Based on Thea von Harbou's novel. *Cinematography*: Karl Freund, Günther Rittau. *Special Effects*: Eugen Shuften. *Art Directors*: Otto Hunt, Rich Kettlehut, Karl Vollbrecht. *Music*: Konrad Elfers, Gottfried Happertz.
Cast: Brigitte Helm as Maria/Mary; Alfred Abel as Jon Frederson; Gustav Fröhlich as Freder Frederson; Rudolf Klein-Rogge as Rotwang; Theodore Loos, Heinrich George, Erwin Biswanger, Fritz Rasp.

Mighty Joe Young (1949). Black and white, 94 minutes, RKO Radio. Also known as *Mr. Joseph Young of Africa*.
Director: Ernest B. Schoedsack. *Producers*: Ernest B. Schoedsack, John Ford. *Screenplay*: Ruth Rose. *Cinematography*: J. Roy Hunt. *Special Effects*: Willis H. O'Brien, Marcel Delgado, Ray Harryhausen, Pete Peterson.
Cast: Terry Moore, Ben Johnson, Robert Armstrong, Frank McHugh, Douglas Fowley, Dennis Green, Paul Guilfoyle, Nestor Paiva, Regis Toomey, Lora Lee Michel, James Flavin.

The Mind-Detecting Ray (1918 Hungarian). Black and white, silent, short, Star. *Director*: Alfred Désy. *Screenplay*: István Lázár.

Missing Husbands see *L'Atlantide*

The Mistress of Atlantis see *L'Atlantide*

Mr. Joseph Young of Africa see *Mighty Joe Young*

The Modern Dr. Jekyll see *Dr. Jekyll and Mr. Hyde*

The Monster (1925). Black and white, silent, 86 miuntes, West.
Director and Producer: Roland West. *Scenario*: Willard Mack, Albert Kenyon. *Cinematography*: Hal Mohr. *Editor*: A. Carle Palm.
Cast: Lon Chaney as Dr. Ziska; Gertrude Olmstead, Hallam Cooley, Johnny Arthur, Charles A. Sellon, Walter James, Knute Erickson, George Austin, Edward McWade, Ethel Wales.

The Monster and the Ape (1945). Black and white, serial, 15 episodes, 30 reels, Columbia.
Director: Howard Bretherton. *Producer*: Rudolph C. Flothow. *Screenplay*: Sherman L. Lowe, Royal K. Cole. *Cinematography*: C.W. O'Connell. *Editors*: Dwight Caldwell, Earl Turner. *Music*: Lee Zahler.
Cast: Robert Lowery as Ken Morgan, George Macready as Professor Ernst, Ralph Morgan as Professor Arnold, Carole Mathews as Babs Arnold, Willie Best as Flash, Jack Ingram as Nordik, Anthony Warde as Flint, Ted Mapes as Butler, Eddie Parker as Blake, Stanley Price as Mead.

The Monster and the Girl (1941). Black and white, 65 minutes, Paramount.
Director: Stuart Heisler. *Producer*: Jack Moss. *Screenplay*: Stuart Anthony. *Cinematography*: Victor Milner. *Editor*: Everett Douglas. *Music*: Sigmund Krumgold.
Cast: Ellen Drew as Susan Webster, Robert Paige as Larry Reed, Paul Lukas as Bruhl, Joseph Calleia as Deacon, Onslow Stevens as McMasters, George Zucco as Dr. Parry, Rod Cameron as Sam Daniels, Phillip Terry as Scott Webster, Marc Lawrence as Sleeper, Gerald Mohr as Munn, Tom Dugan as Captain Alton, Willard Robertson as Lieutenant Strickland, Minor Watson as Judge Pulver, George F. Meador as Dr. Knight, Cliff Edwards as Leon Stokes, Frank M. Thomas as Jansen, Abner Biberman as Gregory, Corbet Morris as Claude Winters, Edward Van Sloan as Warden, Maynard Holmes as Tim Harper, Harry C. Bradley as Reverend Russell, Emma Dunn as Aunt Della, Matty Fain as Wade Stanton, Bud Jamison as Tim the doorman, Anne O'Neal as Julia, Sammy Blum, John H. Dilson, John Bleifer, Jayne Hazard, Ethelreda Leopold, Florence Dudley, Al Seymour, Bert Moorhouse, Paul McVey, Oscar Smith, Al M. Hill, Emmett Vogan, Eleanor Wesselhoeft, Emory Parnell, Ruth Gillette, Fern Emmett.

The Monster Maker (1944). Black and white, 62 minutes, Producer's Releasing Corporation.
Director: Sam Newfield. *Producer*: Sigmund Neufeld. *Screenplay*: Pierre Gendron, Martin Monney. Based on a story by Lawrence Williams. *Cinematography*: Robert Cline. *Art Director*: Paul Palmentola. *Editor*: Holbrook N. Todd. *Music*: Albert Glasser.
Cast: J. Carrol Naish, Ralph Morgan, Wanda McKay, Terry Frost, Glenn Strange, Sam Flint.

The Monster of Fate see *The Golem* (1914)

The Monster of Frankenstein (*Il Mostro Di Frankenstein*) (1920 Italian). Black and white, silent, Albertini Film/UCI.
Director: Eugenio Testa. *Scenario*: Giovanni Drovetti. Based on Mary Shelley's novel. *Cinematography*: De Simone.

Moonstruck (1909 French). Hand-colored, silent, 721 feet, Pathé.

Motor Car of the Future (1910 German). Black and white, silent, 300 feet, Messter.

The Motor Chair (1911 Italian). Black and white, silent, 360 feet, Italia.

The Motor Valet (1906 British). Black and white, silent, short, Alpha. *Director*: Arthur Cooper.

Murder by Television (1935). Black and white, 60 minutes, Imperial/Cameo. *Director*: Clifford Sanforth. *Associate Producer*: Edward M. Spitz. *Screenplay*: Joseph O'Donnell. *Television Technician*: Milton M. Stern. *Technical Supervisor*: Henry Spitz. *Art Director*: Louis Rachmil. *Editor*: Leslie Wilder. *Music*: Oliver Wallace.
    Cast: Bela Lugosi, June Collyer, George Meeker, Hattie McDaniel, Huntley Gordon, Henry Mowbray, Charles K. French, Charles Hill Mailes, Claire McDowell, Allan Jung, Larry Francis, Henry Hall.

The Mysterious Contragrav (1915). Black and white, silent, two reels, Gold Seal.
    Producer and Scenario: Henry McRae.

Mysterious Dr. Satan (1940). Black and white, serial, 15 episodes, 31 reels, Republic. Also known as *Dr. Satan's Robot*.
    Directors: William Witney, John English. *Producer*: Herman S. Brown. *Editors*: Edward Todd, William Thompson. *Music*: Cy Feuer.
    Cast: Eduardo Cianelli as Dr. Satan, Robert Wilcox as Bob Wayne, William Newell as Speed Martin, C. Montague Shaw as Professor Scott, Ella Neal as Lois Scott, Dorothy Herbert as Alice Brent, Charles Trowbridge as Governor Bronson, Jack Mulhall as Chief of Police, Edwin Stanley as Colonel Bevans, Walter McGrail as Stoner, Joe McGuinn as Gort, Bud Geary as Hallett, Paul Marion as the stranger, Archie Twitchell as airport radio announcer, Lynton Brent as Scarlett, Kenneth Terrell as Corwin, Al Taylor as Joe, Alan Gregg as Red, Tom Steele as the robot.

Mysterious Island (1929). Two-color, silent with sound effects, 95 minutes, M-G-M.
    Directors: Lucien Hubbard, Maurice Tournier, Benjamin Christiansen. Based on Jules Verne's novel.
    Cast: Lionel Barrymore as Count Dakker.

Mysterious Island (1941 Soviet). Black and white, Soviet Children's Film Studio.
    Directors: Ev Penziline, B.M. Chelintzev. *Screenplay*: B.M. Chelintzev. M.P. Kalinine. *Cinematography*: M.B. Belskine. *Special Effects*: M.F. Karukov.
    Cast: M.V. Commisarov, A.S. Krasnopolski, P.I. Klansky, R. Ross.

The Mystery of the Lost Ranch (1925). Black and white, silent, serial, Vitaphone.
    Directors: Harry S. Webb, Tom Gibson. Based on a story by Barr Cross.
    Cast: Pete Morrison.

Mystery Plane see *Sky Pirates*

New Adventures of Batman and Robin see *Batman and Robin*

The New Microbe (1912 Italian). Black and white, silent, 420 feet, Cines.

New Voyage to the Moon (1909 French). Black and white, silent, short, Pathé. *Director*: Segundo de Chomon.

Night Key (1937). Black and white, 67 minutes, Universal. *Director*: Lloyd Corrigan. *Associate Producer*: Robert Presnell. *Screenplay*: Tristram Tupper, John C. Moffitt. Based on a story by William Pierce. *Cinematography*: George Robinson. *Special Effects*: John P. Fulton. *Art Director*: Jack Otterson. *Editor*: Otis Garrett. *Music*: Lou Forbes.
   Cast: Boris Karloff as Professor David Mallory, Warren Hull as Travers, Jean Rogers as Joan Mallory; Samuel S. Hinds as Steve Ranger; Alan Baxter as the Kid; Hobart Cavanaugh, David Oliver, Ward Bond, Frank Reicher.

Night Monster (1942). Black and white, 80 minutes, Universal. Also known as *House of Mystery*.
   Director and Producer: Ford Beebe. *Associate Producer*: Don Brown. *Screenplay*: Clarence Upton Young. *Cinematography*: Charles Van Enger. *Art Directors*: Jack Otterson, Richard Riedel. *Editor*: Milton Carruth. *Music*: Hans J. Salter.
   Cast: Irene Hervey, Don Porter, Nils Asther, Lionel Atwill, Leif Erickson, Bela Lugosi, Ralph Morgan.

Niobe (1915). Black and white, silent, five reels, Paramount.
   Producer: Daniel Frohman.
   Cast: Hazel Dawn, Charles Abbe.

Non-Stop New York (1937 British). Black and white, eight reels, Gaumont.
   Director: Robert Stevenson. *Screenplay*: Roland Pertwee, J.O.C. Orton, Curt Siodmak, Derek Twist. *Cinematography*: Mutz Greenbaum. *Editor*: A. Barnes. *Music*: Louis Levey.
   Cast: Anna Lee, John Loder, William Dewhurst, Francis L. Sullivan, Frank Cellier, Desmond Tester, Athene Syler.

Once in a New Moon (1935 British). Black and white, 63 minutes, Fox British.
   Director: Anthony Kimmins.
   Cast: Eliot Makeham, Derrick de Marney, John Turnbull, Wally Patch, Rene Ray, Mary Hinton, Morton Selten, John Clements, Gerald Barry, Richard Goolden, H. Saxon-Snell.

One Hundred Years After (1911 French), black and white, silent, 780 feet, Pathé.

100 Years Hence see *The Airship*

One Million B.C. (1940). Black and white, 80 minutes, United Artists. Also known as *Man and His Mate*.
   Directors: Hal Roach, Hal Roach, Jr., *Producer*: Hal Roach. *Associate Producer*: D.W. Griffith. *Screenplay*: Mickell Novak, George Baker, Joseph Frickert. Based on a story by Eugene Roche. *Cinematography*: Norbert Brodine. *Special Effects*: Roy Seawright, Frank William Young, Fred Knoth, Danny Hall, Jack Shaw, Elmer Raguse. *Art Director*: Charles D. Hall. *Editor*: Ray Snyder. *Music*: Werner R. Heymann.

Cast: Victor Mature as Tumak, Carole Landis as Luana; Lon Chaney, Jr., John Hubbard, Mamo Clark, Jean Porter, Mickell Novak, Grover James, Nigel deBrulier, Ben Hall.

Our Heavenly Bodies (1925 German). Black and white, seven reels, UFA. Also known as *Wonders of Creation*.
Director: Hans Walter Kornblum.
Cast: Theodor Loos, Walter Reinman.

Overcharged (1912 British). Black and white, silent, 350 feet, Hepworth.
Director: Frank Wilson.

Panic on the Air (1936). Black and white, 60 minutes, Columbia.
Director: D. Ross Lederman. *Screenplay*: Harold Shumate. Based on a story by Theodore A. Tinsley. *Cinematography*: Benjamin Kline. *Editor*: James R. Sweeney.
Cast: Lew Ayres, Florence Rice, Benny Baker, Murray Alper, Ann Sothern, Edwin Maxwell, Charles Wilson, Robert Emmet Keane.

Paris Asleep see *The Crazy Ray*

Paris Qui Dort see *The Crazy Ray*

Pawns on Mars (1915). Black and white, silent, three reels, Vitaphone/Broadway Star Feature.
Director: Theodore Marston. *Scenario*: Donald I. Buchanan.
Cast: Charles Kent, Dorothy Kelly, James Morrison, George Cooper.

The Perfect Woman (1949 British). Black and white, 90 minutes, Two Cities/Eagle-Lion.
Director: Bernard Knowles. *Producers*: George Black, Alfred Black. *Screenplay*: Bernard Knowles, George Black. Based on a play by Wallace Geoffrey, Basil Mitchell. *Cinematography*: Jack Hildyard. *Art Director*: J. Elder Willis. *Editor*: Peter Graham Scott. *Music*: Arthur Wilkinson.
Cast: Stanley Holloway, Pamela Devis, Patricia Roc, Nigel Patrick, Miles Malleson, Irene Handle, Patti Morgan, Anita Sharp-Bolster, Fred Berger, David Hurst, Constance Smith.

Peril from Planet Mongo see *Flash Gordon Conquers the Universe*

The Perils of Paris (1924). Black and white, silent, six reels, Anderson Pictures/Fordy's Film/FBO. Also known as *Terror*.
Director: Edward José. *Scenario*: Gerard Bourgeois.
Cast: Pearl White, Robert Lee, Henry Bandin, Arlene Marchalo.

Perpetual Motion Solved (1914 British). Black and white, silent, 300 feet, Hilarity.

The Phantom (1943). Black and white, serial, 15 episodes, 31 reels, Columbia.
Director: B. Reeves "Breezy" Eason. *Producer*: Rudolph C. Flothow. *Screenplay*: Leslie Swabacker, Morgan Cox, Victor McLeod, Sherman Lowe. *Cinematography*: James S. Brown, Jr. *Editors*: Dwight Caldwell, J. Henry Adams. *Music*: Lee Zahler.

Cast: Tom Tyler as Godfrey Prescott/the Phantom, Kenneth MacDonald as Dr. Bremmer, Frank Shannon as Professor Davidson, Jeanne Bates as Diana, Guy Kingsford as Byron Andrews, Joe Devlin as Singapore Smith, Ernie Adams as Rusty, John S. Bagni as Moku, Ace the Wonder Dog as Devil.

The Phantom Creeps (1939). Black and white, serial, 12 episodes, Universal. *Directors*: Ford Beebe, Saul A. Goodkind. *Associate Producer*: Henry Macrae. *Screenplay*: George H. Plympton, Basil Dickey, Mildred Barish. Based on a story by Willis Cooper. *Cinematography*: Jerry Ash, William Sickner.
Cast: Bela Lugosi as Dr. Alex Zorka, Robert Kent as Captain Bob West, Regis Toomey as Jim Daly, Dorothy Arnold as Jean Drew, Edward Van Sloan as Chief Jarvis, Eddie Acuff as Mac, Anthony Averill as Rankin, Jack C. Smith as Monk, Roy Barcroft as Parker, Forrest Taylor as Black.

The Phantom Empire (1935). Black and white, serial, 12 episodes, Mascot. Also known as *Radio Ranch*, *Men with Steel Faces*.
Directors: Otto Brower, B. Reeves "Breezy" Eason. *Producer*: Armand Shaefer. *Screenplay*: John Rathmell, Armand Shaefer. Based on a story by Wallace MacDonald, Gerald Geraghty, H. Freedman. *Cinematography*: Ernest Miller.
Cast: Gene Autry as Gene Autry, Frankie Darrow as Frankie, Betsy King Ross as Betsy, Dorothy Christy as Queen Tika, Wheeler Oakman as Argo, Charles R. French as Mal, Warren Richmond as Rab, Frank Glendon as Professor Beetson, Lester "Smiley" Burnette as Oscar, William Morre as Pete.

The Phantom of the Air (1933). Black and white, serial, 12 episodes, 24 reels, Universal.
Director: Ray Taylor. *Screenplay*: Ella O'Neill, Basil Dickey, George H. Plympton. Based on a story by Ella O'Neill.
Cast: Tom Tyler as Bob Raymond, Gloria Shea as Mary Edmunds, LeRoy Mason as Mort Crome, Hugh Enfield as Blade, William Desmond as Mr. Edmunds, Sidney Bracey as Munsa, Walter Brennan as Skid, Jennie Cramer as Marie, Cecil Kellog as Joe.

Planet Outlaws see ***Buck Rogers***

Plunder (1923). black and white, silent, serial, 15 episodes, Pathé.
Director and Producer: George B. Seitz. *Scenario*: George B. Seitz, Bertram Millhauser.
Cast: Pearl White, Harry Semels, Warren Krech.

Police of the Future (1909 French). Black and white, silent, 540 feet, Gaumont.

The Possibilities of War in the Air see ***The Airship Destroyer***

The Power God (1925). Black and white, silent, serial, 15 episodes, 31 reels, Vital Exchanges/Davis Distributing.
Director: Ben Wilson.
Cast: Ben Wilson, Neva Gerber, Mary Crane, Mary Brooklyn, John Battaglia.

The Prehistoric Man (1914 Hungarian). Black and white, silent, short, Star.
Director: Alfred Désy. *Scenario*: Zoltán Somlyó, Ernö Györf.

Professor Hoskin's Patent Hustler (1913 British). Black and white, silent, 434 feet, Martin.
Director: Dave Aylott.

Professor Oldboy's Rejuvenator (1914). Black and white, silent, 500 feet, Kalem.

Professor Piecan's Discovery (1910 British). Black and white, silent, 580 feet, Cricks and Martin.
Director: A.E. Coleby.

Professor Puddenhead's Patents (1909). Black and white, silent, 404 feet, Kleine. Also known as *the Aerocab and Vacuum Provider*.
Director: Walter Booth.

The Professor's Antigravitational Fluid (1908 British). Black and white, silent, 350 feet, Hepworth.
Director: Lewin Fitzhamon.
Cast: Bertie Potter.

The Professor's Secret (1908 French). Black and white, silent, 614 feet, Gaumont.

The Professor's Strength Tablets (1909 British). Black and white, silent, 450 feet, Clarendon.
Director: Percy Stow.

A Professor's Twirly-Whirly Cigarettes (1909 British). Black and white, silent, 425 feet, B&C.
Director: H.O. Martinek.

Professor Waman (1938 Indian). Black and white, Shree Ranjit.
Director: Manibhai Vyas.
Cast: Mazhar, Sitara, Sunita.

Professor Weise's Brain Serum Injector (1909). Black and white, silent, 300 feet, Lubin.

Professor Zanikoff's Experiences of Grafting (1909). Black and white, silent, 300 feet, Lux.

The Purple Death from Outer Space see **Flash Gordon Conquers the Universe**

The Purple Monster Strikes (1945). Black and white, serial, 15 episodes, 31 reels, Republic. Also known in feature form as *D-Day on Mars* (1966).
Directors: Spencer G. Bennett, Fred C. Brannon. *Associate Producer*: Ronald Davidson. *Screenplay*: Royal K. Cole, Albert DeMond, Basil Dickey, Barney Sarecky, Lynn Perkins, Joseph Poland. *Cinematography*: Bud Thackery. *Special Effects*: Howard Lydecker, Theodore Lydecker. *Editors*: Cliff Bell, Harold Minter. *Music*: Richard Cherwin.
Cast: Dennis Moore as Craig Foster, Linda Stirling as Sheila Layton, Roy Barcroft as the Purple Monster, James Craven as Dr. Cyrus Layton, Bud Geary as Garrett, Mary Moore as Marcia, John Davidson as the Emperor of Mars, Joe

Whitehead as Stewart, Emmett Vogan as Saunders, George Carleton as Meredith, Kenne Duncan as Mitchell, Rosemonde James as Helen, Monte Hale as Harvey, Wheaton Chambers as Benjamin, Frederick Howard as Crandall, Anthony Warde as Tony, Ken Terrill as Andy.

Queen of the Jungle (1935). Black and white, serial, 12 episodes, Screen Attractions.
Director: Robert Hill. *Screenplay*: J. Griffin Jay.
Cast: Reed Howes, Mary Korman, Dickie Jones, William Walsh, Marilyn Spinner, Lafe McKee, George Cheesbro.

The ? Motorist (1905). Black and white, silent, 200 feet, British Films.
Director: Walter R. Booth. *Producer*: Robert William Paul.

Radar Patrol versus Spy King (1949). Black and white, serial, 12 episodes, 24 reels, Republic.
Director: Fred C. Brannon. *Associate Producer*: Franklin Adreon. *Screenplay*: Royal K. Cole, William Lively, Sol Shor. *Cinematography*: Ellis W. Carter. *Special Effects*: Howard Lydecker, Theodore Lydecker. *Music*: Stanley Wilson.
Cast: Kirk Alyn as Chris Calvert, John Merton as Baroda, Jean Dean as Joan Hughes, George J. Lewis as Manuel, Eve Whitney as Nitra, Anthony Warde as Ricco, Tristram Coffin as Lord, Dale Van Sickel as Ames, Tom Steele as Gorman, Eddie Parker as Dutch.

Radio Mania (1923). Black and white, 3-D, silent, five reels, Teleview/Hodkinson. Also known as *M.A.R.S.*, *Mars Calling*, *The Man from Mars*.
Director: R. William Neill. *Producer*: Herman Holland. *Scenario*: Lewis Allen Brown. *Cinematography*: George Folsey.
Cast: Grant Mitchell, Margaret Irving, Peggy Smith, Isabelle Vernon, Gertrude Hillman, W.H. Burton, J.D. Walsh, J. Burke, Betty Borders.

Radio Patrol (1937). Black and white, serial, 12 episodes, 24 reels, Universal.
Directors: Ford Beebe, Cliff Smith. *Producers*: Barney Sarecky, Ben Koenig. *Screenplay*: Wyndham Gittens, Norman S. Hall, Ray Trampe. Based on a comic strip created by Eddie Sullivan, Charlie Schmidt.
Cast: Mickey Rentschler as Pinky Adams, Grant Withers as Pat O'Hara, Catherine Hughs as Molly Selkirk, Adrian Morris as Sam, Max Hoffman, Jr. as Selkirk, Monte Montague as Pollard, Frank Lackteen as Thatta, Leonard Lord as Franklin, Dick Botiller as Zutta, Silver Wolf as Irish.

Radio Ranch see *The Phantom Empire*

The Radium Mystery see *The Great Radium Mystery*

Ramper the Beast Man see *The Strange Case of Captain Ramper*

Rays That Erase (1916 British). Black and white, silent, 567 feet, Martin.
Director: E.J. Collins.

The Return of Batman see *Batman and Robin*

Return of Captain America see *Captain America*

The Return of Dr. Fu Manchu (1930). Black and white, 73 min., Paramount. *Director*: Rowland V. Lee. *Screenplay*: Florence Ryerson, Lloyd Corrigan. Based on Sax Rohmer's novel. *Cinematography*: Archie J. Stout.
Cast: Warner Oland as Fu Manchu; O.P. Heggie, Neil Hamilton, Jean Arthur, Evelyn Hall.

The Return of Dr. X (1939). black and white, 62 minutes, Warner Brothers. *Director*: Vincent Sherman. *Producer*: Bryan Foy. *Screenplay*: Lee Katz. *Cinematography*: Sid Hickox. *Art Director*: Esdras Hartley. *Editor*: Thomas Pratt. *Make-Up*: Perc Westmore. *Music*: Bernard Kaun.
Cast: Humphrey Bogart as Marshal Quesne, Rosemary Lane as Joan Vance, Wayne Morris as Walter Barnett, Dennis Morgan as Michael Rhodes, John Litel as Dr. Francis Flegg, Lya Lys as Angela Merrova, Huntz Hall as Pink, Charles Wilson as Detective Ray Kincaid, Vera Lewis as Miss Sweetman, Howard Hickman as chairman, Olin Howland as undertaker, Arthur Aylesworth as guide, Jack Mower as Detective Sergeant Moran, Creighton Hale as hotel manager, John Dugley as Rodgers, Joe Crehan as editor, Glen Langan, DeWolf Hopper as Interns.

Return of the Ape Man (1944). Black and white, 60 minutes, Monogram. *Director*: Philip Rosen. *Producers*: Sam Katzman, Jack Dietz. *Associate Producer*: Barney Sarecky. *Screenplay*: Robert Charles. *Cinematography*: Marcel LePicard. *Art Director*: Dave Milton. *Music*: Edward Kay.
Cast: Bela Lugosi as Professor Dexter, John Carradine as Professor Gilmore; Judith Gibson, Michael Ames (Tod Andrews), Frank Moran, Mary Currier, George Zucco.

Return of the Terror (1934). Black and white, seven reels, Warner Brothers. *Director*: Howard Bretherton. *Screenplay*: Eugene Solow, Peter Milne. Based on Edgar Wallace's novel *The Terror*. *Cinematography*: Arthur Todd. *Editor*: Owen Marks.
Cast: Mary Astor, Lyle Talbot, John Halliday, J. Carrol Naish, Frank Reicher, Frank McHugh, Irving Pichel, Etienne Girardot, Charles Grapewin.

The Revenge of Homunculus see *Homunculus*

Revenge of the Zombies (1943). Black and white, 61 minutes, Monogram. Also known as *The Corpse Vanished*.
Director: Steve Sekely. *Producer*: Linsley Parsons. *Screenplay*: Edmund Kelson, Van Noncross. *Cinematography*: Mack Stengler. *Art Director*: David Milton. *Editor*: Richard Currier. *Music*: Edward Kay.
Cast: John Carradine, Robert Lowery, Gale Storm, Veda Ann Borg, Mantan Moreland, Mauritz Hugo, Bob Steele.

Revolt of the Zombies (1936). Black and white, 65 minutes, Medallion. *Director*: Victor Halperin. *Producer*: Edward Halperin. *Screenplay*: Howard Higgins, Rollo Lloyd, Victor Halperin. *Cinematography*: J. Arthur Feindel. *Special Effects*: Ray Mercer.
Cast: Dorothy Stone, Dean Jagger, Roy D'Arcy, Robert Noland, George Cleveland, William Crowell.

Robinson Crusoe of Clipper Island (1936). Black and white, serial, 14 episodes, 29 reels, Republic. Also known in feature form as *Robinson Crusoe on Mystery Island*, *S.O.S. Clipper Island*.

Cast: William Newell as Hank, Momo Clark as Princess Melani, Herbert Rawlinson as Jack, George Cleveland as Goebel, John Ward as Tupper.

Robinson Crusoe on Mystery Island see *Robinson Crusoe of Clipper Island*

Romance of the Inventor of the First Aerial Torpedo see *The Airship Destroyer*

Rural Delivery, Million B.C. (1918). Black and white, silent, five minutes, Manikin Films (Edison).
Director: Willis H. O'Brien.

Sakima and the Masked Marvel see *The Masked Marvel*

The Secret Kingdom (1925 British). Black and white, silent, 5,930 feet, Stoll. Also known as *Beyond the Veil*.
Director and Producer: Sinclair Hill. *Scenario*: Alicia Ramsay. *Cinematography*: Percy Strong. *Art Director*: Walter W. Murton.
Cast: Matheson Lang, Stella Arbenia, Eric Bransby Williams, Genevieve Townsend, Rudolph de Cordova, Robin Irvine, Lilian Oldland, Frank Goldsmith.

The Secret of the Loch (1934 British). Black and white, 80 minutes, Wyndham/British Film.
Director: Milton Rosmer. *Producer*: Bray Wyndham. *Screenplay*: Billie Bristow, Charles Bennett. *Cinematography*: James Wilson. *Special Effects*: J. Elder Wells.
Cast: Seymour Hicks, Nancy O'Neil, Gibson Gowland, Frederick Peisley, Eric Hales, Ben Field, Hubert Harben, Stafford Hilliard, Rosemonde Johns.

The Secret Service in Darkest Africa (1943). Black and white, serial, ten episodes, 21 reels, Republic. Also known in feature form as *The Baron's African War*, *Manhunt in the African Jungle*.
Director: Spencer G. Bennett. *Associate Producer*: W.J. O'Sullivan. *Screenplay*: Royal K. Cole, Basil Dickey, Jesse Duffy, Ronald Davidson, Joseph O'Donnell, Joseph Poland. *Cinematography*: William Bradford. *Special Effects*: Howard Lydecker. *Editors*: Wallace Grissell, Thomas Mallory. *Music*: Mort Glickman.
Cast: Rod Cameron as Rex Bennett, Joan Marsh as Janet Blake, Duncan Renaldo as Pierre LaSalle, Lionel Royce as Baron von Rommier/Sultan Abou Ben Ali.

Shh! The Octopus (1938). Black and white, 60 minutes, Warner Brothers.
Director: William McGann. *Producer*: Bryan Foy. *Executive Producers*: Jack Warner, Hal Wallis. *Screenplay*: George Bricker. Adapted by Ralph Spence from a play by Ralph Murphy, Donald Gallagher. *Cinematography*: Arthur Todd. *Art Director*: Max Parker. *Editor*: Clarence Kolster.
Cast: Allen Jenkins, Hugh Herbert, Marcia Ralston, Eric Stanley, John Eldredge, Margaret Irving, Elspeth Dudgeon.

The Shadow (1940). Black and white, serial, 15 episodes, 31 reels, Columbia.
Director: James W. Horne. *Producer*: Larry Darmour. *Screenplay*: Joseph Poland, Ned Dandy, Joseph O'Donnell. Based on characters created by Maxwell Grant (Walter B. Gibson). *Cinematography*: James S. Brown, Jr. *Editor*: Dwight Caldwell. *Music*: Lee Zahler.

Cast: Victor Jory as Lamont Cranston/Lin Chang/the Shadow, Veda Ann Borg as Margot Lane, Robert Moore as Vincent, Robert Fiske as Turner, J. Paul Jones as Marshall, Jack Ingram as Flint, Charles Hamilton as Roberts, Edward Peil, Sr., as Inspector Cardona, Frank LaRue as Commissioner Weston, "?" as the Black Tiger.

Shadow of Chinatown (1934). Black and white, serial, 15 episodes, victory. Also known as *Yellow Phantom*.
Director: Robert F. Hill. *Producer*: Sam Katzman. *Screenplay*: W. Buchanan, Isadore Bernstein, Basil Dickey. Based on a story by Rock Hawkey. *Cinematography*: Bill Hyer. *Art Director*: Fred Preble. *Editor*: Charles Henkel.
Cast: Bela Lugosi as Victor Poten, Joan Barclay as Joan Whiting, Herman Brix (Bruce Bennett) as Martin Andrews, Luana Walters as Sonya Rokoff, Maurice Liu as Willy Fu, William Buchanan as Healy, Forrest Taylor as Captain Walters, James B. Leong as Wong, Henry F. Tung as Dr. Wu, Paul Fung as Tom Chu.

Shadow of the Eagle (1932). Black and white, serial, 12 episodes, Mascot.
Director: Ford Beebe. *Screenplay*: Ford Beebe, C. Clark, Wyndham Gittens. *Cinematography*: Benjamin Kline, V. Scheurich.
Cast: Edward Hearn as Nathan Gregory, John Wayne as Craig McCoy, Dorothy Gulliver as Jean Gregory, Pat O'Malley as Ames, Roy D'Arcy as Gardner, Walter Miller as Danby.

The Shape of Things to Come see *Things to Come*

Sharad of Atlantis see *Undersea Kingdom*

She (1903). Black and white, silent, 1000 feet, Edison.
Based on H. Rider Haggard's novel (as are all following versions).

She (1911). Black and white, silent, two reels, Thanhouser.
Cast: James Cruze, Marguerite Snow.

She (1916 British). Black and white, silent, 5,400 feet, Barker-Lucoque.
Directors: Will Barker, H. Lisle Lucoque. *Producer*: Will Barker. *Scenario*: Nellie E. Lucoque.
Cast: Alice Delysia, Henry Victor, Sidney Bland, Blanche Forsythe, J. Hastings Batson, Jack Denton.

She (1917). Black and white, silent, five reels, Fox.
Director: Kenean Buel. *Scenario*: Mary Murillo.
Cast: Valeska Suratt.

She (1926 British). Black and white, silent, 8,250 feet, Reciprocity.
Director: Leander de Cordova. *Producer*: George Berthold Samuelson. *Scenario*: Walter Summers. *Art Director*: Heinrich Ricther.
Cast: Betty Blythe, Carlisle Blackwell, Marjorie Statler, Henry George, Jerrold Robertshaw, Tom Reynolds, Alexander Butler, Dorothy Barclay.

She (1935). Black and white, 95 minutes, RKO.
Directors: Irving Pichel, Lansing C. Holden. *Producer*: Merian C. Cooper. *Screenplay*: Ruth Rose. *Cinematography*: J. Roy Hunt. *Special Effects*: Vernon Walker. *Art Director*: Van Nest Polglase. *Editor*: Ted Cheesman.

Cast: Helen Gahagen, Randolph Scott, Helen Mack, Nigel Bruce, Gustav von Seyffertitz.

The Sinister Hands of Dr. Orlak see *The Hands of Orlac*

The Ship of Heaven see *Sky Ship*

Sky Bandits (1940). Black and white, six reels, Monogram.
Director: Ralph Staub. *Producer*: Phil Goldstone. *Screenplay*: Edward Halperin. Based on Laurie York Erskine's novel *Renfrew Ride the Sky*.
Cast: James Newell as Renfrew, Louise Stanley.

The Sky Parade (1936). Black and white, 70 minutes, Paramount.
Director: Otho Lovering. *Producer*: Harold Hurley. *Screenplay*: Byron Morgan, Brian Marlow, Arthur J. Backhard. Based on the radio show and comic strip *The Air Adventures of Jimmie Allen*. *Cinematography*: William Mellor, Al Gilks. *Art Directors*: Hans Dreier, Robert Odell.
Cast: Jimmie Allen as Himself, William Gargon, Kent Taylor, Grant Withers.

Sky Pirates (1939). Black and white, 60 minutes, Monogram. Also known as *Mystery Plane*.
Director: George Waggner. *Producer*: Paul Malvern. *Executive Producer*: Scott Dunlap. *Screenplay*: Paul Schofield, Joseph West. Based on Hal Forrest's comic strip *Tailspin Tommy*.
Cast: Jason Robards, Milburn Stone, Marjorie Reynolds, Lucien Littlefield, Polly Ann Young.

Sky Ship (1914 Danish). Black and white, silent, feature, Nordisk (Great Northern). Also known as *Heaven Ship*, *Fourteen Million Leagues from the Earth*, *A Trip to Mars*, *The Ship of Heaven*.
Director: Holger-Madsen. *Scenario*: Ole Olsen, Sophus Michaëlis. *Cinematography*: Louis Larsen.
Cast: Zanny Petersen, Gunnar Tolnaes.

The Sky Skidder (1929). Black and white, silent 4,364 feet, Universal.
Director: Bruce Mitchell. Based on a story by Val Cleveland. *Cinematography*: William Adams. *Editor*: Harry Marker.
Cast: Helen Foster, Al Wilson, Pee Wee Holmes, Wilbur McGaugh.

The Sky Splitter (1923). Black and white, silent, one reel, Hodkinson.
Directors: Ashely Miller, J. Norling. *Producer*: John R. Bray. *Scenario*: J. Norling.

Sombra, the Spider Woman see *The Black Widow*

Son of Frankenstein (1939). Black and white, 95 minutes, Universal.
Director and Producer: Rowland V. Lee. *Screenplay*: Willis Cooper. Based on characters created by Mary Shelley. *Cinematography*: George Robinson. *Art Directors*: Jack Otterson, Richard Riedel. *Editor*: Ted Kent. *Gowns*: Vera West. *Music*: Frank Skinner.
Cast: Basil Rathbone as Dr. Wolf von Frankenstein, Boris Karloff as the Monster, Bela Lugosi as Ygor, Lionel Atwill as Inspector Krogh, Josephine Hutchinson as Elsa Frankenstein, Donnie Dunagan as Peter Frankenstein, Emma Dunn,

Edgar Norton, Gustav von Seyffertitz, Lionel Belmore, Tom Ricketts, Ward Bond, Clarence Wilson, Lawrence Grant, Perry Ivins, Michael Park, Caroline Cooke, Lorimer Johnson.

Son of Kong (1933). Black and white, 70 minutes, RKO.
Director: Ernest B. Schoedsack. *Executive Producer*: Merian C. Cooper. *Associate Producer*: Archie Marshek. *Screenplay*: Ruth Rose. *Cinematography*: Edward Linden, Vernon Walker, J.O. Taylor. *Special Effects*: Willis H. O'Brien. *Models*: Marcel Delgado. *Art Directors*: Van Nest Polglase, Al Herman. *Editor*: Ted Cheesman. *Music*: Max Steiner.
   Cast: Robert Armstrong as Carl Denham, Helen Mack, Victor Wong, John Marston, Lee Kohlmar, Frank Reicher, Noble Johnson.

S.O.S. Clipper Island see *Robinson Crusoe of Clipper Island*

S.O.S. Coast Guard (1937). Black and white, serial, 12 episodes, 25 reels, Republic.
   Directors: William Witney, Alan James. *Associate Producer*: Sol C. Siegel. *Screenplay*: Barry Shipman, Franklyn Adreon. Based on a story by Morgan Cox, Ronald Davidson. *Cinematography*: William Nobles. *Editors*: Helene Turner, Edward Todd. *Music*: Raoul Kraushaar.
   Cast: Ralph Byrd as Terry Kent, Bela Lugosi as Dr. Boroff, Maxine Doyle as Jean Norman, Herbert Rawlinson as Commander Boyle, Richard Alexander as Thorg, Les Ford as Snapper McGee, Carleton Young as Dodds, John Picorri as Rickerby, Lawrence Grant as Rabinisi, Thomas Carr as Jim Kent, Allen Connor as Dick Norman, George Chesebro as Degado, Ranny Weeks as Wies.

Space Soldiers Conquer the Universe see *Flash Gordon Conquers the Universe*

Space Soldiers' Trip to Mars see *Flash Gordon's Trip to Mars*

Spaceship to the Unknown see *Flash Gordon*

The Spider Returns (1941). Black and white, serial, 15 episodes, 31 reels, Columbia.
   Director: James W. Horne. *Producer*: Larry Darmour. *Screenplay*: Jesse A. Duffy, George H. Plympton. Based on a story by Morgan B. Cox, Lawrence E. Taylor, John Cutting. Harry Fraser. *Cinematography*: James S. Brown, Jr., *Editors*: Dwight Caldwell, Earl Turner. *Music*: Lee Zahler.
   Cast: Warren Hull as Richard Wentworth, Mary Ainslee as Nina Van Sloan, Dave O'Brien as Jackson, Corbet Harris as Mr. McLeod, Joe Girard as Commissioner Kirk, Kenne Duncan as Ram Singh, Harry Harvey as Stephen.

The Spider Woman Strikes Back (1946). Black and white, 59 minutes, Universal.
   Director: Arthur Lubin. *Producer*: Howard Welsch. *Screenplay*: Eric Taylor. *Cinematography*: Paul Ivano. *Art Directors*: John B. Goodman, Abraham Grossman. *Editor*: Ray Snyder. *Make-Up*: Jack Pierce. *Music*: Milton Rosen.
   Cast: Brenda Joyce, Gale Sondergaard, Kirby Grant, Rondo Hatton, Milburn Stone, Hobart Cavanaugh.

The Spider's Web (1938). Black and white, serial, 15 episodes, 31 reels, Columbia.

Directors: Ray Taylor, James W. Horne. *Executive Producer*: Irving Briskin. *Associate Producer*: Jack Fier. *Screenplay*: Robert E. Kent, Basil Dickey, George H. Plympton, Mort Ramson. *Cinematography*: Allen Sigler. *Editor*: Richard Fantl. *Music*: Morris Stoloff.

Cast: Warren Hull as Richard Wentworth, Kenne Duncan as Ram Singh, Iris Meredith as Nina Van Sloan, Charles Wilson as Chase, Forbes Murray as Commissioner Kirk, Marc Lawrence as Steve, Donald Douglas as Jenkins.

Spy Smasher (1942). Black and white, serial, 12 episodes, 25 reels, Republic. Also known in feature form as *Spy Smasher Returns* (1966).

Director: William Witney. *Associate Producer*: W.J. O'Sullivan. *Screenplay*: Ronald Davidson, Norman S. Hall, William Lively, Joseph O'Donnell, Joseph Poland. *Cinematography*: Reggie Lanning. *Special Effects*: Howard Lydecker. *Editors*: Tony Martinelli, Edward Todd. *Music*: Mort Glickman, Arnold Schwarzwald, Paul Sawtell, Ludwig von Beethoven.

Cast: Kane Richmond as Spy Smasher; Hans Schumm as the Mask; Frank Corsaro as Durand; Marguerite Chapman as Eve Corby; Sam Flint, Tristram Coffin, Tom London.

Spy Smasher Returns see *Spy Smasher*

The Strange Case of Captain Ramper (1927 German). Black and white, silent, 7,534 feet. Defu/First National. Also known as *Ramper the Beast Man*.

Director: Max Reichmann. *Scenario*: Kurt J. Braun, Paul Wegener. *Cinematography*: Herbert Korner, Frederic Weymann.

Cast: Paul Wegener as Ramper; Max Schreck, Mary Johnson, Kurt Gerron, Camilo Kossath.

Superman (1948). Black and white, serial, 15 episodes, 480 minutes, Columbia. *Directors*: Spencer G. Bennett, Thomas Carr. *Producer*: Sam Katzman. *Screenplay*: Arthur Hoerl, Lewis Clay, Royal K. Cole. Adapted by George H. Plympton, Joseph F. Poland from characters created by Jerry Siegel, Joe Shuster. *Cinematography*: Ira H. Morgan. *Art Director*: Paul Palmentola. *Editor*: Earl Turner. *Music*: Mischa Bakaleinikoff.

Cast: Kirk Alyn as clark Kent/Superman, Noel Neill as Lois Lane, Tommy Bond as Jimmy Olsen, Carol Forman as the Spider Lady, George Meeker as Driller, Jack Ingram as Anton, Pierre Watkin as Perry White, Terry Frost as Brock, Charles King as Conrad, Charles Quigley as Dr. Hackett, Herbert Rawlinson as Dr. Graham, Forrest Taylor as Leeds, Stephen Carr as Morgan, Rusty Wescoatt as Elton, Nelson Leight as Jor-El, Luana Walters as Lara, Edward Cassidy as Eben "Pa" Kent, Virginia Carroll as Sarah "Ma" Kent, Alan Dinehart III as young Clark, Ralph Hodges as teenage Clark.

Superspeed (1935). Black and white, 56 minutes, Columbia. *Director*: Lambert Hillyer. *Screenplay*: Harold Shumate. *Cinematography*: Ben Kline. *Editor*: Otto Meyer.

Cast: Norman Foster, Florence Rice, Mary Carlisle, Charles Grapewin, Arthur Hohl, Robert Middlemass, George McKay.

Tarzan's Desert Mystery (1943). Black and white, 70 minutes, RKO. *Director*: William Thiele. *Producer*: Sol Lesser. *Associate Producer*: Kurt Neumann. *Screenplay*: Nancy Kelly. Based on a story by Carroll Young and characters created by Edgar Rice Burroughs. *Cinematography*: Harry Wild, Russ Harlan.

Art Directors: Hans Peters, Ralph Berger. *Editor*: Ray Lockert. *Music*: Paul Sawtell.
Cast: Johnny Weissmuller as Tarzan, Johnny Sheffield as Boy, Nancy Kelly,
Otto Kruger, Joseph Sawyer, Lloyd Corrigan, Robert Lowery.

Television Spy (1939). Black and white, 58 minutes, Paramount.
Director: Edward Dmytryk. *Executive Producer*: William LeBaron. *Associate
Producer*: Edward T. Lowe. *Screenplay*: Horace McCoy, William R. Lipman, Lillie
Hayward. Based on a story by André Bohem. *Cinematography*: Harry Fischbeck. *Art
Directors*: Hans Dreier, Franz Bachelin. *Editor*: Anne Bauchens.
Cast: William Henry, Judith Barett, Anthony Quinn, Richard Denning, John
Eldredge.

Terror see **The Perils of Paris**

Things to Come (1936 British). Black and white, British version: 130 minutes,
U.S. version: 92 minutes, London/United Artists.
Director: William Cameron Menzies. *Producer*: Alexander Korda. *Screenplay*:
H.G. Wells, Lajos Biro. Based on H.G. Wells' *The Shape of Things to Come*. *Cin-
ematography*: George Perinal. *Special Effects*: Ned Mann, Edward Cohen, Harry
Zech, Lawrence Butler, Paul Morell, Ross Jacklin. *Art Director*: Vincent Korda.
Editor: Charles Crichton. *Costumes*: John Armstrong, Réné Hubert. *Music*: Arthur
Bliss, Muir Matheson.
Cast: Raymond Massey as John Cabal/Oswald Cabal, Ralph Richardson as
Rudolph the Boss, Cedric Hardwicke as Theotocopulos, Margaretta Scott as Roxana,
Edward Chapman as Pippa Passworthy/Raymond, Maurice Braddell as Dr. Harding,
Sophie Stewart as Mrs. Cabal, Derrick de Marney as Richard Gordon, Pickles
Livingston as Horrie Passworthy, Pearl Argyle as Catherine Cabal, Alan Jeayes as
Grandfather Cabal, Anthony Holles, Patricia Hilliard.

Tiger Man see **The Lady and the Monster**

The Times Are Out of Joint (1909 French). Black and white, silent, 601 feet,
Gaumont.
Director: Emile Cohl.

Torture Ship (1939). Black and white, 56 minutes, Producer's Releasing Corp.
Director: Victor Halperin. *Associate Producer*: Sig Neufeld. *Screenplay*:
George Sayre. Based on Jack London's story "A Thousand Deaths". *Cinematog-
raphy*: Jack Greenhalgh. *Editor*: Holbrook Todd.
Cast: Lyle Talbot, Irving Pichel, Jacqueline Wells, Wheeler Oakman, Stanley
Blystone, Anthony Averill, Sheila Bromley, Russell Hopton, Eddie Holden, Leander
de Cordova.

The Trans-Atlantic Tunnel (1935 British). Black and white, 94 minutes,
Gaumont-British. Also known as *The Tunnel*.
Director: Maurice Elvey. *Producer*: Michael Balcon. *Screenplay*: Curt Siod-
mak, Clemence Dane, L. du Garde Peach. Adapted by Curt Siodmak from Bernhard
Kellerman's novel. *Cinematography*: Günther Krampf. *Special Effects*: J. Whitehead,
B. Guidobaldi, A. Stroppa. *Editor*: Charles Frend.
Cast: Richard Dix as McAllen, C. Aubrey Smith as Lloyd, Helen Vinson as
Varlia Lloyd, Madge Evans as Ruth McAllen, Leslie Banks as Robbie, Walter Huston
as the President of the United States, George Arliss as the Prime Minister of Great
Britain, Basil Sidney, Henry Oscar, Jimmy Hanley.

Trapped by Television (1936). Black and white, 64 minutes, Columbia.
Director: Del Lord. *Executive Producer*: Robert North. *Associate Producer*:
Ben Pivar. *Screenplay*: Lee Loeb, Harold Buchman. Based on a story by Sherman
Lowe, Al Martin. *Cinematography*: Allen G. Siegler. *Special Effects*: Roy Davidson.
Editor: James Sweenye.
 Cast: Mary Astor, Lyle Talbot, Nat Pendleton, Thurston Hall, Joyce Compton, Henry Mollison, Robert Strange, Marc Lawrence, Wade Boteler, Russell Hicks.

A Trip to Jupiter (1907 French). Hand-colored, 623 feet, Pathé.
Director: Segundo de Chomon.

A Trip to Mars (1903). Black and white, silent, short, Lubin.

A Trip to Mars (1910). Black and white, silent, short, Edison.

A Trip to Mars (1920 Danish). Black and white, silent, four reels, Nordisk/
Tower.

A Trip to Mars (1920 Italian). Black and white, silent, five reels, W.H.
Productions.

A Trip to Mars (1917) see *Sky Ship*

A Trip to the Moon (*Le Voyage dans la Lune*) (1902 French). Black and
white, silent, 825 feet (app. 14 minutes), Star.
Director, Producer, Scenario, Costumes and Sets: Georges Méliès. Based on
Jules Verne's *From the Earth to the Moon* and H.G. Wells' *The First Men in the
Moon*. *Cinematography*: Lucien Tainguy.
 Cast: Georges Méliès as leader of the expedition, Bleuette Bernon as the
woman in the crescent, Ballet Girls of the Théâtre du Chatelet as stars, Acrobats of
the Folies Bergère as the Sélenites, Victor André, Delpierre, Farjaux-Kelm-Brunnet.

A Trip to the Moon (1903 Spanish). Black and white, silent, short, Pathé.
Producer: Segundo de Chomon.

A Trip to the Moon (1914). Black and white, silent, short, 600 feet, Lubin.

The Triple Cross see *The Kaiser's Shadow*

The Tunnel (1933 German). Black and white, Bavaria Film.
Director: Kurt Bernhardt. *Screenplay*: Curt Siodmak. Based on Bernard
Kellerman's novel.
 Cast: (German version) Paul Hartmann, Olly von Flint, Elga Brink, (French
version) Jean Gabin, Madeleine Renaud, Gustaf Grundgens.

The Tunnel (1935) see *The Trans-Atlantic Tunnel*

Tunnelling the English Channel (1907 French). Black and white, silent, 1160
feet. Star.
Director: Georges Méliès.

20,000 Leagues Under the Sea (1907 French). Hand-colored, silent, 930 feet.
Director and Producer: Georges Méliès. Based on Jules Verne's novel.

Twenty Thousand Leagues Under the Sea (1916). Black and white, silent, 11 reels, Universal.
Director and Scenario: Stuart Paton. Based on Jules Verne's novel. *Producer*: Carl Laemmle. *Cinematography*: Eugene Gaudio. *Underwater Cinematography*: J. Ernest Williamson, George M. Williamson.
Cast: Allen Holuber, Matt Moore, Jane Gail, Joe Welsh.

Undersea Kingdom (1936). Black and white, serial, 12 episodes, 25 reels, Republic. Also known in feature form as *Sharad of Atlantis*.
Directors: B. Reeves "Breezy" Eason, Joseph Kane. *Producer*: Nat Levine. *Screenplay*: J. Rathmell, Maurice Geraghty, Oliver Drake. Based on a story by J. Rathmell, Tracy Night. *Cinematography*: William Nobles, Edgar Lyons. *Music*: Harry Grey.
Cast: Ray "Crash" Corrigan as Crash Corrigan, Lois Wilde as Diana, Monte Blue as Khan, William Farnum as Sharad, Boothe Howard as Ditmar, C. Montague Shaw as Professor Norton, Lee Van Atta as Billy Norton, Smiley Burnette as Briny, Frankie Marvin as Salty, Lon Chaney, Jr., as Hakur, Lane Chandler as Darius, Jack Mulhall as Lieutenant Andrews, John Bradford as Joe, Ralph Holmes as Martos, Ernie Smith as Gourck, Lloyd Whitlock as Captain Clinton, David Horsley as Naval Sentry, Kenneth Lawton as Naval Doctor, Raymond Hatton as Gasspon, Rube Schaeffer as Magna.

Unholy Love see *Alraune* (1928).

Unknown Island (1948). Black and white, 76 minutes, Film Classics.
Director: Jack Bernhard. *Producer*: Albert Jay Cohen. *Screenplay*: Robert T. Shannon, Jack Harvey. Based on a story by Robert T. Shannon. *Cinematography*: Fred Jackman, Jr. *Special Effects*: Howard A. Anderson, Ellis Burman. *Art Director*: Jerome Pycha, Jr. *Sets*: Robert Priestley. *Editor*: Harry Gerstad. *Music*: Ralph Stanley.
Cast: Virginia Grey as Carol Lane, Philip Reed as John Fairbanks, Richard Denning as Ted Osbourne, Barton MacLane as Captain Tanowski, Richard Wessel, Dan White, Philip Mazir.

The Unknown Purple (1923). Black and white, silent, 6,950 feet, Truart.
Director and Producer: Roland West. *Scenario*: Roland West, Paul Schofield. *Cinematography*: Oliver T. Marsh. *Art Director*: Horace Jackson. *Editor*: Alfred A. Cohn.
Cast: Henry B. Walthall, Johnny Arthur, Dorothy Phillips, Alice Lake, Frankie Lee, Stuart Holmes, Helen Ferguson, James Morrison, Richard Wayne.

Valley of the Zombies (1946). Black and white, 56 minutes, Republic.
Director: Philip Ford. *Associate Producers and Screenplay*: Dorrell McGowan, Stuart McGowan. Based on a story by Sherman L. Lowe, Royal K. Cole. *Cinematography*: Reggie Lanning. *Special Effects*: Howard Lydecker, Theodore Lydecker. *Art Director*: Hilyard Brown. *Editor*: William P. Thompson. *Make-Up*: Bob Mark. *Music*: Richard Cherwin.
Cast: Robert Livingston, Adrian Booth, Ian Keith, Earle Hodings, Wilton Graff, Thomas Jackson, Charles Trowbridge, LeRoy Mason, William Haade.

The Vampire Bat (1933). Black and white, 63 minutes, Majectic.
Director: Frank R. Strayer. *Producers*: Frank Starrow, Phil Goldstone. *Screenplay*: Edward T. Lowe. *Cinematography*: Ira Morgan. *Art Director*: Dan Hall.

Editor: Otis Garrett.
    Cast: Lionel Atwill as Dr. Von Neimann, Melvyn Douglas as Carl Brech-schneider, Fay Wray as Ruth, Dwight Frye as Herman Glieg, Lionel Belmore.

The Vanishing Shadow (1934). Black and white, serial, 12 episodes, Universal.
Director: Louis Friedlander. *Screenplay*: Het Manheim, Basil Dickey, George Morgan. Based on a story by Ella O'Neill. *Cinematography*: Richard Fyer. *Art Director*: Thomas F. O'Neill. *Editors*: Edward Todd, Alvin Todd.
    Cast: Onslow Stevens as Stanley Stanfield, James Durkin as Professor Carl Van Dorn, Walter Miller as Ward Barnett, Eddie Cobb as Kent, Richard Cramer as Dorgan, Sidney Bracey as Denny, Ada Ince as Gloria, Tom London, William Steele, Monte Montague.

The Violet Ray (1917). Black and white, silent, one reel, General.
Director: Robert Ellis. *Scenario*: Robert Welles Ritchie.
    Cast: George Larkin, Harry Gordon, Robert Ellis.

Voodoo Man (1944). Black and white, 62 minutes, Monogram.
Director: William Beaudine. *Producers*: Sam Katzman, Jack Dietz. *Associate Producer*: Barney Sarecky. *Screenplay*: Robert Charles. *Cinematography*: Marcel LePicard. *Art Director*: David Milton. *Editor*: Carl Pierson. *Music*: Edward Kay.
    Cast: Bela Lugosi, John Carradine, George Zucco, Michael Ames (Tod Andrews), Henry Hall, Wanda McKay, Louise Currie.

The Walking Dead (1936). Black and white, 66 minutes, Warner Brothers.
Director: Michael Curtiz. *Producer*: Lou Edelman. *Screenplay*: Ewart Adamson, Peter Milne, Robert Adams, Lillie Hayward. Based on a story by Ewart Adamson, Joseph Fields. *Cinematography*: Hal Mohr. *Editor*: Tommy Pratt.
    Cast: Boris Karloff, Edmund Gwen, Marguerite Churchill, Ricardo Cortez, Barton MacLane, Warren Hull, Joe Sawyer, Eddie Acuff, Kenneth Harlan, Joseph King, Henry O'Neill, Ruth Robinson, Addison Richards, Milton Kibbee, Wade Boteler.

War of Dreams (1915). Black and white, silent, three reels, Selig.
Director: E.A. Martin. *Scenario*: W.E. Wing.
    Cast: Edwin Wallock, Lillian Hayward, Bessie Eyton.

When the Man in the Moon Seeks a Wife (1908). Black and white, silent, short, Clarendon.
Director: Percy Stow. *Scenario*: Langford Reed.

Whispering Shadows (1933). Black and white, serial, 12 episodes, Mascot Master-Serial.
Directors: Albert Herman, Colbert Clark. *Producer*: Nat Levine. *Screenplay*: George Morgan, Wyndham Gittens, H. Bimberg, Barney Sarecky, Norman S. Hall. *Cinematography*: Ernest Miller, V. Scheurick.
    Cast: Bela Lugosi as Professor Strang, Henry B. Walthall as Bradley, Karl Dane as Sparks, Viva Tattersall as Vera Strang, Malcolm MacGregor as Jack Foster, Robert Warwick as Raymond, Roy D'Arcy as Steinbeck, George Lewis as Bud Foster, Ethel Clayton as the Countess, Lloyd Whitlock as Dr. Young, Bob Kortman as Slade, Tom London as Dupont, Lafe McKee as Martin Jerome.

The White Gorilla (1945). Black and white, 62 minutes, Weiss Global Enterprises/Special Attractions Film Exchange.

Director: Adrian Weiss. *Producer*: Louis Weiss. Based on a story by Monro Talbot. *Cinematography*: Bob Cline.
Cast: Ray "Crash" Corrigan as Crash Corrigan, Lorraine Miller as Allison.

White Pongo (1945). black and white, 74 minutes, Producer's Releasing Corporation. Also known as *Congo Pongo, Adventure Unlimited, Blonde Gorilla, The Challenge of King Kong*.
Director: Sam Newfield. *Producer*: Sigmund Neufeld. *Screenplay*: Raymond L. Schrock. *Cinematography*: Jack Greenhalgh. *Art Director*: Edward C. Jewell. *Editor*: Holbrook N. Todd. *Music*: Leo Erdody.
Cast: Richard Fraser, Maris Wrixon, Lionel Royce, Al Eben, Gordon Richards, Egon Brecker.

Wild Jungle Captive see **Jungle Captive**

Without a Soul (1916). Black and white, silent, five reels, World.
Producer and Scenario: James Young. Based on Owen Davis' play *Lola*.
Cast: Clara Kimball Young, Alec B. Frances, Edward M. Kimball, Irene Tams, Mary Moore.

The Wizard (1927). Black and white, silent, 5,629 feet, Fox.
Director: Richard Rosson. *Scenario*: Harry O. Hoyt, Andrew Bennison, Malcolm Stuart Boylan. Based on Gaston Leroux's novel *Balaoo*. *Cinematography*: Frank Good. *Titles*: Malcolm Stuart Boylan.
Cast: Edmund Lowe, Leila Hyams, Gustav von Seyffertitz, E.H. Calvert, Barry Norton, Oscar Smith, Perle Marshall, Norman Trevor, George Kotsonaros, Maude Turner Gordon.

Woman in the Moon (*Die Frau im Mond*) (1928 German). Black and white, silent. German version: 156 minutes. U.S. version: 97 minutes. Fritz Lang Film/ G.M.B.H.-UFA. Also known as *Girl in the Moon*.
Director and Producer: Fritz Lang. *Scenario*: Fritz Lang, Thea von Harbou. *Cinematography*: Kurt Kourant, Oskar Fishinger, Otto Kanturek. *Special Effects*: Konstantin Tschetverikov. *Art Directors*: Emil Hasler, Otto Hunte, Karl Vollbrecht. *Technical Advisors*: Hermann Oberth, Willy Ley.
Cast: Gerda Marcus as Friede, Willy Fritsch as Helius, Frtiz Rasp as agent, Gustav von Wangenheim as Windegger, Klaus Pohl as Professor Manfeldt, Gustl Stark-Gesettenbaur as Stowaway.

Wonder Pills (1909 Italian). Black and white, silent, short, Cines.

The Wonderful Chair (1910). Black and white, silent, 420 feet, Brockliss.

The Wonderful Electro-Magnet (1909). Black and white, silent, 400 feet, Edison.

A Wonderful Fluid (1908 French). Black and white, silent, 492 feet, Pathé.

The Wonderful Hair Remover (1910 British). Black and white, silent, short, Gaumont.

The Wonderful Rays (1919 French). Black and white, silent, 2,220 feet, Savoia.

A Wonderful Remedy (1909 French). Black and white, silent, 377 feet, Pathé.

Wonders of Creation see *Our Heavenly Bodies*

The World of 1960 (1939). Black and white, nine minutes, Columbia.
Director and Producer: B.K. Blake. *Cinematography*: Don Malkames, James Lillis. *Narrator*: Edgar Barrier.

X-Rays (1897 British). Black and white, silent, 54 feet, G.A. Smith.
Director: G.A. Smith.

Years to Come (1922). Black and white, silent, one reel, Pathé.
Producer: Hal Roach.
Cast: Snub Pollard, Marie Mosquini.

Yellow Phantom see *Shadow of Chinatown*

The Yukon Patrol see *King of the Royal Mounted*

Zambo (1937 Indian). Black and white, 157 minutes, Bhavani.
Director, Producer and Screenplay: M. Bhavani. *Cinematography*: R.M. Master. *Music*: Pandit Bedriprasad.
Cast: S.B. Nayampally, Sarla, Indira Wadker, Mehru the gorilla.

Zeppelin Attack on New York (1917). Black and white, silent, 660 feet, Mutual.

Bibliography

Ackerman, Forrest J, *The Best from Famous Monsters of Filmland*. New York: Paperback Library, Inc., 1964, 184pp. Greatest hits from the greatest monster magazine of them all.

_____. *The Frankenscience Monster*. New York: Ace Publishing Corp., 1969, 181pp. A collection of reminiscences in tribute to Karloff by the father of monsternalism.

Aylesworth, Thomas G. *Monsters from the Movies*. New York: Bantam Books, 1980, 150pp. Indexed. A brief overview by the editor of a science magazine for high school students with a penchant for the origins of cinematic monsters.

_____. *Movie Monsters*. Philadelphia: J.B. Lippincott, 1975, 79pp. Basically for children. Describes some famous movie monsters, how they were created, and the films in which they appeared. Included are *Frankenstein, Bride of Frankenstein, King Kong, The Invisible Man, Island of Lost Souls* and *Dr. Jekyll and Mr. Hyde*.

Barbour, Alan G. *Cliffhanger*. Secaucus, N.J.: Citadel Press, 1980, 248pp. Indexed. Illustrations galore but slight on text. Barbour has a good sense of the serial format and does not try to scrutinize chapterplays. His gingerly style never breaks the fragile structure of his subject matter. Many great stills.

Baxter, John. *Science Fiction in the Cinema*. New York: A.S. Barnes, 240pp. Anecdotal essays on the making of some of filmdom's greatest science fiction.

Brooks, Tim, and Marsh, Earle. *The Complete Dictionary to Prime Time Network TV Shows*. New York: Ballantine, 1981, 1001pp. Indexed.

Brosnan, John. *Future Tense: The Cinema of Science Fiction*. New York: St. Martin's Press, 1978, 306pp. Indexed. Excellent comprehensive history concentrating on cold war and modern science fiction.

_____. *The Horror People*. New York: St. Martin's Press, 1976, 304pp. Indexed. Includes biographical references.

_____. *Movie Magic*. New York: New American Library, 1976, 302pp. Indexed. A scholarly history of special effects including biographical material on noted film magicians and a complete listing of special effects Oscar-winners.

Butler, Ivan. *Horror in the Cinema*. New York: A.S. Barnes, 162pp. Essays by a British playwright.

Cinefantastique. Winter, 1971. Discussions of *The Lost World*.

Clarens, Carlos. *An Illustrated History of the Horror Film*. New York: Capricorn Books, 1968, 256pp. Outstanding history and analysis from a critic's point of view.

Cook, David A. *A History of Narrative Film*. New York: W.W. Norton, 1981, 721pp. A well-constructed overview of film as storyteller from Méliès to the present. Contains an extensive bibliography and glossary of film terms.

Costa, Richard Haver. *H.G. Wells*. New York: Twayne Publishers, 1967, 181pp. Indexed. Biographical and critical study by a Syracuse University professor.

Eames, John Douglas. *The MGM Story*. New York: Crown Publishers, 1982, 408pp. Indexed. Revised and updated big book discusses and illustrates 1738 films, including all films the studio has produced and independent productions distributed since the firm was formed in 1924.

Everson, William K. *Classics of the Horror Film*. Secaucus, N.J.: Citadel Press, 1974, 247pp. Scholarly discussion of subjectively chosen "major" films, admirably holding to the firm belief that there has never been a great movie in color.

"Frankenstein: King Karloff's Greatest Film of the Man who Made a Monster." *Famous Monsters of Filmland*. No. 178, October, 1981, pp. 27–49.

Franklin, Joe. *Classics of the Silent Screen*. Secaucus, N.J.: Citadel Press, 1959, 255pp. Enthusiastic nostalgia from the long-time NYC TV talk-show host. Researched by William K. Everson. Helpful for its discussions on Barrymore's *Dr. Jekyll and Mr. Hyde* and *The Lost World*.

Gifford, Denis. *The British Film Catalogue 1895-1970*. New York: McGraw-Hill, 1971, 14, 161pp. Comprehensive filmography.

_____. *Movie Monsters*. England: Studio Vista/Dutton Pictureback, 1970, 159pp. British view of monsterdom from the silents to the present. Heavily illustrated, lightweight text.

Glut, Donald F. *The Frankenstein Legend: A Tribute to Mary Shelley and Boris Karloff*. Metuchen, N.J.: Scarecrow Press, 1973, 372pp. Indexed. An attempt to "perpetuate the Frankenstein lengend" in a comprehensive volume which includes the monster's depiction in various media.

Harmon, Jim, and Glut, Donald F. *The Great Movie Serials*. Garden City, N.Y.: Doubleday, 1972, 384pp. Nostalgic view of chapterplays with a loving assessment of those who made them.

Hogan, David J. *Who's Who of the Horrors*. Cranberry, N.J.: A.S. Barnes, 1980, 278pp. Indexed. An international personality encyclopedia of the fantastic film, well written and packed with facts. Contains the largest selection of life dates available.

Huss, Roy and Ross, T.J. eds. *Focus on the Horror Film*. Englewood Cliffs, N.J.: Prentice-Hall, 1972, 186pp. Indexed. The editors and noted contributors such as Ray Bradbury, Ernest Jones, and Jack Kerouac offer comments on the horror film and its central myths.

Kine Weekly. Great Britain, March 5, 1925. Discussion of *The Lost World*.

"Lon, Lee, Lorre and — Legendary John Carradine." *Famous Monsters of Filmland*. No. 187, September 1982, pp. 34–42.

Lee, Walt. *Reference Guide to Fantastic Films*. Los Angeles: Chelsea-Lee Books, 1972, three volumes. Indispensible filmography.

McClelland, Doug. *The Golden Age of B Movies*. New York: Bonanza Books, 216pp. Nicely done essays on 50 notable B-features. Illustrated with over 600 photos.

Maltin, Leonard, ed. *TV Movies*. New York: Signet, 1980, 886pp. A listing of the 13,000 films most apt to show up on television, including directorial and cast credits, quickie plot description, and quality rating (**** to "Bomb").

Manchel, Frank. *An Album of Great Science Fiction Films*. New York: Franklin Watts, 1976, 96pp. Indexed. Heavily illustrated brief overview, admirable for its scholarly approach but packaged as kiddie fare. Researched by Vonetta Lapidou.

Mank, Gregory William. *It's Alive!* San Diego: A.S. Barnes, 1981, 196pp. Includes material on the eight *Frankenstein* films by Universal. Makes fine reading for diehard fans. Also contains an extensive biographical index.

Medved, Harry and Michael. *The Golden Turkey Awards*. New York: Perigee Books, 1980, 223pp. A humorous concept pretentiously written, this mockout of Hollywood's worst efforts contains a discussion on the career of William Beaudine.

Moss, Robert F. *Karloff and Company: The Horror Film.* New York: Pyramid Books, 1974, 159pp. Indexed. Near the end of this witty summation of the genre, Moss wisely notes, "... horror films are best approached as unportentously as possible."

Naha, Ed. *Horrors from Screen to Scream.* New York: Avon Books, 1975, 306pp. Witty alphabetical listing of subjectively chosen films by the New York Post film critic.

_____. *Science Fictionary.* U.S.A.: Wideview Books, 1980, 388pp. "An A-Z Guide to the World of Science Fiction: Authors, Films and TV shows."

The New York Times Directory of the Film. New York: Arno Press, 1971, 1243pp. Guide to film reviews appearing in the daily, used too numerously to list individually.

Parish, James Robert, and Pitts, Michael R. *The Great Science Fiction Pictures.* Metuchen, N.J.: Scarecrow Press, 1977, 382pp.

Pohl, Frederik, and Pohl, Frederik, IV. *Science Fiction Studies in Film.* New York: Ace Books, 346pp. Light essays on major science fiction films from the silent era to the present.

Rovin, Jeff. *A Pictorial History of Science Fiction Films.* Secaucus, N.J.: Citadel Press, 1975, 240pp. From *Metropolis* to *Star Wars* in pictures, with a filmography and special section on TV science fiction.

Saposnik, Irving S. *Robert Louis Stevenson.* New York: Twayne Publishers, 1974, 164pp. Indexed. After an introductory biographical sketch, Israeli Saposnik dedicates each chapter to a literary form which Stevenson employed.

Sklar, Robert. *Movie-Made America: A Cultural History of American Movies.* New York: Random House, 1975, 341pp. Indexed. Useful for its information on film copyright laws before 1912 and the pirating techniques of the Edison Company.

Stanley, John. *The Creature Features Movie Guide.* Pacifica, CA.: Creatures at Large, 1981, 208pp. Stanley is the host of a West Coast, monster movie TV show. Unfortunately, his "guide," which lists over 5000 entries, is padded, uninformed, and whimsical to the point of annoyance.

Stedman, Raymond William. *The Serials.* Norman: University of Oklahoma Press, 1971, 513pp. Indexed. Serials in print, radio and film are covered.

Underwood, Peter. *Karloff.* New York: Drake Publishers, 238pp. Indexed. Underwood, a long-standing member of the British Film Institute, researched this biography for four years. The volume contains a look at Karloff both on and off the screen. It includes a chronological listing of the 163 films he made and a discography of his recorded works.

Weiss, Ken, and Goodgold, Ed. *To Be Continued....* New York: Crown, 1972, 341pp. Cast listings and plot summaries of serials dryly presented.

Waite, Ronald N. "The Alphabeast of Horror Part II." *Famous Monsters of Filmland.* No. 187, September 1982, pp. 14–21. Contains information on Albert Dekker, star of *Dr. Cyclops*, Karl Freund, cinematographer for *Metropolis*, and Ray Harryhausen, the veteran special effects expert who bagan his career working for Willis O'Brien in *Mighty Joe Young*.

Zinman, David. *Saturday Afternoon at the Bijou.* Castle Books, 1973, 511pp. Useful for its essays on *Frankenstein* and *The Invisible Man*.

Index

(Page numbers in boldface indicate photographs)